Scales, Thresholds and Dilemmas of Housing Transformations in Istanbul

Nilay Ünsal Gülmez & Ali Devrim Işıkkaya (eds.)

Scales, Thresholds and Dilemmas of Housing Transformations in Istanbul

PETER LANG

Bibliographic Information published by the Deutsche Nationalbibliothek
The Deutsche Nationalbibliothek lists this publication in the Deutsche Nationalbibliografie; detailed bibliographic data is available online at http://dnb.d-nb.de.

Library of Congress Cataloging-in-Publication Data
A CIP catalog record for this book has been applied for at the Library of Congress.

Cover illustration: © Ali Devrim Işıkkaya

Funded by Bahçeşehir University

ISBN 978-3-631-85491-4 (Print)
E-ISBN 978-3-631-85492-1 (E-PDF)
E-ISBN 978-3-631-87166-9 (EPUB)
10.3726/b19591

Peter Lang – Berlin · Bern · Bruxelles · Istanbul · New York · Oxford · Warszawa · Wien

This publication has been peer reviewed.

www.peterlang.com

Acknowledgement

The idea of writing that book was sparked by the discussions we had in the Housing Studies working group at Bahçeşehir University, Faculty of Architecture and Design. These discussions helped shape the structure and content of the book. We would like to thank all the members of this working group, some of whom have contributed to this book as authors of chapters. We would like to thank to Bahçeşehir University for their financial support.

Contents

List of Contributors

Ahmet SEZGİN (Ph.D.)

He completed his BA in Architecture from the Middle East Technical University in 2000; He received his master's degree from the World Heritage Studies Program at Brandenburg Technical University (BTU) (2006), and his Ph.D. from the Art History & Visual Studies Program at the University of Manchester (2012) with his thesis titled "The Historiography of Sinan in Modern Turkey". He is a lecturer at MEF University and serves as the Interior Design Department Head as of 2021. His research interests cover identity and architecture, nationalism studies, and Ottoman architecture.

Ahsen ÖZSOY (Ph.D.)

Ahsen Özsoy studied architecture at Istanbul Technical University, completed her PhD at ITU Faculty of Architecture, continued academic career until 2020 at the same university. She still teaches at Işık University. She has taught architectural design, research methodologies, architectural psychology, and housing. She has research studies and publications on topics of housing quality; earthquake, housing and woman's role; creativity-university, post-occupancy evaluation, and design participation. She has been responsible for the design of educational and residential projects, has received national architectural awards. Administratively, she served as Director of Institute of Social Sciences and Vice Rector of ITU. Currently, she is the President of the Association for Architecture Education (ArchED/MimED).

Ali Devrim IŞIKKAYA (Ph.D)

Assoc. Prof. Ali Devrim Işıkkaya, earned his bachelor's, master's and Ph.D. degree at the Faculty of Architecture, Yıldız Technical University Istanbul in 1999, 2002 and 2008. He worked for national architectural offices in collaboration with international offices between 2001 and 2006. He is awarded with honorable mention in the national "New Social Habitat Erbaa, Tokat Architectural Design Competition" in 2015. Işıkkaya, as full time academician, is teaching architectural and interior architectural design, construction and housing in the undergraduate and graduate programs of the Faculty of Architecture and Design at Bahcesehir University since 2008. He was a visiting academic in Coburg University of Applied Sciences and HTWG Konstanz Hochschule. His research interests include urban and architectural design competitions, housing culture, and adaptive reuse.

Arda ÇALIŞKAN
Arda Çalışkan graduated from Bahçeşehir University, Department of Interior Architecture and Environmental Design in 2017. He started his master's education in Bahçeşehir University Interior Design program and graduated in 2020 with the thesis titled "Place-Making Practices of Z Generation: Case of Dormitory Rooms". During this time, he worked as an interior architect at Uğur Schools and Bahçeşehir College. Since 2019, he has been a teaching assistant at Bahçeşehir University's Faculty of Architecture and Design. He continues his Ph.D. in Architecture and Design at the same university.

Berna SAYAR
Berna Sayar is a teaching assistant at Istanbul Bahcesehir University, Faculty of Architecture and Design. She graduated from Ege University Department of Art History. She received her Master's degree in Mimar Sinan Fine Arts University, Department of Art History, Turkish-Islamic Arts Program. Currently, she is a Ph.D. candidate in the same institution. She participated in the excavations of of Beçin- Milas, Ani-Kars and Edirne Palace. Her research interests are history of architecture, urban history, cultural heritage, Ottoman modernization, archeology of Ottoman period.

Büşra ATAM
Büşra Atam is an architect, who had her bachelor's degree from Mimar Sinan Fine Arts University Department of Architecture in 2015. She completed her master's degree at Istanbul Technical University Department of Architectural Design in 2019. She is a research assistant at Bahçeşehir University Faculty of Architecture & Design since 2019 and studying for Ph.D. for more than a year in this institution. Her research interests are people-environment relationship and environment-behavior studies, child-play relation in built environment, and educational buildings. Within her doctoral studies, she is researching users' spatial perception in literature and cinema.

Canay TUNÇER YILDIRIM
Canay Tunçer Yıldırım is a teaching assistant at Bahçeşehir University, Faculty of Architecture and Design since 2014. She received her Bachelor's degree in Architecture (2012) and Master's degree in Restoration (2016) from Istanbul Technical University with her thesis entitled "Kadıköy Yeldeğirmeni - Tevfik

Tura Apartment Conservation Project". She took part in several projects on restoration, archaeology, and design. She is currently studying on her dissertation in Architectural Design Ph.D. Program at the same university as well as carrying out her academic research on housing, modernization and culture within the framework of architectural history and theory.

Efsun EKENYAZICI GÜNEY (Ph.D.)
She is graduated from Yıldız Technical University Faculty of Architecture (2002). She received her master's degree (2005), and doctoral degree (2013) from the Building Research and Planning Program of the same university. She started working as a research assistant in the Faculty of Architecture and Design of Bahçeşehir University in 2006 and continued her academic career in the Department of Interior Architecture and Environmental Design Department as a faculty member since 2013. She has taken part in design studios; has taught courses on adaptive reuse, visual media in design, introduction to architecture and interior architecture. She has publications on her research topics which are dwelling culture, urban transformation, adaptive reuse, design education and architectural design.

Emine GÖRGÜL (Ph.D.)
Emine Görgül is an associate professor in Istanbul Technical University-ITU Department of Interior Architecture. She has received her B.Sc. (1999), M.Sc. (2002) and Ph.D. (2013) degrees from ITU. She was a visiting academic in TU Delft, AA-London, HKU, Auburn University. Her researches and publications focus on architecture theory and criticism, politics and space, gender and space, design education.

Gizem AKDEMİR
Gizem Akdemir has graduated from Işık University Faculty of Fine Arts, Department of Interior Architecture in which she got in with a special talent exam on drawing skills in 2016. Thereafter she completed her master's degree in Istanbul Technical University (ITU) International Master of Interior Architectural Design in 2019. During her education, she traveled to several countries for her studies including international workshops and exchange programs. She started her academic career as a research assistant in the ITU Faculty of Architecture, Department of Interior Architecture in 2018 and enrolled in Bahcesehir Architecture and Design Doctorate Program. She studies topics such as well-being, urban interior, and tiny houses.

Hande TULUM (Ph.D.)
She received her bachelor degree in architecture from Mimar Sinan Fine Arts University, Faculty of Architecture, Department of Architecture in 2010; her graduate degree in History of Architecture from the same university in 2012 and she worked as an architect in architectural-conservation offices in Istanbul. She received her Ph.D. degree from Bahçeşehir University, Department of Architecture in 2018. She has been a faculty member in Bahçeşehir University, Department of Interior Architecture and Environmental Design since 2018. Her research interests include art and architecture relationship, architecture and cinema, history and theory of architecture and design, modern architecture in Turkey, modern architectural heritage, post-war architectural practice in Turkey, twentieth century residential culture in Turkey, urban transformation in Istanbul.

Hatice SADIKOĞLU ASAN
She received her doctorate in design field from Istanbul Technical University. During her Ph.D. studies, she worked as a design researcher in the Housing Lab, La Sapienza University of Rome. She served as a postdoctoral researcher at UC Berkeley Center for Environmental Design and Research and Stanford University in 2017–2020. She has been teaching at California San Jose State University since 2018. Her research interests include midcentury modernism, housing design, smart home products, design quality and experience design.

Naz GÜMÜŞELİ
Naz Gümüşeli graduated from Bahcesehir University, Department of Interior Architecture and Environmental Design in 2013. The author, who completed her master's program at Istanbul Technical University in the History of Architecture, is still continuing her Ph.D. in Architecture and Design program at Bahcesehir University. The author, who has a thesis named "Cihangir District and Art Deco", academically focuses on architectural styles, adaptive reuse, and store design. She has been working on store design and visual merchandising for various corporate companies since 2013. The author has also written several academic publications about store design.

Nilay ÜNSAL GULMEZ (Ph.D.)
She received her BA in Architecture from the Middle East Technical University in 1997; She completed her master's degree in Istanbul Technical University (ITU) Building Sciences Program (2000) and her Ph.D. in ITU Architectural Design Program (2009) with her thesis titled "Diversified Households and Housing

in the Metropolis". She is an associate professor at Bahcesehir University and has been serving as Architecture Department Head since October 2019. Her research interests include housing studies, design history and theory, gender and space, and place-making practices. Her work has appeared in the METU Faculty of Architecture Journal, the Journal of Interior Design (JID), Home Cultures, and a variety of other international and national publications.

Pınar ŞAHİN (Ph.D.)

Pınar Şahin currently works as an assistant professor at Bahçeşehir University, Faculty of Architecture and Design, Department of Architecture. She received her bachelor's and master's degree from Yıldız Technical University. She completed the second year of her master's education as a thesis student at the Eindhoven University of Technology, Netherlands. She studied on Rotterdam office buildings and urban branding. After returning to Turkey, she worked in various architecture offices and construction firms. She received her Ph.D. from Architectural Design Programme at Istanbul Technical University. Her areas of interest are housing researches, architecture and media, modernity and cultural theories, and Early Republican Period architecture.

Suzan GİRGİNKAYA AKDAĞ

Suzan Girginkaya Akdag, Ph.D. is a full-time lecturer at Bahcesehir University, Faculty of Architecture and Design. She received her undergraduate degree from Middle East Technical University (METU) in 2003. She received her M.Sc. in Architectural Design Computing and her Ph.D. in Architectural Design programs from Istanbul Technical University (ITU). After graduation, she worked in the AEC sector as a full-time and part-time architect. Between 2007 and 2011, she worked at Yeditepe University as a research assistant. Since 2011, she has been lecturing at Bahcesehir University, as an assistant professor. Her research interests are digital technologies and their influence on the interior, architectural and urban design theories, practice and education.

List of Abbreviations

AB:	Avrupa Birliği (European Union, EU)
AEC:	Architecture, Engineering and Construction
AKP (JDP):	Adalet ve Kalkınma Partisi (Justice and Development Party)
ANAP:	Anavatan Partisi (Motherland Party)
ÇED:	Çevresel Etkinlik Değerlendirmesi (Environmental Impact Assessment)
CEO:	Chief Executive Officer
CIAM:	The International Congresses of Modern Architecture
ÇLD:	Çağdaş Levent Derneği (Contemporary Association of Levent)
CNN:	Cable News Network
COVID 19:	Corona Virus Disease
DOCOMOMO:	Documentation and Conservation of Buildings, Sites and Neighborhoods of the Modern Movement
DOI:	Digital Object Identifier
DP:	Democrat Party
FHA:	Federal Housing Agency
İBB:	İstanbul Büyükşehir Belediyesi (Istanbul Metropolitan Municipality)
ICT:	Information and Communication Technologies
IETT:	İstanbul Elektrik Tramvay ve Tünel İşletmeleri (Istanbul Electric Tramway and Tunnel Establishments)
ITU:	Istanbul Technical University
KAKS:	Floor Area Ratio
KYK:	Kredili Yurtlar Kurumu (Credit and Dormitories Institution)
MoMA:	Museum of Modern Art
MS-DOS:	MicroSoft Disk Operating System
NATO:	The North Atlantic Treaty Organization
PC:	Personal Computer
QEM:	Quality Environment Modules
TBMM:	Türkiye Büyük Millet Meclisi (Grand National Assembly of Turkey)
TDK:	Turkish Language Association

THOW:	Travelers with Tiny House On Wheels
TOKİ:	Toplu Konut İdaresi (Mass Housing Administration)
TRT:	Türkiye Radyo Televizyonları (Turkish Radio and Televisions)
TÜBİTAK:	Türkiye Bilimsel ve Teknolojik Araştırma Kurumu (Scientific and Technological Research Council of Turkey)
URL:	Uniform Resource Locator
USA:	United States of America
YTÜ:	Yıldız Teknik Üniversitesi (Yıldız Technical University)

Introduction

Istanbul is a multi-layered city that provides a laboratory-like environment for researching various aspects of housing and living. Remembering Heidegger's reflection on the mutual existence of being and dwelling, we bear in mind that a house physically and/or mentally attaches human beings on earth and is becoming increasingly the raison d'être of well-being.

At the same time, housing constitutes the majority of the built environment and leads to the formation of cities. The changes and all the factors that stimulate change in housing production evoke dilemmas between its vital and physical purpose of sheltering, its meaning as being the repository of memories, and its value as one of the pioneer assets of neoliberal economies. As housing practices change, so does the way we interact with one another and with the city. On the other hand, architecture is always political, and urban policies and visions for city development influence decisions about and actions related to housing production. In Istanbul, urban transformation and housing production processes are so intricately entwined and intertwined that they elicit a plethora of predictable and unexpected subject matters to be studied holistically. This book intends to offer a glimpse into the scales, thresholds, and dilemmas of housing transformations in Istanbul, with a specific emphasis on cause-and-effect relationships. It presents a tripartite division.

The first part "Scenes and Narratives of Housing (in) Transformation" focuses on scenes and narratives of housing (in) transformation. The chapters in this section cover the period from the 1950s to the 1980s, when Istanbul witnessed major social, cultural, legal, and political milestones in the history of housing transformation. The transformation narratives shed light on the emergence of new housing typologies during this time period, as well as their characteristics and peculiarities, with the goal of contributing to their documentation and conservation.

Istanbul is a city that was extended on the east-west axis until recent developments shifted the direction of urban sprawl towards the north. In the first chapter of Part I, titled "Istanbul During the Glorious Thirty (1945–75): Mobilization of the Middle-Class and Emergence of Motorways as Tools for Re-Shaping Society and the Littoral Periphery," Emine Görgül presents a comprehensive historical review and exploration of the littoral development of the city of Istanbul in the east-west axis and the emergence of leisure culture and dwelling practices, which provides contextual background to subsequent chapters in Part One.

Focusing on the period between 1945 and 1975, which is named "the Glorius thirty" by Foursatié she investigates the spatial-political impact of infrastructural developments, specifically new motorways, in reshaping Istanbul's urban realm. In doing so, she first clarifies the Democrat Party's mélange economic model, which supports Keynesian approaches on the one hand while participating in infrastructure projects on the other, as well as the reflections of this hybrid approach. Her multi-layered reading elucidates how these new motorways have been politically instrumentalized for both re-positioning Turkey's foreign policy in an alliance with the United States as part of the consumerist culture and formulating planning strategies based on the expansion of the city in the east-west axis with littoral developments. Görgül traces the littoral transformation of the city through the emergence of leisurescapes on both the European and Asian sides of the city. While scrutinizing the summer housing and public economic enterprises' summer camps/holiday complexes, she also depicts the modernization narrative of the period, addressing the changing habits of the citizens in use of the city triggered by mobilization policies and car-use. In the following chapter, titled "Suburban Neighborhoods in Transformation: Unveiling the Modern Architectural Heritage in Pendik" Canay Tunçer Yıldırım picks up from where Görgül left off. She focuses on the east coast (Kadıköy), specifically Pendik, addressing its transformation process from a sayfiye to a suburban neighborhood. Tunçer Yıldırım marks the thresholds of this transformation through the development plans. She emphasizes the neighborhood's shift from industry to the service sector, as well as its designation as a commercial zone, and its dramatic consequences in accelerating the scale and scope of the transformation, as well as the risks in conservation of the modern heritage.

Tunçer Yıldırım unveils the Pendik's lower-middle-class housing typology of the 1950s, which formed the dominant urban texture of the neighborhood during those years. She reveals the characteristics of this modern heritage through on-site observation, mapping, and interviews. Her efforts are critical in terms of documenting the remaining houses, tracing the footprints of this typology in the existing multi-layered urban texture, and comprehending the impact of the accelerated urban transformation process on this modern heritage.

Indeed, Istanbul is home to many housing examples of mid-century modernism worth conservation. Among them, Levent Houses has a special place. Built as a suburban mass-housing project and now having a presence in Istanbul's hot commercial core, Levent Houses represent an authentic interpretation of "other modernisms." The chapter titled "The Ethos of Mid-Century Modern in Istanbul and San Francisco: A Comparative Reading on Levent Houses and Eichler Homes" by Ahsen Özsoy and Hatice Sadıkoğlu Asan sheds light on 1950s residential culture in two different locations, representing two forms of "other modernisms" influenced by European modernism.

Identity and ethos/value systems of various geographies are critical in the creation of authentic and creative adaptations of the translation of modernism. In line with that, this chapter unfolds how modernism, which flourished in the 1920s in Europe, has been adapted in Istanbul and San Francisco in response to local conditions and resources. The authors uncover the ethos of the selected suburban projects of the 1950s: Levent Houses in Istanbul and Eichler Homes in San Francisco, both of which targeted middle-income groups through archival research, interviews, and site observations. The architectural value of the projects has been scrutinized through planning and design principles as well as representation and public visibility of the projects in media and publications of the period. That is followed by the analysis of the social and cultural value of the projects that comprise the conservation efforts and the perception of both dwellers and citizens. Özsoy and Sadıkoğlu Asan pursue the question of what does help to create and sustain the ethos of a project and put emphasis on the complex nature of such efforts.

While presenting authentic and unique examples of housing from various periods, Istanbul also struggles with the sameness of the built environment, and residential apartments take the lead as homogenizing agents in this regard. The last chapter of Part One, written by Hande Tulum Okur and Efsun Ekenyazıcı Güney, titled "Documenting the Evolutionary Process of Apartments in Kadıköy, Moda Between 1960–1980," aims to reveal the variety of apartments in Moda built between the 1960s and 1980s, ranging from unique and distinguished cases by prominent architects of the period and the repetitive standard productions of the build-and-sell strategy.

This chapter contributes to the historiography and documentation of housing, particularly the apartment typology of a specific era in Moda through archival research. Changes in laws and development plans cause social, demographic, and economic changes in the built environment, which are accompanied by changes in architectural features. The authors initially define the contextual background of urban transformation in Kadıköy district and relatively belated but recently accelerated transformation process in Moda. Stressing the impact of the property ownership (1964) law that triggered the production of apartments in the whole country, they trace the modernist architectural language of the period and its reflections on facades, spatial organization, and interior atmosphere through the selected showcases. Tulum Okur and Ekenyazıcı Güney draw attention to the fact that the Moda neighborhood is losing its character as the unique examples of 4–5-story apartments from the 1960 to 1980 period are demolished and facing the thread of homogenization.

The second part of the book includes chapters on the urban transformation of Istanbul from the past to the present, specifically through mega-projects and the ideology behind them, with a special emphasis on the twenty-first century. The chapters in this part scrutinize Istanbul from new angles as the primary scene, target, and playground for neoliberal market acts and actors.

The first chapter of Part II, "Mega Projects and Urban Transformation" by Ali Devrim Işıkkaya, "Eternal Now of Urban Metastasis in Istanbul," narrates the bewildering transformation of the city of Istanbul, referring to the thresholds defined by İhsan Bilgin but reinterpreting them through powerful biological metaphors, metastasis and metamorphosis in a multi-layered and stimulating way. Considering Istanbul as an alive metabolism, he uses the metaphors of urban metastasis and metamorphosis to explain, epitomize, and discuss the fragmented, divisible, patch-work like spatial growth of the city, alluding to the destructive nature of the medical-architectural analogies he employs.

Işıkkaya's narrative invites the reader to re-imagine the thresholds through metaphors referring to the political, social, and economic turning points and actors involved in decision-making processes; the investments, urban scenarios, projects, and implementations that have so far contributed to the erasing-rewriting policies proposed by Işıkkaya. He asserts that this vicious cycle, besides the reductionist way of re-imagining and re-designing the city as a brand in the competitive global market, erodes the physical and social identity and urban memory of Istanbul. Işıkkaya proposes the conceptualization of another biological metaphor, "urban tropism," alluding to its responsive and positive connotations instead of urban metastasis, for a more sustainable, peaceful, democratic development and growth. This chapter provides fertile ground and a fresh, holistic perspective for more focused readings of Istanbul's urban transformation in the subsequent chapters.

Infrastructure projects have a significant impact on the macro-form of cities, and Istanbul is no exception. Water-related projects, such as the Bosphorus bridges and the recent Istanbul Canal project, which has been on the agenda for the last decade, are especially important for Istanbul, which separates and extends two continents.

The following chapter, titled "From Infrastructural Developmentalism to Mega-Projects: "The Istanbul Canal,"" by Ahmet Sezgin and Nilay Ünsal Gülmez, investigates how the politicization of infrastructure projects, their scope and scale, as well as motivations and promotion methods, have evolved in Turkey from the 1950s to the present. The authors argue that the Istanbul Canal is a forerunner of a new approach to mega-projects not only due its goals and scale, but also because it conforms to a recent global trend of new city construction aimed at boosting real-estate markets. After summarizing the right-wing legacy of infrastructure projects as part of developmentalist rhetoric, particularly through the Bosphorus bridges, and examining the shifting context of mega-projects where real-estate meets gigantism, Sezgin and Ünsal Gülmez conduct a concise discourse analysis to decipher the codes of this new approach to mega-projects and the Istanbul Canal narrative.

The chapter assesses Istanbul Canal's global positioning in the context of ongoing city branding strategies. According to the authors, the concept of "smart cities" emerged in Turkey at the same time as the initial announcement of the Istanbul Canal project. Since its inception, the project's public promotion has relied on the concept of "smart city," as well as a more recent one, "horizontal urbanism," as indicators of its main goal, besides its infrastructural value as a continuation of the right-wing developmentalist tradition as a supporting theme. In line with this new approach to mega-projects, the authors pose critical questions for the City's future.

Istanbul, as the center of social, cultural, political, urban and housing developments have been redefined in parallel with the globalization discourses, and in the 2000s, housing came onto the scene with different forms of presentation. In the chapter entitled "Urban Development Processes and the Changing Housing Pattern in Istanbul: The Case of Fulya Neighborhood" Pınar Şahin mentions that urban space has become the place where capitalism manifests itself in its most concrete form, and housing has become a commodity structured with rent-oriented strategies for the reproduction of capital. Accordingly, the Fulya neighborhood, this in-between region, as a remarkable representative of the multi-layered urban and housing development, located in the core of the city, is subject to this chapter. In this context, this chapter aims to examine the changing morphology of the housing patterns in the Fulya neighborhood through the phenomenon of the urbanization of Istanbul divided into thresholds, where significant changes are experienced in the political, socio-cultural, and spatial contexts in Turkey.

In the beginning of a new era of urban and housing concepts, high-rise buildings have been very popular particularly in the last period of the twentieth century. The vertical housing projects located particularly in Istanbul, Ankara and Izmir metropolises of Turkey, offer a new domestic safe and isolated lifestyle for people from new upper-middle class that emerged in the twenty-first century, who started to prefer high-rise residential buildings as accomodational space for many reasons such as security, location close to the financial center, and the inclusion of services likewise in many metropolises of the world. The aim of the chapter, entitled "A Comparative Study of Contemporary Strategies in High-Rise Housing Markets in Istanbul, Ankara and Izmir" written by Naz Gümüşeli, is to analyze Istanbul's high-rise residential marketing strategies, which consist of four variables namely price, product, promotion, and place, and compare them with other metropolitan areas, Izmir and Ankara in Turkey. Within the scope of the chapter, high-rise residential buildings of twenty floors or more that have been completed and entered the market in the last seven years, are examined.

Last but not least, the third part of the book "What Is Next? Future Reflections" seeks to shed light on future prospects with regards to housing practices. The needs and expectations of new generations as a source of progressive approaches, as well as the ways in which some recent trends have been translated and experienced, are discussed here. When we first started thinking about how to structure a book about housing transformation in Istanbul, pandemics were not on the World's agenda. However, since the end of 2019, it has revived long-forgotten memories about the impact of plaques on the built environment, paving the way for rethinking housing. As a result, some chapters in Part III discuss the effects of the pandemic and other potential crisis scenarios on certain groups' dwelling practices and housing production.

Considering the variety of accomodational options for students in metropolis Istanbul and specific needs/wants of the new generation "Z" born between 1995 and 2010, and having different behaviors and desires, in the chapter entitled "Housing Preferences for Generation Z Students: A Case Study in Istanbul" Arda Çalışkan focuses on two main questions: "Which of the many accommodation options offered for students is more suitable for Generation Z?," and "What kind of a place do they want to live in?". The study is based on outcomes of the survey on generation Z students attending a university in Istanbul, in order to better understand their wishes and desires, to make inferences on their housing preferences. This chapter also aims to make a brief definition and overview of generation Z characteristics in case of the transformation and types of student accommodations around the world, Turkey and particularly in Istanbul. Moreover, Arda Çalışkan in his chapter discusses on how twenty-first century houses and accommodation types should be adapted to new generations' preferences which might include a nomadic tendency and preference to live in motion rather than belonging to a place.

During the pandemic situation home space has taken on the meaning and functions of working, learning, playing, feeling safer, opening up to the world, and exploring the environment virtually. This transformation can be described as a total center of human life, the reflection of individualization in home space where many different functions overlap, expansion of the household into the city while transforming into a self-referenced independent space, and the change of the interior spatial setup. In this context the changing student-home-school relationship, between home and person in terms of sense of belonging, social interaction, and place-making practices is the main conceptual triad of the chapter entitled "From School to Home: Changing of Home-School Relation in Architecture and Design Students in Istanbul with The Pandemic" written by Büşra Atam. As a result, the following chapter discusses the transformation of education, as well as the transformation of home settings and the meaning of home due to pandemics, in order to shed light on the student-home-school relationship based on the survey conducted with 193 students who are all studying at Bahçeşehir University Faculty of Architecture and Design.

The chapter entitled "Smart Transformation of Housing in Istanbul as a Resilience Response to Crises Scenarios" written by Suzan Girginkaya Akdağ and Berna Sayar, deals with the crisis scenarios that may cause problems on the social, political, and economic systems, as well as contemporary metropolitan solutions such as smart city concepts and technologies branding. As Girginkaya Akdağ and Sayar mention, in addition to smart city applications, smart buildings and smart spaces using advanced ICT enabling sustainable design, construction, operation and maintenance of buildings, are increasingly becoming a necessity. Moreover, the smart home has become a key solution for fulfilling different customer needs and expectations including sustainable (active-passive), green, environmental-friendly, certificated, age-friendly, assisted and/or healthy housing and architecture along with urban development. This chapter firstly underlines the need for smart cities and buildings with increasing intelligence which is urgent for all cities in Turkey and Istanbul.

In this context, this chapter explains the transformation of housing architecture in Istanbul to smart and intelligent buildings as a resilience response to crisis scenarios and investigates the impact of safe life scenarios on the smart housing market and trends in Istanbul. Accordingly, it does focus on the "smart" transformation of housing in Istanbul and conduct a pilot study on three smart housing projects in Anatolian side district Kadıköy, located along the Istanbul-Baghdad railway line that has always been an indicator of the modernization process of the city. The outcomes of the mapping and comparison of projects demonstrate the strengths and weaknesses of the existing smart home and intelligent building practices in responding to disaster scenarios such as major earthquakes, rapid climate change, new migration waves, recurrent pandemic waves, and subsequent economic crises expected in the metropolitan region of Istanbul, as well as the opportunities and threats in the real estate market.

The tiny house concept as one of the alternative ways of living today, became a valid topic amongst recent housing discussions particularly during the times of Covid-19 pandemic. Motivations such as environmental concerns, the cycle of debt related with contemporary, primarily American lifestyles, frustration concerning excessive materialism, and its potential as a small structure for housing the homeless and poor are considered as reasons for the growth of the tiny house movement which has been also criticized for promoting an overly romantic outlook for down-sizing, sustainability, and affordability. Consequently, according to Gizem Akdemir who investigates the tiny house movement in Istanbul in the chapter entitled "Tiny Living in A Megacity: Exploring the Emergence of Tiny-House Movement in Istanbul," this also affected the increase of tiny houses as temporary and mobile housing concepts in urban areas in Turkey and in its most crowded city, Istanbul.

Therefore, this chapter mainly aims to understand the tiny house movement and its manifestations in Istanbul. After providing a brief history of the concept's emergence, the study intends to explore how the situation differ or reflect in Istanbul by sharing the outcomes of a short survey about Istanbul's leading tiny house developers such as Vagoon House, Gorgor House, Yako Groups. It is hoped to shed light on the situation in Istanbul and a discussion is initiated about the future of tiny homes, in terms of examination of the existence of affordable, sustainable and mobile housing concepts in Istanbul.

Nilay Ünsal Gülmez & Ali Devrim Işıkkaya

Part I
Scenes and Narratives of Housing (In) Transformation

Emine Görgül

1 Istanbul During the Glorious Thirty (1945–75): Mobilization of the Middle-Class and Emergence of Motorways as Tools for Re-Shaping the Society and the Littoral Periphery

Introduction

Doubtlessly, the long twentieth century encompassed infinite technological, social, political, ideological, and economic advancements that were all leading us to today's modern society. Besides, the mid-century also addressed to a significant interval, a relief-full breakthrough in this broader history. During the recuperation processes, the destructive consequences of World Wars and socio-political struggles and economic difficulties were resolved and replaced with wealthy and peaceful days of the 1950s. Foursatié (1979) named this exact interval as the Glorious Thirties -*Les Trente Glorieuses*-, with multiple emphases counting the heydays of a *dolce vita*, in the free-liberal world of capitalism (Hobsbawm, 1995). On one side, this critical interval acted as a subliminal realm by seeding the expedient characteristics of the capitalist approach contrary to the partaker communist half of the globe. Then again, this interval also appeared as a transition from modern societies into consumerist societies in the liberal world. So, the *zeitgeist* of the post-war epoch deepened the evident split between two-polar world order, while fueling the dialectics between the liberal ideologies and capitalist economies contrary to the communist ideology and the statist economies. However, in each camp, architecture became the retainer of this neck-to-neck race between the sides via the construction of various infrastructure and capacity-building projects together with housing, mobility, leisure, and hospitality. Evidently, during the mid-century, these projects became the key features of the broader rivalry, acting as spatial-political agents of the states, shaping the physical and social realm in each ideological camp.

Indeed, both the Truman Doctrine and the establishment of the Marshall economic aid program for the beneficiary alliances of the US were the fundamental acts that were not only shaping this polarization in the global realm (i.e. the birth of NATO and Warsaw Pact) but also boosting the economies and production systems of the alliance countries. Nevertheless, they also influenced the policies of architecture, urbanism, engineering, and infrastructure webs. Being a member of NATO, Turkey was also a recipient of the Marshall economic aid and the pursuer of the liberal economic policies. Thus, the 1950s also signaled the epoch when the socio-economic transformation of Turkish society was highly under the influence of the American culture. Hence the modernization of Turkish society almost became the Americanization of the nation (Adalet, 2018; Gürel, 2019). Again, following the transatlantic impact, the production of both the public sphere and the construction of the welfare state was actualized through the ways and means of the architectural realm.

In light of these policies emerging in the 1950s Turkish socio-political scene, this chapter aims to discuss how the mobility-based urban development policies of the DP-Democrat Party in the mid-century re-shaped the urban periphery, significantly the littoral developments. So, while focusing on the drastic impetus of these macro-strategies in the re-organization of the society as well the city of Istanbul (Akpınar, 2010a), the chapter aims to decipher the littoral transformation of the city via examining the emergence of novel dwelling sites for summer housing and leisure spaces -like beach clubs and sea-resorts or hybrid leisure accommodations like KİT- Public Economic Enterprises' summer camps or holiday complexes-.

In this scope, the two major inter-city motorways, the coastal roads along the waterfront and the European transit road D100 are taken as reference lanes in tracing the spatial and socio-political transformation. More specifically, the southern coastal line of the city, both on the south-east axis of Maltepe, Kartal, Dragos, Tuzla, Bayramoğlu, İzmit axis, and on the south-west axis of Çekmece, Avcılar, Güzelce, Silivri, Tekirdağ are the spotlighted destinations revealed. Besides, the impact of the mobility policies both on the modernization of the society and the middle class also constitute the complementary discussion of this chapter.

In other words, by developing a multiple-reading based on Istanbul's transforming urban condition between the 1950s until the 1970s, this chapter scrutinizes the spatial-political impact of the new motorways as political instruments of both the liberalist policies of the time and the state's apparatus in re-shaping the urban realm of Istanbul. On the meta-level, the chapter investigates how these infrastructures work as state apparatuses to re-position Turkey in alliance with American politics and fueling the consumerist policies as a part of dolce-vita welfare state processes. Besides, on the mezzo-scale, the chapter investigates how these infrastructure projects steered the urban planning policies for population growth and expanding land use. In addition, the triggering capacities of infrastructural growth were also dismantled following both the formation of urban sprawl areas and the emergence of summer houses/

secondary housing phenomenon. Accordingly, the re-defined dialectics of center-periphery, labor, and leisurescape tensions are opened into a discussion. Finally, on the micro-level of the citizens' realm, this chapter argues how the consequences of mobilization and motorway infrastructures contributed to the modernization of the individual. In this respect, the transformation of mid-century Turkish society is discussed concerning the transfiguring metropolitan-life via the introduction of novel outdoor leisure spaces, urban mobility, and the car-ownership and mapping the driveways out from the city.

The Postwar Condition and the Birth of a New Era: The 1950s' Turkey on the Crossroads

The post-war condition addressed to an epoch of a quick but fundamental recuperation giving birth to novel political strategies, alliances, and economic growth models. These were also decisive in the modernization of the social realm, everyday life, and finally in spatial change. So, during this period, in the liberal world, we encounter two relatively distinct but colliding aspects of the states in the constitution and implementation of the economic policies: the welfare state and the consumerist liberal state. These two aspects were also effective in the establishment of the physical and social infrastructures of modern society during the post-war period.

Fundamentally, the notion of *welfare state* politics became the vision for the post-war governments within the trans-Atlantic bloc, advocating the necessity of "social support [for the citizens] extending from the cradle to the grave" (Gough, 2008). As this inclusive model defined the basis of the post-war order, it also introduced the essentials of the contemporary society such as; wage regulations, pension fund, free education, healthcare, and even further the well-being of the citizens claiming the paid vacation.[1] The idea of paid vacation further triggered the notion of leisure and the mobility of the middle-class during the mid-century.[2] The growing importance of leisure has been a long-going discussion within

---

1 Beveridge's seminal report from 1942 emphasized the essences of the overall transition and the shifting relations in each approach but mostly buttressing to the welfare state policies. In this respect, he marked the reward and scarification principles as the essences of this novel era and the contemporary modern society (Beveridge, 1942).

2 The welfare state is crucial in the development and fostering of the middle-class and its consumerist tendencies. Consequently, these tendencies also impacted the global tourism movements of the mid-century, together with all leisure-related activities in the practical level of both hospitality as a sector and second-house/vacation-house ownership.

the frame of modernization. In this respect, Lefebvre's (1991) critique against the everyday life and the modernization of the mid-century western societies also emerged as another milestone criticizing the intertwined relations of the production, inhabitation, and leisure. While advocating the latter as the essence of the individuation processes of the modern subject, Lefebvre further positions the leisure spaces as a core milieu in the modernization processes of the society. According to Lefebvre, leisure spaces enable the production of the "contemporary other" which is the formation process of the modern individual (Lefebvre, 1991: 29–42). As a result, the self emerges in-between spatiality of leisure among the former clustering milieus of work and family.

So, during the post-war period, this vision of extensive support by the state comprehensively recovered the fundamental lack of physical and social infrastructures such as housing, education, healthcare, nursery, production spaces, motorways, transportation systems, and many other major capacity-building projects, as well as the web of leisure infrastructures. So, the new spatial programs being introduced by these emerging infrastructures further blended with the physical and socio-economical mobilization of the middle class. This interaction gave way to the birth of modern aesthetics of the mid-century, so did the numerous spatial typologies encompassing leisure hospitality and summer/vacation houses. Unquestionably, this vast web of novel infrastructures either directly or indirectly served to the institutionalization of the soft and subliminal emergence of the state through this developed nexus.

On the other hand, simultaneous with the welfare state policies and state-driven organization of the post-war society, the impact of the Keynesian macro-economic model and the throw-away culture was also the key strategies in the trans-Atlantic bloc, fueling the liberal capitalist approach (Bullock, 2015; Whiteley, 1987). The birth of throw-away culture was closely tied with the aftermath of the 1920s economic crisis, whereas the promotion of consumption was seen as the key to increasing productivity and boosting economic growth.[3] The practical mechanism of leading the society to consume more was resolved through the introduction of the notion of fashion and being up-to-date via seasonally changing design of goods even very essentials from refrigerators to cars etc. (Whiteley, 1987). Whilst, the advertisement of each novel model of products via reproduced images either in the printed media or other publicity milieus emerged as the creative way of marketing and manipulating the consumption

3 Pursuing the Great Depression, in 1936 John Maynard Keynes introduced his macro-economic model for economic growth based on the consumption-production chain and the market strategies (Keynes, 1936).

trends of the society (Figure 1.1a and 1.1b). Remarkably, each targeted user profile was professionally defined and addressed in the ads so that a clear definition of gender roles was also visible. As the American local market was the initial goal of this economic growth, later the global market became the ultimate target of the producers, superposing the capitalist structure of the Industrial movement.

Figure 1.1 a and 1.1b: Vintage advertisements of 1956 Cadillac Sixty Special Sedan Classic and a Hi-Fi from the 1950s. Source: https://www.pinterest.fr/pin/824581012994192454/ and https://tr.pinterest.com/pin/742108844829133785/ (Open source).

In short, during the interval between 1945 and 1975, on the global scale, on one side, the welfare state policies took care of citizens via its extensive web of infrastructure and provided fair accessibility and rights almost in a socialist manner while securing equity in the distribution of wealth to every stakeholder in the broadest sense. On the other hand, the consumerist aspects promoted the liberal capitalist transformation of society while mobilizing and stratifying it based on varying socio-economical standards. These two aspects of a non-communist but affordance-based welfare utopia model melted in the presence of the societal modernization of the 1950s until the 1970s, and apparently through the spatial agency of architecture and numerous infrastructure projects with motorways and leisure infrastructures.

Subsequently, these blended tendencies of both the welfare state and American consumerism transmitted and molded into a merely hybrid model in the Turkish context. This hybrid model intermingled both the earlier statist principles of the 1930s Republic and the Democrats' novel political manifestations. In other words, while re-positioning the 1930s republican-state into a liberalist welfare-state, the DP also applied keen consumerist policies, supporting merely the Keynesian approach.[4] In this respect, pursuing the post-war economic policies and trans-Atlantic Marshall aid, Turkey became part of the global export and import policies. So, shifting from a statist economic model of growth into an import-substitution industrialization model, the American cars and the motorways became the macro-import materials of Turkey, during the 1950s (Beylan, 2011) (Figure 1.2a and 1.2b).

However, again during the DP turn, we also observe the supportive presence of the state being as the planner, organizer, and regulator in the constitution of fundamental physical and social infrastructures from the perspective of the statist aspect while enhancing the social standards of its citizens and articulating the vision of over-all wealth.

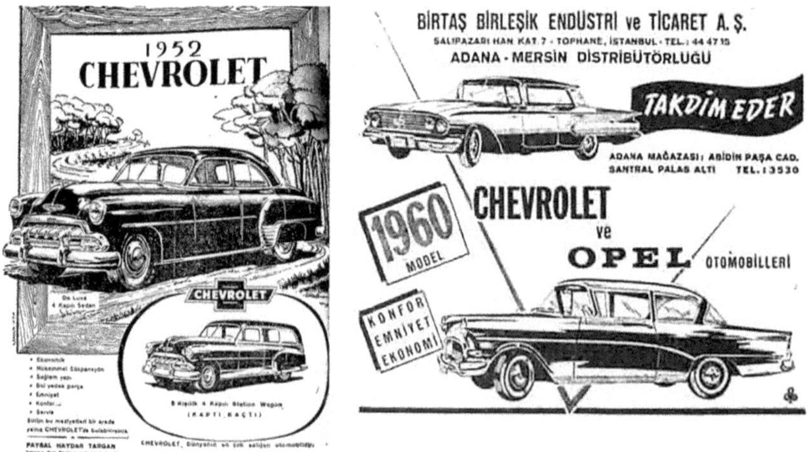

Figure 1.2 a and 1.2b: Automobile advertisements appearing on Turkish newspapers during the 1950s–1960s. Source: https://www.haberturk.com/eski-istanbul-un-zarafeti-1766079 and http://gazetearsivi.milliyet.com.tr/Arsiv/1960/03/ (Web source).

4 To do so, they looked for international capital holders and transnational investments in Turkey. For instance, local investments of Ford automotive, Pfizer pharmaceuticals, General Electronics, Hilton chains, etc. could be asserted within this scope.

This *mélange* model of the DP and its multi-fold strategies could be traced via its nationwide infrastructure projects (Akpınar, 2010a).[5] In addition to the extensive scope of modernization implementations in diverse fields such as agriculture and tourism, the government's defined focus on maintaining the physical and social mobility of the classes and individuals through constructing new motorways and leisure infrastructures was a significant attempt in concretizing interfaces for fostering and manipulating the desires and behavior of the middle-class, which further acted as the apparatuses of state-space-nexus. Gülhan (2014) defines the presence of the state-space nexus as "the ultimate agent of redistribution" of the sovereign power, operating through regulations drawn by the state-power. Accordingly, concerning the built environment, as an omnipresence apparatus of the state and its controlling role, Brenner (2004) acknowledges the inter-dependence and transitive power relations of state and urban space after the 1960s. He further reveals how systematic territorialization and nationalist discourses in reciprocity were knitted with the utilization of architectural space to develop a broader web of spatio-political relations (Brenner, 2004). In this respect, the sovereignty of the state emerged through the nexus or web of concrete spatiality that it constituted.

Therefore, to discuss the critical role of architecture in forming the post-war state-space-nexus, the DP's web of mobility projects in Istanbul, and its consequences on the littoral development around the city are asserted within this perspective. So, departing from Blau's (2015, pp. 29–47) question of "what did the welfare state do for architecture and what did architecture do for the welfare state?," the mélange economic and political model of the DP, the spatio-political agency of mobility and leisure became the essential apparatus in reshaping and representing the post-war state and the society in Turkey.

Transformation of Istanbul and Changing Urban Condition

Following the global impact of postwar politics, the 1950s addressed a significant interval in Turkey's political scene, giving way to the alteration of the early-republican single-party-ruling social-state mechanism into the multi-party parliamentary system. Based on its political agenda, the new ruling party the

5 As it is known, the party's president Menderes, put a stamped mark on mid-century Turkey with extensive construction projects of motorways, dams, factories, real estate development, and novel public spaces, which all aimed to serve the modernization of the society of its time. About the immense urban transformation operations of the Democrat Party please see Akpınar (2010a).

DP operated in a three-fold pattern to stratify and organize the spatio-political realm. First, the geopolitical manifestation of growth and leadership is constituted via reconstructing the image of modernization and wealth through the big cities (while extensively utilizing image-making strategies). Second, concerning the national economic policies, urban growth was prioritized in the big cities. Thus, real estate projects and the development of the urban periphery were promoted. Third, novel master planning facilities were performed to legitimize and regulate the future growth of the cities. Whilst, pursuing this three-fold strategic plan, the DP oversaw the three functional programs *of housing, mobility, and leisure* as infrastructural elements or tools to re-design the spatio-political realm and maintain the continuity of state-space nexus via their presence. Hand in hand with each functional program, the DP further utilized novel planning tactics to activate and maintain its effectiveness. In this way, implementations such as; developing novel districts and dwelling sites, enhancing urban inter-connectedness among these new nodes via developing motorways, rising interest and appetize for mobility through promoting the notion of leisure, and manipulating users' desires via the reproduced image of the leisure experience in the milieus of popular culture, printed media and everyday life could be all taken into account as the basic tactical interventions that the DP utilized. Evidently, similar to the three-fold strategic plan, a strong cohesion is visible among the tactics, so that each tactic also existed in an intertwined way to connect the functional program elements of *housing, mobility, and leisure* into a broader unity of mentioned three-fold pattern to stratify and organize the spatio-political realm.

When the planning strategies of the DP are elaborated more into detail, as an initial step, on the geopolitical level, it emphasized modernization, global integration, and internationalization of Turkey as its precise goal. Then, envisioning the country as an oasis between the east and the west (Akpınar, 2010b). Turkey projected as the new leader and the peaceful state of the Balkans and the Middle East. Accordingly, the DP's visionary breakthrough lit the fire for an extensive makeover movement all around the country, paving the way to a series of drastic changes in every field of life from everyday standards and individuals' lifestyles to major infrastructure and urban redevelopment projects. Albeit, due to Turkey's involvement in the North-Atlantic bloc and to the Truman Doctrine as an alliance, definite regulations and constraints applied to the national development and infrastructure projects[6]. These parameters

6 Marshall aid plan introduced not only financial support to the associating countries for the post-war recuperation, but also it regulated the content and the capacity of industrialization, production, and market economy among the countries within Europe and the Middle East.

were affective tools in constituting and fueling the DP's political and economic program as well as their immense spatio-political applications during the mid-century.[7]

Accordingly, Istanbul appeared as the epicenter of all these extensive transformations, and the scene of systematic de/reterritorialization operations of the DP government. Similarly, the DP leader and the prime minister Adnan Menderes appeared as the chief architect of these stamp marking urban renewal operations. The systematic planning and functional transformation of both the metropolitan realm and the coastline of Istanbul are shaped during this interval, based on the DP's premises for global modernization and integration, ideological transformation to liberalism, and finally the mobilization of classes. The extensive inland discharges and reterritorializations, or littoral landfills in Istanbul and vast infrastructure constructions were the significant projects in the actualization of the state-space-nexus in the Istanbul scale during the DP reign. Like Akpınar argues, the demolition and replacement of old neighborhoods inside the old-city and shifting demographic structure of the settlements, or likewise, the construction of main arteries of Millet and Vatan avenues in a Haussmannian fashion could be countable as the initial attempts in changing the existing layout and organization of the city (Akpınar, 2010b) (Figure 1.3a and 1.3b). Besides, the reproduced images of demolitions and motorway constructions appeared along with the chief architect Menderes' image from the construction sites were acted as genuine promotions of the progress and the modernization (Figure 1.4a). Nevertheless, these reproduced images of both the politicians and the spatio-political operations were not only limited in the local scale, but it also turned into an extensive image reproduction that depicted the overall national projects as well as the international contacts and global synchronization. For instance, apart from Menderes' local visits to the construction sites for capacity building projects like dams, airports, etc. (Gülmez, 2015), his foreign visits to international projects' sites were also emerged as the circulating images to enhance the image-maker and constructor role of the political leader at the time (Figure 1.4b).

7 It is also worth mentioning that -from the counter perspective- Turkey was unable to mobilize the Marshall fund neither to any investment in technology development nor on heavy industry, other than agriculture, infrastructure projects -such as housing, mobility, and capacity building projects- and basic service sectors. Thus, the prioritization of tourism as the major sector in national economic development derives from these global constraints and motivations.

Figure 1.3 a and 1.3b: Menderes's demolitions and the construction of Vatan and Millet Avenues inside the old-city. Source: http://www.eskiistanbul.net (Open source).

Figure 1.4 a and 1.4b: Menderes's reproduced image on the printed media, a planner, a diplomat, the prominent figure of the post-war period. Source: https://v3.arkitera.com/h53810-istanbula-vurulan-darbeler.html, and https://egazete.cumhuriyet.com.tr/oku/192/1955-05-06/1 (Web source).

In addition to geopolitical concerns and reconstructing the image of modernization, the construction of novel motorways also emerged as an essential tactic in enhancing mobility and urban interconnectedness. So, as a functional apparatus, the motorway infrastructures simply orchestrated the interconnection between different parts of the city and enabled the vicinity and coherence among the districts. Hence, the shifting spatial syntax of the city was the broader impact that the mobilization provided for the urban realm. In this respect, the mobility and the increasing velocity affected the regimes of perception via ways and means of moving images. Thus, the mobility of either the eye of the passenger or

Figure 1.5 a and 1.5b: Construction of the littoral roads and infills by the Bosporus and Marmara coastline. Source: https://kassamstrateji.files.wordpress.com/2013/01/sahil-yolu.jpg (Web source) and https://commons.wikimedia.org/wiki/File:Tarabya,_%C4%B0stanbul_(12966899674).jpg (Open source).

the driver being encapsulated within the cabin of the automobile provided novel perception and cognition of the city and its image. In addition to the movement and speed, the presence of novel pathways or trajectories also became important. Both the constructed littoral and land roads provided novel trajectories presenting fresh viewpoints of the cityscape and enabled the citizens to develop a novel awareness of the city and the waterfront (Figure 1.5a and 1.5b).

When it is asserted from a macro-perspective, Turkey demonstrated a similar lane of progress in comparison to the mid-century European context, on behalf of rehabilitation of the big cities and improving the standards of mobility and motorway infrastructures (Üngür, 2017). This inevitably triggered both the realm of infrastructure -the motorway network- and the vehicles -significantly the individual car ownership and the motorways- which at the end shaped and enhanced the mobility of the mid-century society.[8] In this case, both the impact of Americanization and the trans-Atlantic funds purposefully boosted individual mobility and vehicle ownership among the middle-class (Üngür, 2017). Mid-century Turkey also marked itself within these economic and political strategies. So, initially in the 1950s the imported American cars -like Ford, MG, etc.-,

8 This is a multifaceted process, related to both the articulated wealth of the country, so the citizens, and the egalitarian accessibility of the resources in the market condition in resonance with the consumerism.

later in the 1960s, local productions -like Anadol, Tofaş, etc- emerged as the principal actors of the nation's mobilization (Bedir, 2002; Yılmaz et al., 2017). Besides, the implicit and explicit visibility of the cars were the decisive factors in the promotion of the products while seeding and forming the user demand for ownership. For instance, dating back to the late 1920s, the earliest Ford Cars' Company assembly hall and showroom in Istanbul, which was located at Tophane, right after the Karaköy pier, in the very heart of the city could be mentioned in this way (Odman, 2011) (Figure 1.6). Consequently, the growing network of car distributors became visible in the popular spots of the city, mostly in the vicinity of entertainment and nightlife leisure escapes. For instance, the auto gallery at the Taksim square right under the famous nightclub and restaurant *Kristal Gazinosu*; emerged as the central spot of novel intertwined relations and subliminal coding of leisure and mobility, car ownership, and entertainment, modernization, and wealth. Nevertheless, the reproduced images of people posing with the fashionable cars and mobility of the modern subject among the view of Istanbul motorways became the iconic visual narratives circulating on the magazines and movies of the time (Figure 1.7).

Figure 1.6: Ford Motor car assembly hall and gallery in Karaköy 1925–1944. Source: https://otomobil.haber7.com/otogundem/haber/2328163-kucuk-detroit-tophane (Web source).

Figure 1.7: Promotion of mobility and car ownership in mid-century Turkey via magazines and popular culture. Source: *Hayat* Journal cover from 1959 https://tr.pinterest.com/pin/399413060696417966/ (Open source).

Undoubtedly, the use of media and diverse milieus of popular culture and everyday life, to promote and circulate the reproduced images of mobility, leisure, and their experiences were the key tactics of the liberal state policies that were also deployed by the DP, to foster an interest and an appetizer within the society. On the other hand, going beyond the fetish of woman figure as a gendered appetizer for consumerist policies towards car ownership and mobility; from a feminist perspective, the visibility of modern Turkish women image associated with the car image and her driver persona could be further read following the societal modernization of the nation and the established gender equity in the mid-century Turkish society. Even articulating the discussion into a further level, for instance, the iconic persona of a very well-known mid-century Turkish movie *Şöför Nebahat*-Driver Nebahat initially performed by Sezer Sezin and later re-performed by Turkey's most renowned actress Fatma Girik was a typical example of this feminist articulation of the roles (Figure 1.8).[9]

Figure 1.8: Scene from *Şoför Nebahat*-Driver Nebahat movie, 1960, dir. Metin Erksan. Source: https://www.haberturk.com/sofor-nebahat-maskulen-kadinin-mucadelesi-2654202 (Web source).

Beyond the popularization of the automobile image and its subliminal seeding into the contemporary life of the mid-century Turkish society -concerning multiple perspectives of global political concerns, national policies of the DP, economics, gender, and class-; the DP's policies for constant and purposed growth of the city emerged as the second fundamental plan or strategy in shaping the spatio-political realm. As Mattsson (2015) discusses, the mid-century European

9 The first *Şoför Nebahat* movie was shoot by director Metin Erksan in 1960, https://www.haberturk.com/sofor-nebahat-maskulen-kadinin-mucadelesi-2654202, https://film.iksv.org/tr/otuzyedinci-istanbul-film-festivali-2018/sofor-nebahat, whereas the second was re-shoot by director Süreyya Duru in 1970, https://www.tsa.org.tr/tr/film/filmgoster/1647/sofor-nebahat.

urban design and real-estate policies were also influenced and shaped in the presence of the growing availability of transportation facilities. The increased mobility of the middle-class either via motorway infrastructures and via promoting car ownership was enabling factors of urban growth and the development of both the suburbia and the satellite cities. These global consequences were felt in the mid-century urban transformation of Istanbul. In this respect, the visible impact of novel real-estate development projects just outside the city's existing footprint marked the existential transformation of the city and the emergence of the suburbia phenomenon and novel dwelling sites. For instance, the establishment of the Levent district in 1951 with the conceptualization of European garden-city life but mostly an American suburban family-style two-story houses, or Ataköy neighborhood in 1954 with another conceptualization of mass-housing or a satellite city of modern apartments were the projects to be stated. As each could be the focus of numerous academic studies, the most critical difference in-between the two housing projects was the emergence of the integrity between the housing and leisurescapes, which was introduced innovatively in the Ataköy project. So, using the advantage of being located both on the periphery and by the sea -in the vicinity of Bakırköy and Yeşilköy districts, where have been the renowned epicenter of sea-based activities with its golden seascape dating back to even the Byzantine times; the Ataköy project also introduced a modernly designed and constructed beach complex serving for the leisure activities that were open to the use of all Istanbulites at the time. This groundbreaking project became very popular among the citizens, whereas the reproduced images of the experiences were also effective in manipulating the leisurescapes around the city. Thus, beyond the conventional and institutional mass-housing developments of the time, the Ataköy project rendered the inception of modernly combined housing and seaside activities for the citizens, which was also being triggered by the rising mobility and wealth of the middle-class. Hand in hand with these possibilities, and the state's land development and construction strategies, by the mid-1950, immense littoral development projects were observed both on the east and west coasts of the Marmara Sea. This turn immediately objectified the accommodation of leisure-based activities and secondary housing move for summer or weekend use of the citizens. So, like the earlier planners and analysts of the city, Wagner or Prost envisioned, the citizens were enabled to access the overall hinterland of the city and fully experience the leisure after the articulation of a certain wealth, a certain ratio of car ownership and realization of motorway infrastructure. This transition immediately addresses the modernization of society, via its changing habitudes, seasonal use of the center, and periphery dialectics. This is discussed more in detail in the next section.

Nevertheless, following the two intertwined plans or strategies of geopolitical manifestation and urban renewal projects for the modernization of the city and the society, as well as the development and constructional move for constant and purposed growth of the city; on the third level the DP also utilized urban and regional planning facilities to institutionally legitimize the urban renewal actions and regulate the future growth of the city. Accordingly, the novel master plan of Istanbul was developed in 1956 to re-shape the city as a contemporary metropolitan area. This interdisciplinary and contemporary planning process of its time was executed through a broader dialog with international experts like Luigi Piccinato -the renowned architect, urban planner, and professor from La Sapienza University, Rome- and with the integration of local institutions and a group of experts comprising professors of urban planning departments from both Istanbul Technical University and the Academy of Fine Arts together with professionals and members of chambers. Pursuing the open city principles of CIAM Athens charter, -and also the former predictions of both Wagner and Prost-, Piccinato proposed a linear growth for the future of the city, consisting of diverse sub-centers for generating de-intensified settlements based on human-centered aspects. Doubtlessly, the re-planning and development of the coastline were also executed as part of this meta-planning. As Piccinato's master plan proposes the linear growth of the city in an east-west direction along the motorways (in-land and littoral), he further proposed the use of southern-coastline -the Marmara Sea shores- and the northern-coastline -the Black Sea shores- of the city as the potential destinations for leisure facilities and sea-based activities. Hand in hand with the institutional envisions and with the existing motorway infrastructures and the tendency of the citizens expanding towards both ends of the east-west urban fringe of the city, the districts beyond Maltepe on the west and Büyükçekmece on the east became the central spots for the littoral based peripheral development of the city.

Littoral Developments as the Way Out to the Sea

In resonance with global policies and the welfare turn, together with the DP's strategies and tactics for urban growth, the littoral periphery of Istanbul was reshaped under the impact of the sea and summer-based activities. Thus, the mid-1950s conceptualization of the waterfront of the Marmara Sea was envisioned as a destination reserved for leisurescapes, recreation facilities, and sea-based activities, beach clubs, resorts, and mostly summer houses or holiday complexes for an affordable vacation.

In this respect, two ends of the motorway axis, from Maltepe to Erdek shoreline on the west and from Büyükçekmece to Silivri shoreline on the east, became the epicenters of the littoral developments for the leisure activities. Yet, following the previously discussed mélange economic model of the DP period, these developments emerged through a blended financial model ranging from private ownership to public investors and state enterprises. For instance, privately invested summer houses designed in the modern fashion of the time by the well-known Turkish architects of the period, or summer housing cooperatives by groups of individuals of collectives, or recreation complexes or camps of the public enterprises of the state were the dominant archetypes on the sites.

The late nineteenth century was the interval when Istanbulites began to commute for the beach activities outside the city (Evren, 1994). Based on multi-cultural background and modernization, beach culture and sea hamams became popular social infrastructures for leisure among the citizens during the earlier decades of the twentieth century. And with the birth of the Republic and changing politics of the body, intimacy, and public sphere, the nakedness freed from the cultural and theological pressures, so that the modernly dressed bodies with swimming suits and robes became the indispensables of the beach culture and modern urban life. As it is acknowledged, during the 1900s, due to their coastline with natural beaches, Erenköy on the east, Yeşilköy, and Florya on the west, and Büyükdere-Sarıyer on the north were the initial districts of Istanbul, being popular among the citizens with their leisure and sea-based activities (Akçura, 2018). Despite their remote locations from the city center, the public transportation facilities, initially Şirket-i Hayriye ships, then commuter trains enabled the accessibility of the broader crowds to the site for their daily travels to the beach.

However, the fundamental transformation in the use of the urban waterfront and re-configuration of littoral planning along the southern coastline of the city emerged during the 1950s, together with the shifting moral and political climate as well as socio-economical possibilities of the time. The notion of the weekend, weekend-mobility and weekend-houses were the frequent issues that were appearing on the professional journal *Arkitekt* as well as popular culture magazines such as *Yedigün* and *Hayat* beginning with the late 1930s (Arkitekt, 1935), but with an increased emphasis in the 1950s (Arkitekt, 1952a and b). The images depicting the modernist aesthetics of the weekend-houses or summer-houses were also associated items of these articles, that were, directly and indirectly, shaping the taste of the readers at the same time (Figure 1.9a and 1.9b). Pursuing these descriptive briefs, by the mid-century we begin to witness both the acceleration of constructions around the coastal periphery of Istanbul, simultaneously with the publication of the private weekend or summer house projects on the *Arkitekt* journal (Figure 1.10).

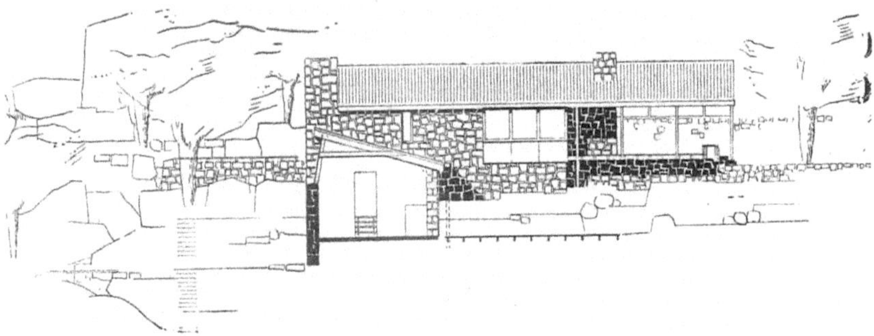

Figure 1.9 a and 1.9b: The images appearing on Arkitekt journal depicting the modernist aesthetics of the weekend-houses. Source: 1935 *Arkitekt*, 4 (52) (Open Source).

Probably the initiation of this established movement for summerhouse ownership and seaside vacation around the Marmara coastal line was not only triggered by the translocation of Istanbulites to the seaside but also due to the rising interest of the bureaucrats from Ankara to access the waterfront for leisure activities. Like Kuru and Halu (2020) acknowledges, the initiation of *Ankara Housing Cooperative* in Maltepe-Dragos in 1947 was probably the first attempt in the emergence of the summer house cooperatives phenomenon, not only as a financial role model for the following cooperatives but also as an initial settler of the site -pursing the Maltepe Sürreya Beach-, attracting attentions of the following dwellers such as individual housing projects, cooperatives, camps and holiday complexes of the public enterprises.

Figure 1.10: A Cottage house in Küçükyalı, 1950. Source: *Arkitekt*, 5–6 (221–222) (Open Source).

In the late 1950s, the dwellings on the eastern coastline gradually expanded from Maltepe to Pendik, Tuzla, and then to Bayramoğlu districts. Havacılar Housing cooperative (Figure 1.11), at Çavuşoğlu-Cevizli, emerged as the second-largest summer house dwelling site at Kartal, on the neighboring of Maltepe. Apart from the motorway infrastructure, the existing railway system was also effective in the growth of the population on the site. In addition to the cooperative housing projects, the private housing projects significantly around Maltepe-Dragos district constituted the bigger portion of the settlements on the eastern coastline. The axis between Orhantepe-Dragos to Tuzla became the showcase of mid-century modern aesthetics of leisure and also the stage for professional visibility of the noteworthy Turkish architects of the time such as; Emin Necip Uzman, Feridun Akozan, Mehmet Ali Handan, Ercümend Bigat, Abdurrahman Hancı, Alpay Aşkun, Ali Muslubaş, Ersen Gürsel, Mehmet Konuralp in chronological order of their practices on the site (Kuru, 2018).[10]

10 Probably Feridun Akozan was one of the most renowned architects working in the Kartal-Orhantepe region and produced many private houses in between the 1950s and 1970s (Arkitekt, 1969).

Figure 1.11: Havacılar Cooperative housing, from 1960s. Source: Author's archive.

Doubtlessly, these private vacation houses not only challenged the profession of architecture but also paved the way to the post-CIAM collaboration of interdisciplinary design aspects, accommodating diverse fields of artistic production into the production of space. For instance, like in the Adnan Kunt House in Pendik (Arkitekt, 1968), the pioneering Turkish ceramic artist Füreya Koral was also included in the team as a "ceramist" among with architects Asım Mutlu, Utarit İzgi, Esat Suher all of whom were also the practicing academicians in State's School of Fine Arts-Istanbul at the time (Figure 1.12). On the other hand, like Sayar (1964) discussed, the mid-1960s was an epoch when the inquiry of "luxurious housing" became a question in the field of the construction industry, after the gradual saturation of affordable and mass-housing projects of the 1950s. Unquestionably, the private summer housing projects on the Maltepe-Pendik axis addressed these inquiries of the time. This tendency towards building -relatively- luxurious vacation houses of their times by the renowned architects was a long-term demand until the late 1980s (Table 1.1), when the district lost its leisurescape identity in the face of urban development areas due to the rising population threat of the big city.

Figure 1.12: Adnan Kunt House. Source: 1968 *Arkitekt*, 4 (332) (Open Source).

Table 1.1: Some stamp marking projects. Source: Prepared by the author.

Axis	Group	Name of the House/project	Date of Construct.	Location	Architect /Constructor
Maltepe-Tuzla Axis	Cooperatives and Housing Projects	Ankara Housing Cooperative	1947	Kartal-Orhantepe	
		Havacılar Housing Cooperative	late 1950s-1960s	Kartal-Çavuşoğlu	
		Petroliş Housing Cooperative	The 1970s	Kartal	
		Aydın Shoreline Housing	1976	Yalova	Cafer Bozkurt, Mustafa Kavadarlı
		Yüksel Shoreline Housing	1976	Yalova	Yüksel Okan
		Balıkçıkoyu Housing	1979	Tuzla	İlhan Arguvangil,Semih Kaya
	Private Houses	A Cottage House in Küçükyalı	1950	Küçükyalı	Hidayet Nejat Erer
		A Summer House in Pendik	1958	Pendik	Ercümend Bigat
		Maruf Önal House	1958	Bayramoğlu	Maruf Önal
		Feridun Akozan House	1963	Kartal-Orhantepe	Feridun Akozan
		Dr. İlhami Masar House	1963	Kartal-Orhantepe	Feridun Akozan
		A House in Maltepe	1964	Maltepe	Firuzan Baytop
		A Summer House in Orhantepe	1966	Kartal-Orhantepe	Ercümend Bigat and Alpay Aşkun
		Uzunoğlu House	1967	Küçükyalı	Muhteşem Giray
		Özgür House	1967	Küçükyalı	Muhteşem Giray
		Adnan Kunt House	1968	Pendik	Asım Mutlu, Utarit İzgi, Esat Suher
		Namık Yolga House	1971	Bayramoğlu	Çelik Alatur
		Ali Aksel house	1972	Kartal-Orhantepe	Abdurrahman Hancı
		Melih Esenbel House	1972	Kartal-Orhantepe	Mehmet Ali Handan
		A Summer House in Orhantepe	1980	Kartal-Orhantepe	Prof. Emin Necip Uzman
		A Summer House in Tuzla	1980	Tuzla	Prof. Emin Necip Uzman
		Zümrüt Akkoyunlu Villası	1987	Kartal-Orhantepe	Mehmet Konuralp
		B. Atabey House	1989	Kartal-Orhantepe	Ali Muslubaş and Sasnuhi Muşlıyan
		G. Çağlayan house	2008	Kartal-Orhantepe	Ali Muslubaş
		M. Naibi House	1993	Kartal-Orhantepe	Ersen Gürsel
	Public Enterp. for Holiday Resorts and Complex	PTT Summer Camp	1968-69	Kartal-Orhantepe	
		DSI Summer Lodgings	1968-69	Kartal-Orhantepe	
		Tekel Summer Camp	1970	Kartal-Orhantepe	
		SSK Summer Camp	1968-69	Kartal-Orhantepe	
		TEK Summer Camp	1968-69	Kartal-Orhantepe	
		T.C. İş Bank Holiday Complex	1970	Bayramoğlu	Yelken Kaya, Çelik Alatur
Büyükçekmece-Tekirdağ	Coopera tives and Housing Projects	Selimpaşa Touristik Shoreline Housing	1964	Selimpaşa	Yılmaz Sanlı, Yılmaz Tuncer, Güner Acar, Aydın Boysan
		A Holiday Resort Project	1978	Küçükçekmece	Necati İnceoğlu, Reşit Soley
		Kumburgaz Terrace Houses	1978	Kumburgaz	Hamdi Şensoy
	Private Houses	Three Houses in Kumburgaz	1964	Kumburgaz	Yılmaz Sanlı, Yılmaz Tuncer, Güner Acar
		A Summer House in Kumburgaz	1969	Kumburgaz	Osep Sarafoğlu
		A Summer House in Enez	1978	Enez	Ruşen Dora
		Başak Sigorta Recreation Resort	1970	Tekirdağ	Çelik Alatur

In addition to housing cooperatives and the fashionable private houses; the holiday complexes of the public enterprises constituted the other portion of the littoral developments for leisure facilities along the Kartal-Tuzla even down to the Erdek axis (Figure 1.13). As these complexes proposed relatively affordable leisure solutions, they also contributed to the collective amusement culture of the districts in which they existed with their evening facilities. Moreover, these resorts also served to the multiplicity of the user background in the districts, via accommodating guests coming from diverse cities but working for the same enterprises. In this way, these resorts also act as interfaces of the extended state-space-nexus one more time, a melting pot in re-arranging the habits of the society.

Figure 1.13: T.R. İş Bankası holiday complex, Bayramoğlu-Istanbul, the 1970s.
Source: Salt Archives, TMGCH00880002.

Simultaneous to the littoral developments on the east end of the Marmara Sea, the west end of the waterfront was also shaped similarly. The housing cooperatives or *sahil siteleri*-shoreline housing sites were the dominant typology shaping the Büyükçekmece-Silivri axis. Significantly, districts of Celaliye, Selimpaşa, and Silivri-Parkköy were developed in this way during the 1960s and 1970s (Arkitekt, 1964a and b). It is also traceable that the topic became fashionable even being translated into studio briefs at the universities like in the case of ITU by Prof. Necati İnceoğlu and Reşit Soley's studios (Arkitekt, 1977) (Figure 1.14). Besides, Kumburgaz appeared as a more popular destination for private houses, whereas the renowned architects of the time also took part in the site (Arkitekt, 1964a and b). Nevertheless, the holiday resort typology of the public enterprises equally emerged as a relevant model for this side as well. For instance, Başak Sigorta's holiday complex in Tekirdağ could be mentioned in this way (Arkitekt, 1970).

Figure 1.14: An Under-graduate Design Studio Project in İTÜ, Küçükçekmece-Istanbul. Source: 1977, Arkitekt, 2 (366) (Open Source).

To sum up, during the littoral development of Istanbul's coastal line between the 1950s and 1970s, all the three different categories of ownership models and the associating dwelling characteristics -private houses, cooperative houses, and holiday complexes of the public enterprises- appeared to be applied both on the east end and west end of the Marmara Sea. However, based on affordance, location, and user profile; private houses and holiday complexes of the public enterprises were more intense on the Maltepe-Tuzla axis. Doubtlessly, the peripheral vicinity of the site both to Istanbul and Ankara might be a reason for the agglomeration. In this scope, both the bureaucracy of Ankara and the leading figures of Turkish politics, diplomacy, and popular culture were the inhabitants of the site, as were the users of both the holiday complexes and the owners of the private houses. Yet, the transportation infrastructures of both motorways and railways were the further possibilities that enabled the easy and rapid transfer to the site. On the other side, along the Büyükçekmece-Silivri axis, housing cooperatives or shoreline housing sites were more popular than the experimental private housing practices. The socio-economic status of the users -mostly middle to middle-low income groups which are still the current owners of the houses- was also decisive in the development of the site (Yazgan, 2018). Besides, the D100 motorway and the commuters' bus lanes from Topkapı to Silivri were the only infrastructure and transportation options aside from the private cars. From a speculative perspective, the lack of an alternative in transportation probably enabled the development of a cooperative housing schema on the west end.

Concluding Remarks

Similar to the global changes, the post-war interval and its three-following decades were also a transition period both for Turkey and the Turkish society, based on multiple advancements in economic growth, reception of liberalism and capitalist policies as well as changing lifestyles due to increased wealth and mobility. Based on these multi-faced improvements, the social standards of the society were also re-transformed while affecting the perception and spaces of leisure and amusement and vice versa. Thus, on one side, as the motorway infrastructures acted as the interfaces of mobility and became both the mediums and tools for connecting and designing the urban periphery; on the other side, following the shifting notion of leisure and novel perception of living in a big city, the enhanced urban mobility paved the way to the weekend escapes and the inquiry of vacation houses.

So, hand in hand with the urban development projects of the DP and national policies, the coastal development of Istanbul was also shaped by the rising importance of leisure and mobility notions, so that the summer housing phenomenon became the symbol of mid-century modernization of the society living in the big cities. Doubtlessly, the two motorways axis, both the littoral motorway on the southern coastline overarching towards Izmit and shaping the coastal inhabitation and secondary/summer houses on the Eastern periphery of Istanbul, as well as the trans-European motorway-D100 starting from Tekirdağ and overarching towards Ankara and shaping the littoral accumulation on the Western periphery of Istanbul, became the two essential actors of the urban transformation during the mid-century Istanbul.

As both motorways turned into the two-core spine of the urbane organism, they also became the regulators of the urban growth in the following decades, providing a schema or lane of expansion. The mid-century motorway constructions of Istanbul, and the coastal development of the city concerning the enhanced mobility, also introduced further spatio-temporal and socio-economical dialectics in the urban life such as the center-periphery, work-leisure dualities. However, around the late 1980s, with the construction of the second Bosporus bridge and its connection roads and second trans-European-motorway, the former west-east expansion direction changed heading to the north instead. And during this re-urbanization period of the 1990s, the discussed locations and the settlements of the mid-century secondary/summer housing phenomenon became part of the big-city territorial footprint in the latter urban expansion.

Nevertheless, the critical turn in the 1950s also gave birth to further consequences, including the seeding of modern aesthetics of leisure within the Turkish society, as well as visibility of architectural discipline and renowned architects of mid-century Turkish architecture. As it is observed from the examples, during this significant interval, the global influences of Modernism in architecture and housing design found their relevant spot in the national practice while enabling the experienced and the young architects to practice in the same environment. It is also influencing to examine how the international trends were also pursued and interpreted into the local realm with creative adaptations. Last but not least, it is also worth mentioning that during the *Glorious Thirty* in Turkey, based on the articulated wealth and societal modernization, the middle-class families were also able to afford to receive professional architectural service and commission their vacation houses, which became quite impossible for them in today's standards.

References

Adalet, B. (2018). *Hotels and Highways: The Construction of Modernization Theory in Cold War Turkey*, Stanford University Press.

Akçura, G. (2018). Istanbul Plajlarında Yaşam [Life on the Beaches of Istanbul], in Z. Ögel, G. Tanman, E. Alışık (Eds.), *İstanbul'da Deniz Sefası: Deniz Hamamından Plaja Nostalji* [Istanbul's Seaside Leisure: Nostalgia From Sea Baths to Beaches] (pp. 86–129). Pera Museum.

Akpınar, İ.Y. (2010a). Remapping the Mid -20th Century Urban Demolitions: Representation of the Rebuilding of Istanbul, in T. Saner, C. Kozar (Eds.), *History and Destruction in Istanbul: Ghost Buildings* (pp. 174–183).

Akpınar, I.Y. (2010b). The Making of a Modern Pay-I That in Istanbul: Menderes' Executions After Prost's Plan, in C. Bilsel, P. Pinon (Eds.), *The Imperial Capital to the Republican Modern City: Henri Prost's Planning of Istanbul (1936–1951)* (pp. 167–199). İstanbul Research Institute.

(1935). Yabancı Dergilerden [From International Journals]. *Arkitekt*, 4 (52), 121–132.

(1950). Küçükyalı'da Bir Kır Evi [A Cottage House in Küçükyalı]. *Arkitekt*, 5–6 (221–22), 96–97.

(1952a). İsviçre'de bir Tatil Evi [A Vacation House in Switzerland]. *Arkitekt*, 9–10 (253–254), 152.

(1952b). Tatil Evleri [Vacation Houses]. *Arkitekt*, 9–10 (253–254), 186–187.

(1964a). Kumburgaz'da Üç Villa [Three Houses in Kumburgaz]. *Arkitekt*, 1 (314), 6–7.

(1964b). Turistik Tatil Sitesi Projesi-Selimpaşa [Touristik Holiday Housing-Selimpaşa]. *Arkitekt*, 3 (316), 118–121.

(1968). Adnan Kunt Villası [Adnan Kunt House]. *Arkitekt*, 4 (332), 151–153.

(1969). Bir Yaz Evi Kumburgaz [A Summer House in Kumburgaz]. *Arkitekt*, 4 (336), 154–155.

(1969). Feridun Akozan Mimar D.G.S.A. [Feridun Akoza, Architect]. *Arkitekt*, 2 (334), 52–53, 58.

(1970). Başak Sigorta Tekirdağ Dinlenme Tesisleri [Başak Reinsurance Tekirdağ Holiday Complex]. *Arkitekt*, 3 (339), 128–131.

(1977). Küçükçekmece'de bir Tatil Köyü Projesi-İTÜ Mimarlık Fakültesi Proje 1 [A Holiday Village in Küçükçekmece, İTU School of Architecture-Project 1]. *Arkitekt*, 2 (366), 81–84.

Bedir, A. (2002). Türkiye'de Otomotiv Sanayi Gelişme Perspektifi [Automotive Industry Development Perspective in Turkey], DPT- Devlet Planlama Teşkilatı Raporları. https://www.sbb.gov.tr/wp-content/uploads/2018/11/Turkiyede_Otomotiv_Sanayii_Gelisme_Perspektifi.pdf, S. Yılmaz.

Beveridge, W. (1942). Social Insurance and Allied Services (Cmd. 6404).

Beylan, C. (2011). "Korumacı İktisat Politikalarının Kalkınma Sürecindeki Etkileri Ve Türkiye Çözümlemesi [The Effects of Protectionist Economic Policies on the Development Process and Turkey Analysis]", [Unpublished M.Sc. thesis]. Binghamton University.

Blau, E. (2015). From Red Superblocks to Green Mega Structures, in M. Swenarton, T. Avermaete, D. van der Heuvel (Eds.), *Architecture and the Welfare State* (pp. 29–47), Routledge.

Brenner, N. (2004). *New State Spaces: Urban Governance and the Rescaling of Statehood*, Oxford University Press.

Bullock, N. (2015). West Ham and the Welfare State 1945–70, a Suitable Case for Treatment?, in M. Swenarton, T. Avermaete, D. van der Heuvel (Eds.), *Architecture and the Welfare State* (pp. 93–110), Routledge.

Evren, B. (1994). Plajlar [Beaches], in *İstanbul Ansiklopedisi* [Istanbul Encyclopedia], (vol. 6, pp. 261–262), Türkiye Ekonomik ve Toplumsal Tarih Vakfı.

Foursatié, J. (1979). *Les Trente Glorieuses, ou la révolution invisible de 1946 à 1975*, Fayard.

Gough, I. (2008). European Welfare States: Explanations and Lessons from Developing Countries, in A.A. Dani and A. den Haan (Eds.), *Inclusive States: Social Policy and Structural Inequalities World Bank*, Washington DC.

Gülhan, S.T. (2014). *The Honorable Exception: State and The Social Production of Concrete Space in Istanbul* [Unpublished Ph.D. thesis], Binghamton University.

Gürel, M. (Eds.). (2019). Mid-century Modernism in Turkey: Architecture Across Cultures in the 1950s and 1960s, Routledge.

Hobsbawm, E. (1995). *Age of Extreme: The Short Twentieth Century 1919–1991*, Abacus Book.

Keynes, J. M. (1936). *The General Theory of Employment, Interest, and Money*, Palgrave Macmillan.

Kuru, Z. (2018). *A Study on Villa Type Housing in Sayfiye Settlements: Dragos, Orhantepe Neighbourhood as a Case Study*, [Unpublished M.Sc. thesis], Yeditepe University.

Kuru, Z., and Yazıcıoğlu Halu, Z. (2020). Resort (Sayfiye) Settlements in the Historical Process: The Case of Dragos, Ortantepe Neighborhood. *MJH-Mediterranean Journal of Humanities*, 339–361. http://doi.org/10.13114/MJH.2020.535

Lefebvre, H. (1991). *Critique of Everyday Life*. Verso Books.

Mattsson, H. (2015). Were the Motorways Meet: Architecture and Corporatism in Sweden 1968?, in M. Swenarton, T. Avermaete, D. van der Heuvel (Eds.), *Architecture and the Welfare State* (pp. 155–175), Routledge.

Odman, A. (2011). Serbest Mıntıka'dan Amerikan Pazarına Tophane Rıhtımı: Ford Motor Company Exports Inc., İstanbul Otomotiv Montaj Fabrikası 1925–1944 [Tophane Pier from Free Zone to American Market: Ford Motor Company Exports Inc., Istanbul Automotive Assembly Factory 1925–1944]. *Tarih ve Toplum Yeni Yaklaşımlar* [History and Society New Approaches], 12, 71–93.

Sayar, Z. (1964). Lüks Konutlar [Luxurious Houses], *Arkitekt*, 3 (316), 99–100.

Üngür, E. (2017). Kentsel bir altyapının biyopolitikası: D-100 karayolu [Biopolitics of an urban infrastructure: D-100 highway], [Unpublished Ph.D. thesis]. İstanbul Technical University.

Ünsal Gülmez, N. (2015). Ege Taşrasında "Modern" in Mitleşmesi: Kemer (Bozdoğan, Aydın) ve Demirköprü (Salihli, Manisa) Baraj Siteleri ve

Lojmanları [Mythification of the "Modern" in the Rural Aegean: The Case of Kemer (Bozdoğan, Aydın) and Demirköprü (Salihli, Manisa) Dam Sites and Lodgings], *METU JFA*, 2015/2. 19–43, http://doi.org/ 10.4305/METU.JFA.2015.2.2

Whiteley, N. (1987). Toward a Throw-Away Culture. Consumerism, 'Style Obsolescence' and Cultural Theory in the 1950s and 1960s. *Oxford Art Journal*, 10 (2), 3–27.

Yazgan, A. (2018). İstanbul Kıyı Alanlarında İkinci Konutun Değişim ve Gelişimi [Change and Development of the Second House in Istanbul Coastal Areas], *Megaron*, 3 (13), 422–430. http://doi.org/10.5505/MEGARON.2018.57338

Yılmaz, S., Taştan, K., Ecek, N., and Çınar, E. (2017). Otomotiv Sektörünün Dünyadaki ve Türkiye'deki Değişimi [Change of the Automotiv Sector in the World and in Turkey].*Journal of Social Science Research*, 7 (3), 685–695. https://dergipark.org.tr/tr/download/article-file/372677

Canay Tunçer Yıldırım

2 Suburban Neighborhoods in Transformation: Unveiling the Modern Architectural Heritage in Pendik

The Implicit Architectural Heritage of the Modern Period

Modernist perspectives and relevant architectural productions are recently being subject to an increasing number of studies regarding both international scale and local variety. During the twentieth century, modernization processes in Turkey have shown themselves in various scales and various parts of the urban fabric, generating a variety of architectural heritage. Whereas large-scaled modern dwellings designed for high-income households by prominent architects are more acknowledged, small-scaled modest dwellings designed for lower- or middle-income households do not meet the same fate. Productive and bold Turkish architects or foreign architects invited to the country as well as iconic residential buildings/mass housing examples are deservedly yet frequently being subject to research in detail[1]. Additionally, publications with wider scopes also refer to these[2]. Nevertheless, as Altan Ergut (2009) states, the historiography

---

1 Sedad Hakkı Eldem, Seyfi Arkan, Ernst Egli, Bruno Taut may be counted among the mentioned architects scrutinized in particular publications, some of which are listed below, together with an example of mass housing projects—Ataköy:
Bozdoğan, S., Özkan, S., & Yenal, E. (Eds.). (1987). *Sedad Eldem: Architect in Turkey*. Literatür Yayıncılık.
Cengizkan, A., Cengizkan, M., & İnan, D. (Eds.). (2012). *Modernist açılımda bir öncü: Seyfi Arkan*. TMMOB Mimarlar Odası Yayınları.
Cengizkan, M., & Cengizkan, A. (Eds.). (2017). *Haluk Baysal - Melih Birsel rasyonalizmi: 20. yüzyılın ikinci yarısında mimarlık pratiği*. TMMOB Mimarlar Odası Yayınları.
Atalay Franck, O. (2015). *Politika ve mimarlık: Ernst Egli ve Türkiye'de modernliğin arayışı (1927–1940)*. TMMOB Mimarlar Odası Yayınları.
Nicolai, B. (2011). *Modern ve sürgün: Almanca konuşulan ülkelerin mimarları Türkiye'de 1925–1955*. TMMOB Mimarlar Odası Yayınları.Baturayoğlu Yöney, N. (2018). Modern Bir Planlama Deneyimi: Ataköy, İstanbul. *Mimarist*, 18(61), 58–68.

2 Bozdoğan, S. (2013). Residential Architecture and Urban Landscape in Istanbul since 1950. In P. Pyla (Ed.), *Landscapes of Development* (pp. 118–141). Harvard University Press.

of modern architecture is getting more comprehensive and pluralist with the contributions of diverse studies, especially after the 1990s. For instance, a recent issue of *Betonart* journal displays various planning processes for large-scale affordable housing projects throughout Istanbul following the World War II as a response to the consequential housing problem[3]. Besides such planning examples, modern vernacular architectures should also be considered as a part of modern heritage. Only in this way, an overarching assessment of dwelling practices of the era can be made. Moreover, as a result of globalization and neoliberal policies, urban transformation in Istanbul is affecting small-scaled housing units dramatically—especially if they are located in former suburban areas of the city, which raises the importance of potential observations on them.

Pendik is an outlying suburban district of Istanbul on its Anatolian Side, that formerly had a *sayfiye* character. The term *sayfiye* corresponds to a rural place at the outskirts of the city for resting as well as a summer house or resort, according to *TDK* [Turkish Language Association]. Despite its distance from the center of the metropolitan area, it is observed in recent years that Pendik is also being affected by the transformation at issue. The district is considered as a continuation of other suburban settlements along the Marmara coast towards the east of Kadıköy, which were also *sayfiye* areas from the 1930s to 1970s and have been suffering similar transformation processes. Even though cities experience changes in various scales constantly and somehow lose their previous layers, urban transformation in the last few decades is getting more accelerated and severe. Alterations in development plans promote transformation in these areas and cause the creation of a new, distinct physical environment. Especially civil architecture examples of the modern period are being demolished before documented or even noticed by the public, which are not perceived as old or historical, ultimately leading to their extinction.

The main aim of this chapter is to discover Pendik's lower-middle-class housing typology in terms of mid-twentieth century modern architecture, which dominantly formed the suburban texture of the district in the past. By finding out existing and demolished examples, it is expected to define the present footprint of this housing pattern as well as to diagnose the impact of the recent transformation process and relate it with processes experienced in similar but more

---

Holod, R., Evin, A., & Özkan, S. (Eds.). (2005). *Modern Turkish Architecture*. Chamber of Architects of Turkey.

3 Salman, Y. (Ed.). (2020). 1950'ler İstanbulu. *Betonart* 65.

centralized suburban areas. On-site observation, mapping, and interview are used for the methodology besides literature review.

Urban Transformation in Istanbul as an Overall Phenomenon

The concept of urban transformation has various aspects according to the region or culture, which includes notions such as urban renewal, urban regeneration, and urban redevelopment. Although cities are bound to change since the inception of urbanization, research on planning history reveals how dimensions of urban change outgrew with its multifaceted structure in the twentieth and twenty-first centuries (Zeren Gülersoy & Gürler, 2011). Modernist architectural approaches in the twentieth century tended to treat urban texture as *tabula rasa*. In the 1980s, modern industrial cities worldwide started to transform into post-modern cities of the Information Era by eliminating industrial production methods (Tekeli, 2013). After the 1980s, post-modernist and post-industrial global cities emerged with new central business districts and new types of workers with higher socio-economic backgrounds. In these cities, industrial sites have been reused by designating other functions—mostly due to political and economic concerns.

Being one of the globalizing cities, Istanbul has also been facing political and economic changes since the 1950s, followed by neoliberal policies in the 1980s and consequently rapid urban transformation. Craving for economic growth has been putting pressure on surrounding urban areas. Beside drastic changes in terms of public spaces in different eras, the texture of the city has mostly been transformed via urban housing stock.

As the city is expanding day by day, its various regions have been experiencing transformation processes carried out with different causes. After the 1999 Gölcük Earthquake, the earthquake risk that the city beholds was represented as the main cause, resulted in Urban Transformation Law (No.6306: Transformation of Areas under Disaster Risk) in 2012. According to the law, "at-risk" declaration can be made both in the scale of urban areas and individual parcels, by the ministry and the municipalities respectively (Aydın Gök & Çınar Çıtak, 2021). Low-rise dwellings older than few decades or squatter settlements [*gecekondu*] on economically valuable land are the most common targets in sake for potential high-end places and high-rise residential buildings in the city centers. Neighborhoods like Süleymaniye, Tarlabaşı, Sulukule, Fener-Balat, Fikirtepe experienced massive demolitions accordingly.

In the recent years following the regulations, the intense pressure of transformation has been spreading towards the Anatolian Side of Istanbul, starting from the surroundings of Üsküdar and Kadıköy, mostly in individual parcel scale. Pendik exists as a continuation of former *sayfiye* settlements at the shore of Marmara Sea, reaching until Kadıköy, and is representing almost the edge of the city near the neighboring city of Izmit. Therefore, the history and ongoing urban transformation processes of the whole area between Kadıköy and Pendik should be assessed correlatively.

From Kadıköy to Pendik

Since its inception, the settlement in Istanbul has been concentrated on the tripod of the Historical Peninsula (*Sarayburnu*), Pera/Galata, and Üsküdar, split by major waterways of Bosphorus and Golden Horn (*Haliç*). While the settlement center with main commercial functions and urban dwellings were located at these three tips of land, suburban residential buildings such as summer palaces or waterfront mansions (*yalı*) scattered mostly along the coastlines of Bosphorus, Prince Islands, and partially of Marmara Sea, all composing loose urban spaces. After *Şehir Hatları* [Cityline] company started its ferry services in the 1840s and Haydarpaşa–İzmit railway was constructed in 1872–3, transportation to Marmara Seashore became more convenient and this triggered urban development in the region (Akbulut, 1994). The Anatolian Side of the city began to develop along the railway and consequently Bağdat Road (*Bağdat Yolu*—the old name of Bağdat Avenue) parallel to it, reaching until the seashore. This road dates back to the Ottoman period and is the main transportation axis of the region (Yazıcıoğlu, 2001).

In 1935, the road was paved with asphalt and a tramway was constructed. Renamed as Bağdat Avenue, its two sides were split into parcels and construction of mostly two-storey detached houses (villas) started around old mansions (Yazıcıoğlu, 2001). Some of these modern period villas, constructed in *kübik* [cubic] style as from the 1930s can be found in the renowned journal *Arkitekt*, characterizing the dominant architectural taste of the Early Republican period. Beaches in Fenerbahçe, Suadiye, Caddebostan and Maltepe (Süreyya Beach) among others reflect *sayfiye* culture developed in the region between the 1930s and 1970s, peaking in the 1950s (E. Güney & Tulum, 2019). In the 1950s, mansions started to be demolished and the number of modern villas gradually increased, reinforcing the image of *sayfiye* (Berkmen & Turgut, 2019; Yazıcıoğlu, 2001).

Internal migration increased drastically in the 1950s due to political and economic circumstances and rising industrialization, with relation to capitalist government policies of the Democrat Party. With the construction of the D100 (E5) highway in the 1960s, squatter settlements began to emerge along this axis. After the 1960s, settlement areas between Kızıltoprak and Bostancı that developed parallel to or in relation with Bağdat Avenue started to lose their *sayfiye* character—basically augmented with the effects of Flat Ownership Law (*Kat Mülkiyeti Yasası*) in 1965 and construction of Boğaziçi Bridge in 1973 (Yazıcıoğlu Halu, 2010). Flat Ownership Law encouraged the semination of apartment buildings by allowing multi-owners, and development plans of Kadıköy in 1952 and 1972 encouraged constant escalation in the construction area.

Revisions in Flat Ownership Law in 1983 paved the way for a new form of housing supply called *yap-sat*, literally meaning build and sell, including the contractor to the ownership of the property at stake either by the purchase of an individual apartment or the whole site in exchange of the construction work (Aydın Gök & Çınar Çıtak, 2021). Following the last development plan of Kadıköy in 2005, high-rise apartment buildings with liberated heights emerged in the region, until restricted with 15 floors in 2016 (Berkmen & Turgut, 2019).

All these processes have been creating a multi-layered housing pattern in the region, demonstrating *sayfiye*–suburban–urban transition, continuing until Pendik lately. Pendik is one of the suburban districts in Istanbul that recently face this sort of rapid transformation.

Settlement History of Pendik

Located at the southeast of Istanbul on its Anatolian Side, Pendik District is bordered by Kartal, Sultanbeyli, and Sancaktepe at the west; Çekmeköy and Şile at the north; Tuzla and Kocaeli at the east; and the Marmara Sea at the south (Figure 2.1). Pendik is geographically characterized by Pendik Cape and bay at the shore, and with its hills towards the north. Due to the previously mentioned tripodal settlement type of Istanbul that remained for centuries, most of the documents like old maps, photos, etc. excluded the far located geography of Pendik. Nevertheless, it is possible to trace the settlement history of Pendik from several sources.

Figure 2.1: Location of Pendik in the City. Source: From Istanbul Metropolitan Municipality, Urban Map (https://sehirharitasi.ibb.gov.tr/).

Settlement in Pendik dates back to Neolithic Age. This settlement was deserted due to a decrease in Marmara Sea level and oversalinization; then in 1200 BC invading tribes that are assumed to be Macedonians settled in the region; subsequently, Romans ruled the area in the eighth century BC, followed by Byzantines after the establishment of East Roman Empire (Aksel, 1994). The oldest known name of Pendik is *Pantikapaion*, converted into *Pantecion* in the Byzantine period, and into *Peninda-kot* under Latin rule (Pendik Municipality, 2020). When the Ottoman Empire conquered the region in 1329, the settlement area shifted to Dolayoba, which is located at the northeast of today's waterfront center of the district. Meanwhile, *Rum* [Greek] people established a small-scale fishing village at the shore of the bay (Aksel, 1994). In time, this *sayfiye* area became the center of Pendik. Consisting mainly of wooden buildings, Pendik survived three sequential fires, beginning from the end of the eighteenth century. The last fire took place in 1889, which destroyed 1,200 houses and commercial buildings. Chairman of Senate Council of Foreign Affairs Azaryan [Azerian] Efendi was commissioned for the redevelopment of the area in 1900. He employed French architects and engineers to prepare a plan for Pendik, for which the settlement is known to be the first planned town of Turkey (Pendik Municipality, 2019). Completed previously in 1873, Haydarpaşa–İzmit railway has also been an efficient catalyst for the development of the district.

The small-scale seafront village started to be filled with villas of English and French people with one or two storey and garden at the beginning of the twentieth century, at the eastern and western part of the settlement respectively (Aksel, 1994). The whole village was mainly settled by English, French, *Rum*, and Armenian communities, comprising of 1,500–2,000 people before the First World War (Suri, 2002). Even though *Rum*s and Armenians were dominating the population, *Rum*s had to leave the country after the population exchange in 1924, replaced by incoming Turks from Preveza (*Preveze*) and especially Ioannina (*Yanya*) (Tezcan, 1999; Tarcan, 2020). Moreover, there were immigrants from Anatolia in the 1930s (Pendik Municipality, 2019).

The density of the settlement began to increase as a result of continual immigration to Istanbul after the mid-twentieth century, leading to urban growth and consequential sprawl towards the outskirts. In 1950, Pendik's center split into two neighborhoods: Batı [West] and Doğu [East]. After 1955 and following the 1960s, Yugoslavian immigrants settled in Yeni Neighborhood (*Yenimahalle*—New Neighborhood), established at the northern part of the center beyond the railway, especially in the large part of today's Sapan Bağları Neighborhood (Suri, 2002; Kara, 2010). Initially, Sapan Bağları was part of Yeni Neighborhood. Bahçelievler split from Yeni Neighborhood in 1967, and Yeşilbağlar emerged in 1968 as a continuation of Yeni, which generally developed with the continuation of immigration. As recorded by Evliya Çelebi during his journey in the seventeenth century, Pendik was so full of orchards and gardens until the 1950s that it supplied Istanbul with fruits and vegetables (Aksel, 1994; Tezcan, 1999). Belonged to the minority of nonimmigrant households in the neighborhood, Berin and Bedri Alpar—former residents in Sapan Bağları Neighborhood—state that in 1960, while their house was being constructed, the surrounding area was covered with olive groves and fruit gardens. Regarding this rural landscape preserved until 1960 and the mentioned urban growth towards 1970, the majority of the characteristic houses in the Sapan Bağları Neighborhood that are subject to this study must have been built by the immigrants.

Industrialization, corresponding internal migration, and the emergence of squatter settlements after 1950 were crucial steps for Pendik's transformation (Aksel, 1994). Industrial Areas Plan in 1966 initiated industrial development in Pendik as well as Maltepe, Kartal, and Tuzla (Yazıcıoğlu Halu, 2010). Factories emerged along the D100 highway after its construction at the north of the settlement. Nevertheless, Pendik did not face a relevant population increase until after 1973, when squatter settlements started to form due to improper execution of the urban development plan (Güçlü, 1999). A comparison between the decentralization of the industry and the population in the Anatolian Side of Istanbul—from Kadıköy towards Pendik—from the 1960s to 1980s reveals this temporal shift due to capital-based industry type developed in Pendik instead of labor-based as in the European Side, which requires less workers (Ataş, 2013). Following the industry sector, service sector started to develop in Pendik. With the new development plan in 1976, the center of the district was proposed for a commercial zone remaining until today, which gradually altered its scale and scope.

As a second phase of industrialization after 1966, the construction of Ömerli Dam in 1975 and the Pendik Shipyard in 1982 turned Pendik into one of the most significant industrial centers of the region (Ataş, 2013). Augmenting facilities were followed by informal housing shaping around them. 1980 onwards, a sharp and constant increase in Pendik's population can be observed. Whereas the population of Pendik was not even 10,000 in the 1950s, it almost reached 300,000 in 1990 (Aksel, 1994). Comprised of villages with low population densities, Pendik used to be a part of Kartal since Kartal's constitution as a district at the end of the 1920s, yet it split from Kartal in 1987 as a separate district (Şahin, 2015). In 2001, Istanbul's second airport Sabiha Gökçen was built in the northeast of central Pendik, beyond the D100 highway. The density of the district has been raising more and more, consequently transforming the built environment and threatening the local identity of the region.

Constituting a crucial step of this transformation, the development plan in 1976 caused Pendik to lose its *sayfiye* qualifications entirely (Suri, 2002). However, *sayfiye* character was still being preserved at the east of the center, and the northern part of the center—Yeni Neighborhood with its suburban character—was consisting of one- or two-storey dwellings, mostly inhabited by the immigrants (Suri, 2002). Sapan Bağları had been within the borders of Yeni Neighborhood until the year 1990. Therefore, it can be deduced that these one- or two-storey villa-type houses were prevalent also in Sapan Bağları after 1976, which makes these two neighborhoods the focus of the study.

Looking at Pendik through the Lens of Architecture: An In-Between Scale

Comprehension of the process of Pendik's transition from *sayfiye* settlement to a suburban area requires an understanding of its urban development and housing typology. However, Pendik appears to be neglected in that sense, since the existing limited number of studies on Pendik concentrate on many issues such as means and impacts of urban transformation, demographics, socioeconomic aspects, etc. but not on housing characteristics of the district, architectural features of its residential buildings or their background[4]. Lack of architectural information may be linked to the low socioeconomic profile of the district when various internal and external immigrations throughout its history is considered.

In order to trace the urban growth, it is essential to make an architectural analysis of the physical environment. Observations in the area reveal a prevalent housing typology pertaining to the modern period in terms of architectural language. Within this context, it is aimed to define the existing pattern of modern suburban dwellings in the central neighborhoods of Pendik, where the examples of mid-century modern architecture emerged collectively. Accordingly, the individual houses in the area will be detected and mapped, and their common features will be presented.

The earliest settlement pattern of Pendik may be found on Goltz Pascha's (*Golç Paşa*) map in 1897, most possibly showing the built environment right before the redevelopment plan of Azaryan Efendi in 1900, following the settlement-wide fire (Goltz, 1897). The boundaries of the settlement are approximately overlapping the new plan, which is the center of the district, situated in the northeast of Pendik Cape, between the train station and seashore. Except for this settlement, there were only the Turkish villages Dolayoba, Yayalar, Şeyhli, and Kurtköy in the northeast. Maps published in 1900 and 1911–12 roughly indicates the same waterfront area as the only settlement in Pendik (Fitzner, Tiedemann, Volckmann & Wette, 1900; Erkân-ı Harbiye-i Umûmiye, 1911). Another map produced in 1909 represents the same layout, yet the settlement expanded slightly to the north and transcended the railway (Great Britain War Office, 1909).

A broad map of Istanbul prepared by the General Directorate of Mapping in 1941 shows that a scattered layout of buildings was developed around the center

4 Please see: Aslanoğlu, C. (2011). *Gecekondu dönüşümü: Pendik örneği* [Master's thesis, Marmara University]. DSpace, Marmara University Open Access System. http://dspace.marmara.edu.tr/handle/11424/24966?locale-attribute=en.
Başkan, B. (2015). *Kentsel dönüşüm işleyişinin mekansal planlama, ulaşım ve toplum algısı kapsamında değerlendirilmesi; Pendik Taşlıbayır ve Batı burnu örneği* [Master's thesis, Istanbul Technical University]. DSpace, ITU Academic Open Archive. https://polen.itu.edu.tr/handle/11527/13860.
Paşali, K. (2013). *Arazi ve arsa düzenlemelerinde hisselendirme problemleri: Pendik - Sapanbağları örneği* [Master's thesis, Bahçeşehir University]. *YÖK* (Council of Higher Education) Thesis Center. https://tez.yok.gov.tr/UlusalTezMerkezi/tezDetay.jsp?id=mc9MTGvKJDcuIQM-FvXZCA&no=bGVBldUd2ihcdp7OMdkqZw.
Yeniçare, E. (2013). *Sancaklı Boşnakların yerel demokratik katılımı: Pendik örneği* [Master's thesis, Bahçeşehir University]. *YÖK* (Council of Higher Education) Thesis Center. https://tez.yok.gov.tr/UlusalTezMerkezi/tezSorguSonucYeni.jsp.

of Pendik—namely Pendik Cape in the south, coastlines on the east and west of the cape, and beyond the railway in the north (Harita Umum Müdürlüğü, 1941). Pendik Cape was roughly shown as covered with buildings on a map with the date 1967 (Union of Soviet Socialist Republics, 1967). It might be stated that the built environment on the cape was developed within this time span. Nevertheless, the cape must have been a part of *sayfiye* at the beginning of the twentieth century, since some civil architectural examples are known to exist. One of them is Burla Brothers' Mansion, located on the grove with the same name, which is a First Degree Natural Protected Area including French Catholic Church (Arkitera Mimarlık Merkezi, n.d.; Olgar, 2020). This church used to serve the French community in the Batı Neighborhood in that period.

Retaining its central position in the district up until today, the historical settlement of Pendik was mainly comprised of the planned area between the railway at the north and seashore at the south, and the residential areas on Pendik Cape and along the eastern and western coastlines, with more of a rural character (Figure 2.2). When this region between the railway and the coastline got denser, the settlement started to shift towards the north, forming a suburban character for the district. The first satellite map of Pendik captured in 1970 shows that the settlement was developing around the central bazaar, at the cape, and at the northern part of the railway (Figure 2.3). Concurrently, Yugoslavian immigrants settled mostly in Sapan Bağları ve Yeni neighborhoods. Coastline and especially Pendik Cape have been the high-end places of the region. On the other hand, the bazaar area was occupied with commercial buildings. Accordingly, they settled on the northern side of the railway. Cemal Yılmaz, the mukhtar of Sapan Bağları and an immigrant, states that the land was parcelled and as a newly-arrived immigrant household in 1966, they bought one of the lots (Başiç Başsaray, 2016). Thereby, the settlement expanded towards the D100 highway along the south–north axis as the immigration continued. Yılmaz also notes that the north of Süreyyapaşa Avenue was full of orchards and gardens when they arrived, but immigration continued and created Yeşilbağlar Neighborhood there. This type of development should be shaped by geographical or governmental factors such as Gözdağı Hill and D100 route converging to the shore at the east, and the boundary of the Kartal District at the west.

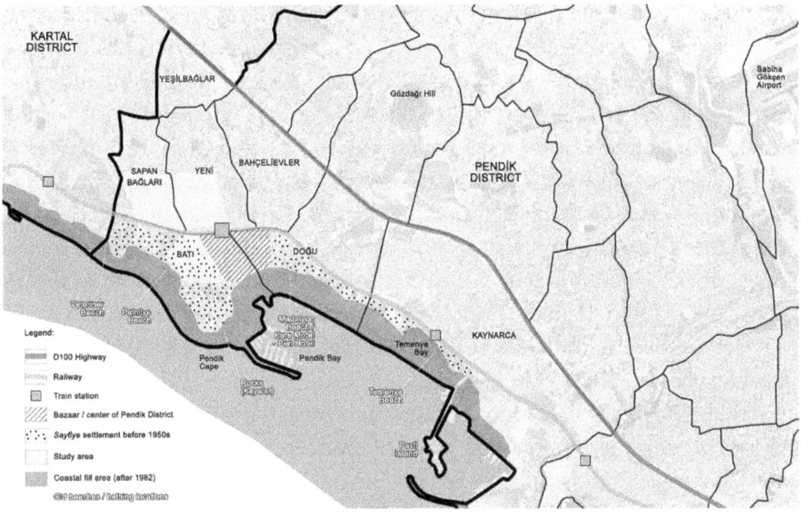

Figure 2.2: Visual Representation of Pendik's Important Elements for Settlement Analysis. Source: By the author, 2021. Base map from Google Maps (https://www.google.com/maps); district information from Pendik Municipality, Urban Information System (https://cbs.pendik.bel.tr/); coastal fill area information from 1970 to 1982 Satellite Maps of Pendik, Istanbul Metropolitan Municipality, Urban Map (https://sehirharitasi.ibb.gov.tr/).

Figure 2.3: 1970 Satellite Map of Pendik. Source: From Istanbul Metropolitan Municipality, Urban Map (https://sehirharitasi.ibb.gov.tr/).

Becoming popular as a part of daily life practice in the modern period, beaches were essential components of *sayfiye* areas along with other social activity venues like cinemas or *gazino*s—places that offer food, drinks and musical entertainment, usually located on shore in Pendik. Although no complete list of beaches or bathing locations is to be found, information gathered from the interviewed former residents and some digital sources put together leads to approximate locations of some of them (Figure 2.2) (Pendik Duyuru, 2018; Yazıcı, 2021). During the 1970s, the coastal strip of Marmara started to be filled with recreation facilities in central parts of the city, repelling the public and shifting citizens' search for *sayfiye* to Maltepe, Kartal, and Pendik (E. Güney & Tulum, 2019). Yet the speed of the urban transformation was higher, which coincided *sayfiye* and suburban characters in 1970s Pendik.

As the suburban houses represent the majority of the modern period housing in Pendik today, there were other types of modern residential buildings in the district as well. Photographs from after the mid-twentieth century demonstrate the modernist features of attached buildings in the bazaar zone; the most remarkable feature being their prolonged, cantilevering balconies (Figure 2.4). It is legible from the pictures that there were also detached houses in the same period, surrounded by their narrow gardens. One of these houses that used to be located at the intersection of 23 Nisan Avenue and Papatya Street resembles the mentioned suburban houses with its design features such as external open stairs or garden walls (Figure 2.5). Even though there are few preserved examples of these attached and detached building typologies, their designs are differing from the suburban houses developed outside of the bazaar. Among the modern structures in the bazaar, wooden buildings dating before the 1930s were also to be found here at least until the 1970s, creating a multi-layered urban environment similar to the surroundings of Bağdat Avenue. Since the bazaar zone has been the most crowded part of the district from its inception, wooden residential buildings of the district that mainly emerged here were the primary objects of transformation. Substitutes such as villas or apartment buildings—especially after the Flat Ownership Law in 1965—reinforced the transition from *sayfiye* to suburb.

Figure 2.4: Modern Architectural Character of the Bazaar Zone. Source: Top left from 70'li Yıllar Balıkçı Sokağı sahil [Photograph], by Yazıcı, E. (2021), Pendik Gazetesi. https:// www.pendikgazetesi.com.tr.
Top right from Balıkçı Sokak arkada Ortanca Sokak [Photograph], by Yazıcı, E. (2021), Pendik Gazetesi. https:// www.pendikgazetesi.com.tr.
Bottom left from 70'li yıllar - Balıkçı Sokağı [Photograph], by Yazıcı, E. (2021), Pendik Gazetesi. https:// www.pendikgazetesi.com.tr.
Bottom right from PENDİK [Photograph], by Yazıcı, E. (2021), Pendik Gazetesi. https:// www.pendikgazetesi.com.tr.

Figure 2.5: Figure 2.5: The House at the Intersection of 23 Nisan Avenue and Papatya Street.

Source: From 23 Nisan Caddesi ile Papaptya Sokak Köşesindeki Ev [Photograph], by Yazıcı, E. (2021), Pendik Gazetesi. https:// www.pendikgazetesi.com.tr.

There were more prestigious houses at the cape, and along the eastern and western coastlines, designed by prominent architects of the period and owned by upper-middle-income households. With their relatively avant-garde design approaches, three of these modern villas were published in the *Arkitekt* journal: Villa of Engineer Arif Saltuk and a summer house in 1958, and Villa of Adnan Kunt in 1968—yet was built in 1964 (Bigat, 1958; Bigat & Bilgesü, 1958; Mutlu, İzgi & Suher, 1968). While the first two were summer houses located on the cape, Adnan Kunt's villa was built as a permanent residence—used both in summer and winter—at the coastline of Temenye Bay, which forms the east of Pendik Bay. Although the other two houses hold *sayfiye* characteristics, this villa might be considered to indicate that permanent housing began to emerge in the area and the settlement was experiencing the process of transformation from *sayfiye* towards suburb. This transformation refers to a turning point for Pendik, since the population and urban sprawl started to shift from Bağdat Avenue and its surroundings until this region.

Study Area and Features of Its Modern Dwellings

Prior to the description of the study area and related housing stock, the term "modern" within this scope must be clarified since it has held various connotations over time. Modernization processes have been reflecting on the geography of Turkey since the mid-nineteenth century during the reign of the Ottoman Empire, mostly blended with local ideologies and practices. After the establishment of the Republic of Turkey, Western modernist approaches adopted from Europe started to dominate in all possible fields. Among others, urban and architectural developments were as well associated with being contemporary (*asri*), neat and hygienic. Beyond these immaterial values, the aesthetic approach was also transmitted in the 1930s via invited foreign architects' productions and thereby influenced Turkish architects. This influence was concretized and popularized as *kübik* [cubic] style in Turkey, showcasing the effects of Austrian modernism, symbolized with the Sezession building in Vienna. This *kübik* style was mainly characterized by abstract and plain geometric masses. Parallel to the political and economical changes in the 1950s, the course of modernization was changing with a direction towards the USA, named American modernism (Balamir, 2003). The political stance of the period was imposing a social Americanization, consequently altering lifestyles and cultures.

In the neighborhoods of Pendik that are identified with immigrants, countless suburban houses with gardens and similar scale, building technology, and elements were built, having some features of the mid-twentieth century modern architecture. On-site observations point out that the area between the bazaar, cape, and railway, within the bounds of Batı Neighborhood, also involves housing examples of this type. Therefore, the neighborhoods of Sapan Bağları, Yeni, and Batı are chosen for the study. The boundaries of the study area are defined by the areas, in which this housing type seems prevalent and constitutes a meaningful whole. This typology represents the housing sprawl that exceeded the center in the 1960s (Figures 2.6 and 2.7).

Figure 2.6: Aerial Photo Displaying the District Center (Bazaar) and Early Developments at its Periphery. Source: In the source article, these two photos are dated to different periods (1950s and 1970s from left to right). However, they appear to be completing each other and dating between the mid-1950s and mid-1960s. Another source includes the left photo, noting its date as the end of the 1950s and the beginning of the 1960s (Güçlü, 1999). From "Urban vascular flora and ecologic characteristics of the Pendik District (Istanbul-Turkey)," by B. Eskin, V. Altay, İ. İ. Özyiğit, and M. Serin, 2012, *African Journal of Agricultural Research*, *7*(4), p. 632 (https://doi.org/10.5897/AJAR11.2188).

Figure 2.7: Photographs from Sapan Bağları Neighborhood in 1963 (left) and 1975 (right). Source: From the photo archive of Alpar family.

The study area is restricted with the boundaries of Sapan Bağları Neighborhood at the west; Süreyyapaşa and Ulubatlı Hasan Avenue at the north; Plevne Avenue and Begonya Street at the east; and bazaar zone at the south, separated from the rest of the area due to the location of Pendik Train Station and the railway. Sabri Taşkın Avenue defines the east end of this zone; Kızılay Avenue defines its west end; and Erol Kaya Avenue defines its south end, which cuts through the joint between Pendik Cape and the rest of the district (Figure 2.8). The housing pattern continues beyond the Süreyyapaşa Avenue until reaching D100, including the Yeşilbağlar and Bahçelievler neighborhoods. Although these parts could also be evaluated correlatively, they are not included to the study area due to the rarity of the mentioned type of houses detected there. The selected neighborhoods are scrutinized via field survey and Google Maps tools to create a mapping of the modern dwellings, presenting their existence and preservation status.

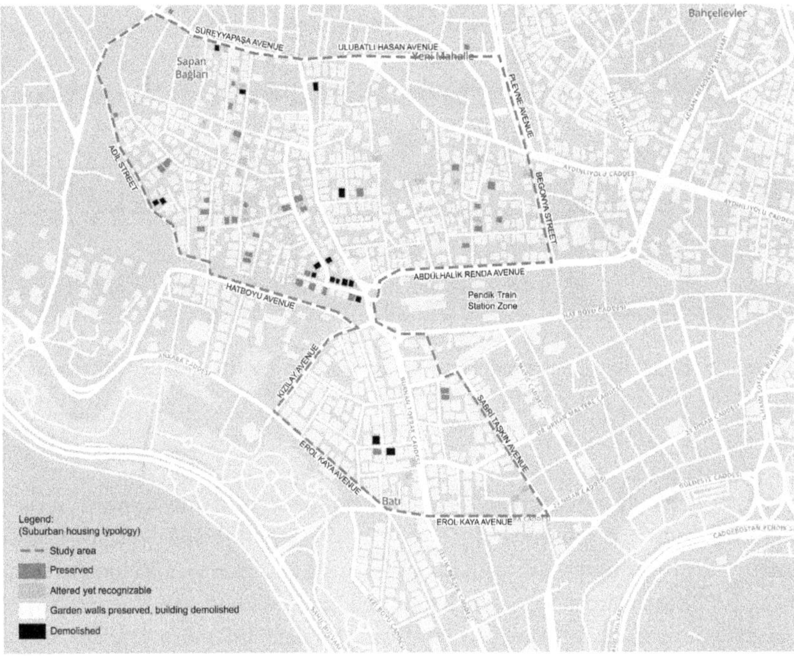

Figure 2.8: Boundaries of the Study Area and Mapping of the Examined Suburban Housing. Source: By the author, 2021.

An evaluation in the study area reveals that the prevalent housing typology in the area and its architectural features refer to several aspects of modern architecture (Figure 2.9). While masses of these houses were designed in such forms that remind *kübik* architecture, some of these houses—most probably owned by lower-middle-income households—had space in the front garden and a wide door opening for car entrance, peculiar to an American lifestyle. Even though the examples of this housing typology are far from constituting an integrative pattern nowadays due to the ongoing urban transformation process, several existing buildings can be observed with their original or altered state, or some traces of the demolished ones can be pursued.

Figure 2.9: Preserved Examples of Housing Typology in the Area. Source: By the author, 2018.

Mentioned housing examples observed in the area are mainly minimalist rectangular prisms with hipped roofs. These low-rise, small-scaled detached houses usually have two storeys, although few of them are one-storey. Additionally, some examples have a third storey as an annex. All of these houses are surrounded by a private garden, as the satellite map from the date 1970 also displays. These gardens are separated from the streets and neighboring houses by garden walls, which are mutual when they are located between two neighboring houses. The entrance door to the garden is usually located at one end of the wall facade, and houses with a garage way have a garage entrance at the other end. The axis of the garden entrance leads to the entrance of the house, usually being on one of the lateral facades. Generally, the houses have separate entrances for both floors. Attached to lateral facades and in some cases enclosed underneath, external open stairs made of terrazzo reach the upper floor entrance, mostly ending with an enclosed porch (Figure 2.10). The front facades are characterized by long balconies on both floors leaning to one edge of the building, sometimes turning around the corner.

Figure 2.10: External Open Stairs, Mostly Ending with an Enclosed Porch. Source: By the author, 2018.

One of the common features of the houses is the existence of enclosed porches (Figure 2.11). These spaces are surrounded by a modular window system made of thin metal grids (muntins) and glazing, applied on top of the balcony parapets. This construction technique was used both for creating a vestibule between the staircase and the entrance door on the upper level and for enclosing a balcony. According to the interviewed former residents in the area, some of the balconies or entranceways were covered with this system after the construction of the houses.

Figure 2.11: Enclosed Porches with Common Modular Window System. Source: By the author, 2018.

Another remarkable feature in the area is the formation of similar garden walls. Low masonry walls are decorated with fences on top between piers. The most common fence type is metal wire mesh panel with a frame, which is also observed on some garage doors (Figure 2.12). The more ornamental elements of the garden walls are garden gates with metal arches, made of two parallel metal strips that are crossed and connected by short metal strips on top with curved ends (Figure 2.13). These arches are entwined with plants as if representing the strong relationship between the houses with the gardens.

Figure 2.12: Garden Walls with Metal Wire Mesh Panels. Source: By the author, 2018.

Figure 2.13: Garden Gates with Metal Arches. Source: By the author, 2018.

All these mentioned features can be found in civil architecture examples of other districts as well (Figure 2.14). Apart from Pendik, the window system of enclosed porches, in general, was used in many other districts or cities of the country at that time, especially in the staircase windows of low-rise apartment buildings. Garden walls with ornamental arches and metal mesh panels on top are also rather generic; some of the examples are still present today in Salacak Neighborhood in Üsküdar District, and at Paşabahçe Ucuz Evler in Beykoz District (Akbulut & Akay, 2020). Enclosed porches can be detected for instance in Salacak; or among Koşuyolu mass housing typologies in Kadıköy developed after the 1950s, along with external stairs for the upper floor, attached to lateral facades (Suoğlu, 2009). Hence it would not be insubstantial to assume that these elements were used in the whole region between Üsküdar and Pendik. Other building materials and construction techniques that are used in Pendik also fit in the context of mid-century modern architecture in Turkey, such as sprayed concrete as plaster for the facades, or terrazzo stairs.

Figure 2.14: Examples for Building Elements in Residential Area of Salacak, Üsküdar. Source: By the author, 2021.

To represent the entity of this suburban housing type, the examples that are still existing in the determined study area or the demolished ones that could be detected are pieced together by mapping, based on on-site observations and examinations in Google Maps panoramas via Street View technology (Figure 2.8). According to the map; 33 houses are still preserved with their authentic features; 27 houses were partially altered but their authentic features are readable; 14 houses are demolished but their authentic garden walls are recognizable, and 17 are demolished. The demolished houses have been replaced mostly with out-of-scale contemporary apartment buildings. Besides these mapped houses, there are also many other examples resembling this typology. However, they are either newly built similar to the type or altered beyond recognition. These are not included in the mapping to achieve precision.

Pendik as a Recent Scene for Urban Transformation

The physical environment of the examined neighborhoods of Pendik along with their surroundings started to change a few years ago due to developing means of transportation and services. Such developments drew population to the district, whereas the land values started to increase. Previously, industrialization after the 1950s, immigrations and suburban sprawl towards the periphery of the center, commercial zone planning for the central Batı and Doğu neighborhoods in 1976 following the growth, construction of Pendik Shipyard in 1982 have been main turning points for the district in the transformation process from *sayfiye* to suburban. The opening of Sabiha Gökçen Airport in 2001 represents another crucial change, not only for the district, it has been affecting the wide coastal region and the land around D100 highway until Kadıköy as well. Consequently, these existing urban areas have become more valuable, including Pendik as it has been more connected to the metropolitan center.

Despite the similarity of the urban transformation process of Pendik with the mentioned other suburban settlements along the Marmara Sea coast towards Kadıköy, there are several differences. The degree of proximity to the metropolitan center is the main factor. It determines land values and therefore diversifies the socioeconomic status of the residents. While the industry was decentralized from the city center to as far as Pendik between the 1960s and 1980s, the population shifted only until Bostancı, as Ataş mentions (2013), causing Pendik to sustain its *sayfiye*—suburban character whereas Kadıköy's neighborhoods got crowded and represented a more direct transition from *sayfiye* to urban. Mid-century modern housing held *sayfiye* qualification in Kadıköy while being related to immigrants and the suburban environment in Pendik. As the city grew after the 1980s, industrial development and the low-income population that it brings along identified more neighborhoods as squatter settlements in Pendik region than the districts towards west, due to the underpopulated nature of the district. Additionally, housing co-operatives were intensely operating in the region for the same reason (Ataş, 2013).

The most complete transformations in Pendik have been in the bazaar and the cape. In the mid-twentieth century, the attached housing pattern comprised of modern low-rise apartments emerged in the bazaar area, among wooden mansions of the nineteenth century and modern villa-type dwellings of the 1930s. The same typologies of the late nineteenth and early twentieth centuries existed at the cape's loose settlement as well. Due to the privileged locations of these areas, existing building stock was replaced with multi-storey apartments and fulled their capacities in terms of further renewal. Consequently, Pendik's suburban settlement area with its lower-middle-income residents became a new target regarding its neighboring location.

Alterations in development plans over the last few years accelerated the transformation of the region by creating opportunities for the municipality and construction companies to gain profit. *Yap-sat* method has been encouraging the local contractors used as a convenient and profitable way of construction. Within this context, Sapan Bağları and Yeni neighborhoods have been changing rapidly and radically in recent years. New plan notes in the development plan allowed a much higher floor area ratio and bigger construction area in the selected neighborhoods of Pendik, causing a dramatic scale shift in terms of the built environment and thus erasing the suburban memory of the place.

The legal base of this process is Implementary Development Plans and their revisions. As a recent example from Sapan Bağları with the date 12 June 2015 reveals, the building's garden width is allowed to be decreased and individual parcels are allowed to be merged to increase *emsal* (*KAKS*—floor area ratio). Consequently, the existing houses in the neighborhood are disappearing rapidly, replaced with residential buildings on an extremely different scale, and the silhouettes of almost every street have been changed until this day.

Beyond Pendik, the development has been continuing towards the east of the city. As a part of the industrial development area, Tuzla also continues to transform and grow, connecting stronger with Gebze—a district of Izmit, reinforcing the ecumenopolis character of the city. Regarding these urban transformation processes with a holistic approach, it may be stated that they tend to constitute a threatening factor against the heritage elements of the city as well as the quality or functionality of the urban environment. It is hoped that this study would contribute to the appreciation and documentation of modern suburban housing patterns in Istanbul and Turkey.

References

Akbulut, R. (1994). Kadıköy. In Tekeli, İ. (Ed.), *Dünden Bugüne İstanbul Ansiklopedisi* (Vol. 4, pp. 329–339). Türkiye Ekonomik ve Toplumsal Tarih Vakfı.

Akbulut, R., & Akay, Z. (2020, March 8). *Halk için tasarlamak: Seyfi Arkan'ın 1950'lerdeki "ucuz konut" planlama çalışmaları*. Arkitekt.modern. https://zaferakay.blogspot.com/2020/03/rfat-akbulut-zafer-akay-seyfi-arkan.html

Aksel, A. (1994). Pendik ilçesi. In Tekeli, İ. (Ed.), *Dünden Bugüne İstanbul Ansiklopedisi* (Vol. 6, pp. 237–239). Türkiye Ekonomik ve Toplumsal Tarih Vakfı.

Altan Ergut, E. (2009). Cumhuriyet Dönemi mimarlığı: Tanımlar, sınırlar, olanaklar. *Türkiye Araştırmaları Literatür Dergisi*, *7*(13), 121–130.

Arkitera Mimarlık Merkezi (n.d.). *Burla Biraderler Korusu*. https://kulturenvanteri.com/yer/burla-biraderler-kosku/

Ataş, Z. (2013). *İstanbul'da 1987–2007 dönemi için bir konut tarihi anlatısı* [Doctoral dissertation, Istanbul Technical University]. DSpace, ITU Academic Open Archive. http://hdl.handle.net/11527/6342

Aydın Gök, S. F., & Çınar Çıtak, C. (2021). Konut Politikalarının Fiziksel Yansımaları; Kadıköy Örneği. *Mimarlık ve Yaşam*, *6*(1), 165–197. DOI: https://doi.org/10.26835/my.742288

Balamir, A. (2003). Mimarlık ve kimlik temrinleri-I: Türkiye'de modern yapı kültürünün bir profili. *Mimarlık*, (313), 24–29.

Başiç Başsaray, A. (2016, May 6). *Pendik Sapanbağları Boşnakları*. Boşnak Medya. https://www.bosnakmedya.com/pendik-sapanbaglari-bosnaklari/

Berkmen, N. H., & Turgut, S. (2019). Kentsel dönüşüm kıskacında "Bağdat Caddesi". *Megaron*, *14*(1), 155–166. https://doi.org/10.14744/megaron.2019.35467

Bigat, E. (1958). Yazlık Bir Ev. *Arkitekt*, *1958–02*(291), 68–69.

Bigat, E., & Bilgesü, İ. (1958). Mühendis Arif Saltuk Villası. *Arkitekt*, *1958–02*(291), 55–60.

Ekenyazıcı Güney, E., & Tulum, H. (2019). İstanbul'un Anadolu yakasında sayfiye deneyimi. *Arredamento Mimarlık*, (336), 94–99.

Erkân-ı Harbiye-i Umûmiye (1911). *İstanbul Boğazı ve civarı haritası (1:25000) – The Bosphorus and surroundings map (Scale 1:25000)* [Map]. Erkân-ı Harbiye-i Umûmiye. https://archives.saltresearch.org/handle/123456789/100256

Eskin, B., Altay, V., Özyiğit, İ. İ., & Serin, M. (2012). Urban vascular flora and ecologic characteristics of the Pendik District (Istanbul–Turkey). *African Journal of Agricultural Research*, *7*(4), 629–646. https://doi.org/10.5897/AJAR11.2188

Fitzner, R., Tiedemann, J. G., & Volckmann & Wette (1900). *Karte des Bosporus und der Bithynischen Halbinsel* [Map]. C.J.E. Volckmann-Verlag. http://id.lib.harvard.edu/alma/990119714200203941/catalog

Goltz, C. Frh. v. d. (1897). *Karte der umgegend von Constantinople – İstanbul ve çevresini gösteren harita – Map showing Istanbul and surroundings* [Map]. Schall & Grund. https://archives.saltresearch.org/handle/123456789/102289

Great Britain War Office (1909). *Constantinople & surrounding country, G.S.G.S. no 2390 (Sheet 1)* [Map]. Great Britain War Office, Geographical Section, General Staff. http://www.bl.uk/onlinegallery/onlineex/maps/europe/5011928u1u1909.html

Güçlü, S. (Ed.). (1999). *Pendik: Türkiye Cumhuriyeti'nin 75. yılı Osmanlı İmparatorluğu'nun 700. kuruluş yılı anısına*. Pendik Belediyesi Kültür Yayınları.

Harita Umum Müdürlüğü (1941). *İstanbul [1:100.000]* [Map]. Harita Umum Müdürlüğü. https://archives.saltresearch.org/handle/123456789/123857

Kara, M. (2010). *İstanbulum 59: Pendik'li yıllar, sine-masal anıları*. Heyamola Yayınları.

Mutlu, A., İzgi, U., & Suher, E. (1968). Adnan Kunt Villası. *Arkitekt, 1968-04*(332), 151–153.

Olgar, İ. K. (2020, December 18). *Burla Biraderler Köşkü*. Kültür Envanteri. https://medium.com/t%C3%BCrkiye/bilinmeyen-i%CC%87stanbul-pendik-ve-burla-biraderler-5a5eddd1611

Pendik Duyuru. (2018, August 4). *Bir zamanlar Pendik'te bulunan Plajlarımız.🏖⛱✓• Kaynarca Temenye plajı 1990 yıllar (şimdiki The Green Park Hotel Pendik olduğu)* [Images attached] [Status update]. Facebook. https://www.facebook.com/1050536974997290/posts/1942671012450544/

Pendik Municipality (2019, October 31). *Pendik Belediyesi 2015–2019 Stratejik Planı*. https://www.pendik.bel.tr/data/dokumanlar/5457688dd3bb0_2015-2019-stratejik-plan-kapakli.pdf

Pendik Municipality (2020, November 11). *Pendik Tarihi*. https://www.pendik.bel.tr/sayfa/detay/pendik-tarihi

Suoğlu, R. (2009). *Koşuyolu yerleşmesinin oluşumu ve gelişimi* [Master's thesis, Istanbul Technical University]. DSpace, ITU Academic Open Archive. http://hdl.handle.net/11527/3271

Suri, L. (2002). Mahalle belediye bağlamında İstanbul ve Pendik. *İstanbul*, (40), 87–92.

Şahin, C. (2015). İstanbul'un ilçeleri. In Yılmaz, C. (Ed.), *Antikçağ'dan XXI. yüzyıla büyük İstanbul tarihi* (Vol. 3, pp. 246–324). İBB Kültür A.Ş. & İSAM.

Tarcan, B. H. (2020). *Türk-Yunan nüfus mübadelesinde İstanbul'a gelen Türk göçmenlerin uyum ve entegrasyon süreci* [Master's thesis, Karabük University]. DSpace. http://acikerisim.karabuk.edu.tr:8080/xmlui/handle/123456789/819

Tekeli, İ. (2013). *İstanbul'un Planlanmasının ve Gelişmesinin Öyküsü*. Tarih Vakfı Yurt Yayınları. https://www.academia.edu/30440029/%C4%B0stanbulun_Planlamas%C4%B1n%C4%B1n_ve_Geli%C5%9Fmesinin_%C3%96yk%C3%BCs%C3%BC

Tezcan, S. (1999). *Pendik (Başlangıçtan 1924'e kadar)*. Pendikliler Kültür ve Dayanışma Derneği Yayınları.

Union of Soviet Socialist Republics (1967). *148. Dardanelles. Bosporus. The World Atlas*. [Map]. Union of Soviet Socialist Republics. https://www.davidrumsey.com/luna/servlet/view/search?sort=Pub_List_No_InitialSort%2CPub_Date%2CPub_List_No%2CSeries_No&q=148.+Dardanelles.+Bosporus.+The+World+Atlas.&search=Go

Yazıcı, E. (2021a). *23 Nisan Caddesi ile Papaptya Sokak Köşesindeki Ev* [Photograph]. Pendik Gazetesi. https://www.pendikgazetesi.com.tr/?s=23+N%C4%B0SAN+CADDES%C4%B0+%C4%B0LE+PAPATYA+SOKAK+K%C3%96%C5%9EES%C4%B0NDEK%C4%B0+EV

Yazıcı, E. (2021b). *Balıkçı Sokak arkada Ortanca Sokak* [Photograph]. Pendik Gazetesi. https://www.pendikgazetesi.com.tr/?s=BALIK%C3%87I+SOKAK+ARKADA+ORTANCA+SOKAK

Yazıcı, E. (2021c). *Foto Galeri*. Pendik Gazetesi. https://www.pendikgazetesi.com.tr/?s=plaj

Yazıcıoğlu, Z. (2001). *1950–1970'lerde İstanbul'da konut mimarisi: Bağdat Caddesi örneği* [Master's thesis, Istanbul Technical University]. DSpace, ITU Academic Open Archive. http://hdl.handle.net/11527/10389

Yazıcıoğlu Halu, Z. (2010). *Kentsel mekan olarak caddelerin mekansal karakterinin yürünebilirlik bağlamında irdelenmesi: Bağdat Caddesi örneği* [Doctoral dissertation, Istanbul Technical University]. DSpace, ITU Academic Open Archive. http://hdl.handle.net/11527/8495

Zeren Gülersoy, N., & Gürler, E. (2011). Conceptual challenges on urban transformation. *A|Z ITU Journal of the Faculty of Architecture*, *8*(1), 10–24.

Ahsen Özsoy

Hatice Sadıkoğlu Asan

3
The Ethos of Mid-Century Modern in Istanbul and San Francisco: A Comparative Reading on Levent Houses and Eichler Homes

Introduction

The 1950s witnessed an increase in the developments of large-scale suburban settlements which were built within similar design approach in terms of layout, clustering, and the use of new materials and the latest technology. The development of modern technology in building and construction became a central factor in shaping domestic architecture. In Germany, after the First World War, during a period of political revolution and severe housing shortages, new technologies began to be the focus for a new and modernist style (Lane, 2007). A large-scale settlement, addressing social issues, shows how far Bauhaus concerns had shifted and expanded over the course of the school's existence. The production line was introduced at Bauhaus Dessau and by the international community of architects, CIAM, in the beginning of the century to become a detailed industrial production system.

The heritage of modern movement is considered as a legacy and of considerable value as cultural heritage, including the suburban building stock and works of monumental character such as German Siedlungen and the Unite de Habitation of Le Corbusier in Berlin, Firminy, Nantes, and Marseille. There could be no doubt about the necessity to survey, maintain and improve the quality of the suburban building stock (Di Guilio, 2012).

In Turkey, modern living became synonymous with living in a spacious modern flat and reproduction of mid-rise apartment blocks on small urban lots played a major role in the creation of an urban middle class, with new consumption patterns and a new culture of apartment living (Gönlügür, 2015). In general, mid-century modernism in Turkey displays a visible shift from the Central European 'cubic' modernism, known as the 'New Architecture' of the 1930s, to the more transparent modernism of the 1950s.

American consumers, on the other hand, demanded houses that offered a mixture of traditional and modern components, and thus 'participated in the reshaping of an authentic modernism' (Lane, 2007). If sensitive to people's needs and contemporary living patterns, the architect will necessarily design single-family houses both modern and rooted in the American tradition. These houses, conceived in terms of rational planning, comfort, flexibility, and indoor-outdoor living would result in properly modern architecture.

With recent trends, the popularity of the mid-century modern style was reborn in various countries. Their architectural layout, basic geometric form, interior design elements are still inspiring contemporary architects, designers and developers, too. Today, there is a great number of mid-century housing stock in use and, single-family houses are the most problematic part of this stock in terms of preserving the value as an architectural heritage.

This chapter focuses on the architectural qualities and the value change of this mid-century single-family housing stock in Levent of Istanbul and the Bay Area of San Francisco. It will be explored how twentieth-century modernism and garden city ideal which was born in Europe influenced the modern housing settlements that were built in the same period of time in different locations regarding architectural design and social, cultural and economic value. Changing policies and socio-economic conditions following the Second World War had an impact on architectural design and urban planning ideals in both countries. As the earliest modern housing developments in the 1950s, Levent Houses in Istanbul and Eichler Homes in San Francisco are compared regarding their characteristics and current conditions, it is aimed to understand how they were affected by changes in time.

In this chapter, Levent Houses and Eichler Homes will be comparatively evaluated by questioning the original characteristics of the houses regarding settlement, building and interior details, materials used and construction methods. Finally, their current conditions by different strategies and implementations will be evaluated to understand what is important to preserve and sustain architectural value.

The Ethos of Modernism

Following the rise of modernism in Europe, modern architecture was experimented in other countries, too. Since architecture is an expression of a society as Mumford (1989) states, specifically residential architecture is an essential part of the city to understand how the value systems shaped modernism in different countries.

In spite of being in different countries and formed by different social, cultural and economic motivations and political events, following the World War II, modern mass housing estates were designed and built within similar ideals. Twentieth-century modernists sought to develop a new design approach which focuses on the functionality, simplicity, technology and material quality to create modern homes (Heynen, 1999). In his seminal book 'Towards a New Architecture,' Le Corbusier (1927) emphasized that the new modern housing architecture has responsibility to everyone in the city regarding ethos which was presented in CIAM congresses.

The earlier examples of modern housing were introduced by the architectural exhibitions such as Weissenhof Siedlung in Stuttgart. The housing estate with its 60 units was designed and built to promote new, modern lifestyle by various modernists in 1927. Bauhaus Dessau Masters' Houses are also another example built in 1926 with a modernist vision (Durth, 2014). All these projects and manifestoes by the European modernists were followed by the local architects in different countries. Exhibitions and journals helped to spread these new ideas out of the continent. Moreover, a great number of the European architects emigrated to the other countries to pursue their modernism ideals. It is obvious that European modernism in housing architecture helped to shape other modernisms.

To understand the different motives' modernism ethos in Istanbul and San Francisco, their architectural and social-cultural values will be examined. Literature reviews, archival research, interviews and site observations comprise the methodology of this study. We focused on the following topics to obtain findings: architectural design principles, user profiles, design and development organizations.

Mid-Century Modern Single-Family Houses in Turkey and California

Architecture as a part of our identity and our history, transmits information to the next generations. Modern housing settlements that were designed and built in the mid-century period are one of the most vulnerable members of the built environment today.

European modernism had an influence on 'other' modernisms in different places. Akcan (2012) describes it as a 'cultural flow.' This flow was defined as the process of transformation during the transportation. Mid-century modernism was transformed into new forms and was reshaped by the local, regional characteristics of the places. In this chapter, we explore how European modernism was reshaped in different countries with the examples from Istanbul, Turkey and San Francisco, bay area, US.

Both Istanbul and San Francisco had welcomed modern single-family houses in the beginning of late 40s and early 50s. Although these two cities were shaped by different motives and cultures in time, it can be said that, twentieth century European modernism have had a similar influence on their early suburb and modern single-family housing architecture. We focused on the earlier and the most influential modern mass housing initiatives in both cities that were developed during mid-century: Levent Houses and Eichler Homes. These two projects were designed similarly with a strong twentieth century modernism ideals and visions. However, geographic, economic and social conditions have had different impact following their design, in the last 70 years. This chapter presents a comparative reading focusing on the design and development of these projects, as well as the changes in recent years. The archival research and site observations were carried out in Istanbul and San Francisco during 2017–2019 to understand the design details, dwellers' profile and the NGO activities on the architectural value of the projects.

Modern Single-Family Housing in Turkey in the 1950s: Levent Houses, Istanbul

The idea of modern architecture in Turkey dates back to the 1920s which is at the same time with the establishment of the Republic of Turkey. By the 1930s, new urban planning and modern housing projects were developed in the big cities such as Istanbul and Ankara (Bozdoğan, 2002). Large part of the modern architecture housing projects was completed in the 1950s. The earlier examples of such housing settlements are single-family houses within an urban setting located in the suburbs of the cities. Istanbul Levent, Kosuyolu and Ankara Bahcelievler projects can be listed as the modern mass houses as single-family dwellings (Yıldız & Özsoy, 2016).

Following the World War I, besides local Turkish architects, European architects who were in exile such as Bruno Taut contributed to shape modern cities and residential settlements in Turkey (Akcan, 2012). These 'foreign' architects who emigrated to Turkey were also teaching at the foremost universities in Turkey with a vision of European modernism and it helped to spread the modernism idea in Turkey. At the same time, some architecture and lifestyle magazines and journals such as *Arkitekt* provided information about European and American modernism to the local professionals. There were also some events such as Izmir International Fair to promote modern housing and materials used in other countries (Gönlügür, 2015). With all these contributions, a new mid-century modern housing architecture has been developed which seemed more international than the traditional houses in Turkey.

The period between the 1930s and 1960s also became a prominent time period regarding housing loans and tax reforms to help middle-class families own a house. Emlak Bank, which was founded in 1926 by the state, later joined the production process in the housing development projects with collaborating modernist architects (Güvenç & Isık, 1999). 'Levent Houses' is one of those pioneering projects to provide a modern living environment to the middle-income families with the help of housing loans by the Emlak Bank as a state help. The housing settlement was developed for a suburban area in Istanbul with strong 'garden city' urban planning ideals such as Weissenhof Siedlung, Siemenstadt neighborhoods in Germany (Anon, 2009). The site planning and architectural design was created by the modernist architects Kemal Ahmet Aru and Rebii Gorbon.

'Levent Houses' were designed their built in four stages and completed in 1958. The projects were apart from their predecessors in the country for three reasons: being mass-produced single-family houses promoting modern architecture and modern lifestyle; being marketed with a modern approach; and finally providing an outdoor-indoor living with their front and backyards. So, this project was also a kind of modern architecture laboratory experimentation for Turkey. The houses were designed in different layouts such as 2-bedroom and 3-bedroom houses, one story or two story, with a gable roof. The finishing materials and fixtures of the houses were imported from other countries, main construction materials were listed as brick and stone. There were not any built-in appliances provided in the houses (Aru & Gorbon, 1952; Aru, 1956).

During the design phases of the project, it was promised and targeted to create some sort of similar forms of European modern housing architecture with pure, clean geometries, flexible layout and natural materials. However, construction and supply-chain limitations did not allow the architects and developers to imply their original design approach, and the projects ended up most likely being a combination of local and European architectural styles regarding building forms, materials used and layouts. The Levent Houses Project was an experimental example indicating the translation and interpretation of European Modernism in Turkey in the 1950s.

Modern Single-Family Housing in San Francisco in the1950s: Eichler Homes

In the beginning of the twentieth century, the great depression and the World War II changed the structure of the American cities. By the 1950s, with the help of the developments in the industry, production systems and new urban planning strategies in the 1950s focusing on 'garden city' concept, suburban areas became main residential neighborhoods for the middle-class (Jacobs, 1961). On the other hand, the prominent architects displaced because of the political dynamics of continental Europe came into leading positions in north American schools. The German contribution was much broader, involving city planners like Martin Wagner at Harvard, urban theorists like Werner Hegemann at Columbia, and designers like Konrad Wittmann at Pratt Institute. The influence of the European modernists and Bauhaus ideas was clearly observed on the formation of new residential environments. As a representative of 'American Modern' single family, houses with their indoor and outdoor comfort and amenities became more and more popular. Owning a single-family house was a common target and achievement for middle-income households, it became a symbol of a community-based value system (Serraino, 2006; Smiley, 2007).

In the 1950s, there was an increasing interest and popularity in modern architecture in the United States. Exhibitions by MoMA New York, prestigious magazines such as Fortune, Time and Harper's Bazaar and even Hollywood movies, they all were promoting modernism and modern architecture.

By the late 1930s, modern houses have been built in various locations in the country. New York and California became the two pioneering states in terms of modern architecture. During the 1940s, California became a laboratory for modern housing experimentations by the local modernists and European emigres and exiles such as Richard Neutra, Rudolph Schindler and Eric Mendelsohn (Bahr, 2007). Aside from these architects, architectural photographers such as Julius Shulman and Ezra Stroller worked for the distribution of the modern movement and creating its existence in the architectural memory with their published photographs on the magazines.

As one of the most important contributions to the Californian Modernism, *The Case Study House* program was initiated by the editor John Entenza on behalf of *Arts and Architecture* magazine in 1945. Thirty-six experimental modern single-family house proto-types were designed by the modernists until 1966 (Smith, 2019). Architects remained to design in an experimental way, using functional, flexible layouts and both local and industrial materials. While wood was the primary construction material, they also tried to explore steel and glass.

Large housing developers dominated the housing field in the postwar period, focusing on suburban single-family houses and offering standardized materials to make them more affordable (Adamson & Arbunich, 2002). At the same time, *The Housing Act* was published with the aim of providing a feasible home and a suitable living environment for every American family. Later, large suburban housing developments were promoted and supported by the Federal Housing Agency (FHA). New materials and technics helped with mass production, while low interest rates and tax deductions encouraged people to own a single-family house in the suburbs.

In California, a popular demand for a new lifestyle which promotes individual satisfaction has emerged: causality, indoor & outdoor living, healthy, modern and 'over-scale' design ideas shaped this new culture. Eichler Homes is one of them that liberated lifestyles from traditional patterns and provided more individualized alternatives (Adamson & Arbunich, 2002).

In 1949, as a visionary modernist real estate developer, Joseph Eichler hired modernist architects such as Robert Anshen and Archibald Quincy Jones to bring socially responsive and holistic approaches to suburban community life with the aim of building modern homes for the middle-class. Joseph Eichler had been living in a Frank Lloyd Wright House which inspired him. He also worked with well-known artists, landscape designers, industrial designers in the bay area, in San Francisco to create prototypes for modern living. By 1954, Eichler Homes had built 1.800 modern single-family houses. Both architecture and design magazines and popular press recognized Eichler as one of the leading modernism advocates in the country (Adams, 1995; Adamson & Arbunich, 2002).

Eichler Home layouts mainly included flexible and open plan schema, built-in furnishings and a well-designed landscape. Living area is connected with the kitchen and the garden where children play. Bedrooms are located in apart from the living area to protect the privacy. Most of the models included galleries, atriums and inner courtyards. As a construction method Eichler used post-and-beam structure to provide more flexible layouts. The architects searched for the materials that must be modern, affordable, easy to protect and clean such as Philippine mahogany wall paneling, redwood for exterior and roof systems, heat and scratch resistant plastic laminate counter tops, etc.

The design of Eichler Homes was awarded by various academic and design institutions and press media. The houses were photographed by famous architectural photographers and documented. They created a kind of 'Eichler Identity.' Although Eichler remained to build modern single-family homes in Northern California until the 1970s, the design vision and enthusiasm coined between the 1950s and 1960s were a total gamechanger regarding authentic and regional modern housing design in the Bay Area.

Searching for the Modernism Ethos: Levent Houses versus Eichler Homes

Levent Houses and Eichler Homes are two housing initiatives that were promoted with modernism ideals and realized in the 1950s particularly for middle-income families with the help of bank loans, and both were designed by the influence of European Modernism in different countries. They will be compared regarding their architectural and socio-cultural values to understand how two similar (European) modernism ideals were shaped in two different (non-European) countries.

Architectural Value

Planning and Design

With the aim of providing modern homes to middle-income families in two different countries, both of the projects were designed by the famous architects within a modernist vision in the mid-century. The housing settlements were located in the suburbs in the 1950s. Eichler Homes were located in different parts of the Bay Area, Emlak Bank developed single-family and row houses in Levent and Kosuyolu locations in Istanbul (Figure 3.1).

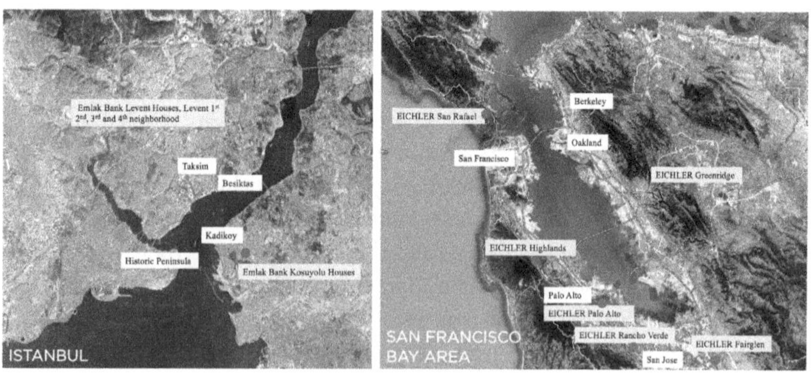

Figure 3.1: Emlak Bank Levent Houses in Istanbul and Some Eichler Homes in the Bay Area, San Francisco. Source: Authors, 2021.

Both Levent Houses and Eichler Homes were planned and realized as a mass-housing settlement including shopping facilities, entertainment, sport facilities, green areas and parks. The settlement layouts were designed by urban planners with the collaborations of architects and landscape designers. They tried to create livable and partially slow streets for dwellers with some cul-de-sacs and small neighborhood clusters (Figures 3.2 and 3.3). The architects of these projects were either apprenticed for several years to European modernist architects or influenced by them during their educations.

Figure 3.2: Levent Houses Map. Source: Aru, 1956 (Open Source).

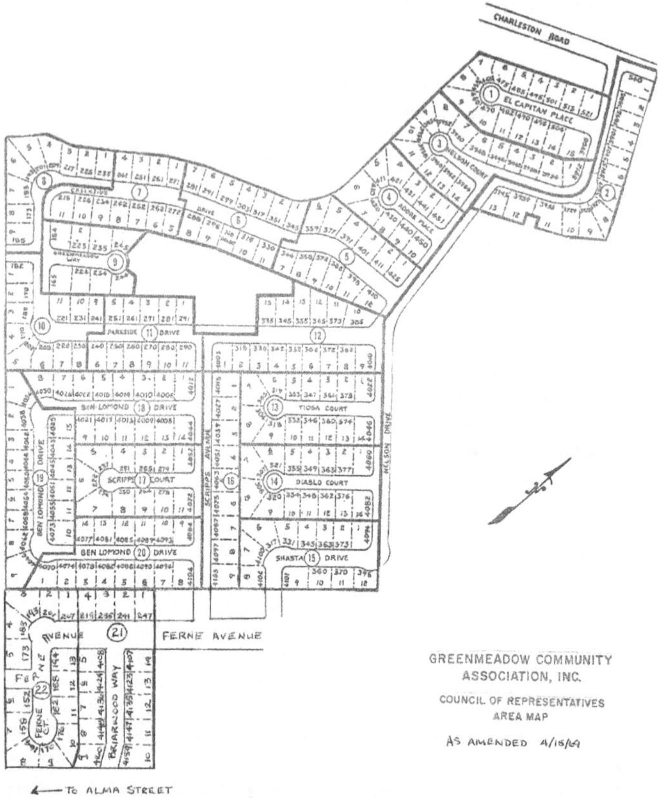

Figure 3.3: Eichler Greenmeadow Community Map. Source: Eichler Greenmeadow Community Map, 2021, September 10 (Open source).

In the 1950s, while there were some bold designs by the modernists, the design of the Levent Houses was more conservative in terms of flexible layout, indoor – outdoor relationship than their American contemporaries. It was mostly caused by the cultural differences, climate, local materials and traditional building technics.

The houses were planned as one or two story depending on the neighborhood: 1st, 2nd, 3rd, and 4th Levent Houses. The houses were designed with gable roofs, some of the facades were covered by the local stone materials

(Figure 3.4). The front yard use was popular like backyard as opposed to Eichler Homes. The layout design was not as flexible as Eichler homes, however, there was an intention to make the rooms more connected and more spacious. Typical houses were designed with two or three bedrooms, a living room, a kitchen, and a bathroom. The materials for the interior were quite limited in that period, some mosaics and fixtures were imported from other countries (Sadıkoğlu & Özsoy, 2016).

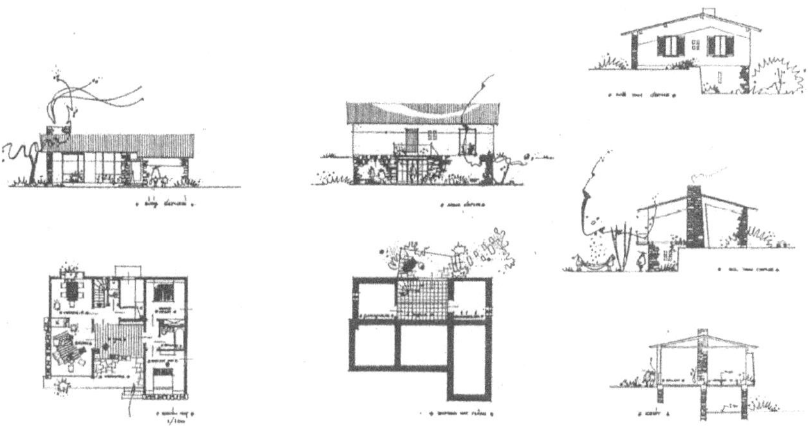

Figure 3.4: N Type House in 4th Levent. Source: Aru, 1956 (Open Source).

Eichler Homes worked with various architects who were well-known modernists including, Claude Oakland, A. Quincy Jones, and Anshen & Allen. Like case study houses organization, Eichler architects tried to develop a perfect prototype for the bay area. They knew how to get inspiration from European Modernism to create Californian Modernism. The designs of the layouts were mostly flexible and functional, and organized according to the Californian climate (Figure 3.5). They mostly designed the houses with gable roofs. While the main street facades were mostly closed, the façade of the backyard was designed more transparent. This shows that the use of backyards by families was more popular rather than the use of front yards.

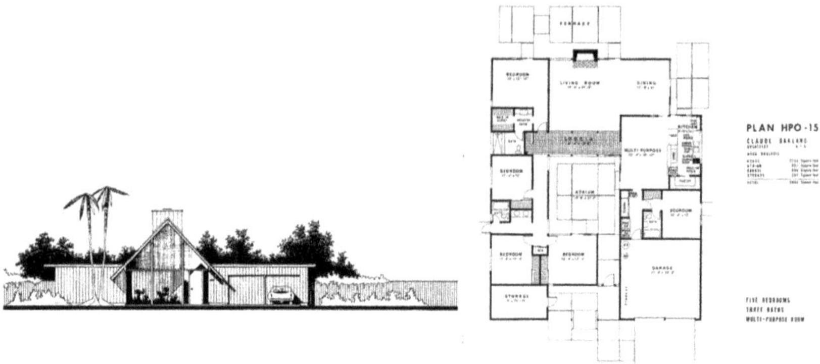

Figure 3.5: A Type plan by Claude Oakland for Eichler Homes. Source: Eichler Network, 2021 (Open source).

Since the company had built many modern single-family houses in the Bay Area from the 1950s to 1970s, they tried to develop new modern designs with the experience they had gotten over the years. Later, atriums, multi-purpose rooms and fire-places in living rooms became inseparable features of the layouts. The materials chosen for exterior, and interior were easy to use and clean and mostly supplied by local providers. The interiors were not made entirely of machine-like materials, which were criticized as being cold and inhumane by their European contemporaries in the 1950s (Figure 3.6).

Figure 3.6: Living Room in an Original Eichler Home in Palo Alto. Source: Authors

Eichler Homes published a value guide to list/explain the materials/features used in the homes (Figure 3.6). In this value guide, all the design details were listed such as '*…the generous use of glass walls, protected by wide overhangs and oriented to private gardens, bring the outdoor beauty into the view the year around.*' (Eichler Network, 2021).

Although they were working toward similar goals, there are differences between Eichler and Levent Homes in the layouts, forms, materials used, and building techniques that formed the design of the houses.

Representation and Public Visibility

The existence of a building in other forms such as media or publications is both essential for the promotion of the building and for extending its life in the built environment. So, representation and public visibility status are quite critical for the ethos of modernism and architectural memory. There was a tendency to publicize the commercial/public projects rather than residential projects, that's why it is hard to reach out to residential projects' publications from the 1950s. Serraino (2018) lists three factors which are important to support the architectural memory; architectural photography, editorial policy and mass-media coverage. When we look at the Levent Houses and Eichler Homes, we see that they had different patterns in terms of representation and public visibility.

Levent Houses were published in some architectural publications and *Arkitekt* Journal; and were not publicized by the professional architectural photographers. There is a limited number of photographs from the 1950s that show the original design of the houses. These photographs were mostly of the exterior and were not showing the house features in detail. Unlike the Eichler Homes professional photo shoot with real figures, the photos of the Levent Houses were not sufficient to provide information about the layout, materials used and other design details.

Despite the fact that Emlak Bank collaborated with private sector or the building industry, the initiative to build houses was still a state initiative, which may have resulted in some financial constraints for promotion. While Eichler Homes' promotional materials included 'modern life' captured photos for both exterior and interior spaces, the architectural drawings of Levent Houses were much more detailed to represent the 'modern life' rather than photographs (Figure 3.7). The original architectural projects were detailed with human figures, a luxury automobile and landscape drawings to narrate the new modern life in the settlement.

Figure 3.7: Single-Family House Drawings. Source: Aru, 1956 (Open Source).

When we look at the figure details, in the front elevation drawing, we see a couple about to go to play tennis. In the other elevation, we see a woman with a modern hat and some mid-century outdoor furniture. All these details were created to express the lifestyle that goes here or to show how to use the indoor and outdoor spaces (Figure 3.7).

The representation and the public visibility of the Levent Houses were not wide as much as Eichler Homes. In the 1950s, there was a limited architecture media in Turkey. As an architecture journal for professionals *Arkitekt* was the only one which promoted and searched about new styles such as modern architecture in that period. Some photos and the architectural projects of Levent Houses were published by *Arkitekt* in 1952 and 1956 with an informational text by the architects (Aru & Gorbon, 1952; Aru, 1956).

Eichler Homes had been photographed by the photographer Ernest Braun for 14 years. Although, the photographs were taken primarily to use as promotional material such as flyers, booklets and advertisements, all of them included dramatic modern architectural scenes. Braun tried to represent how to use an Eichler House with placing real people in the scenes such as kids playing on the ground, people dining by moonlight (Figure 3.8). To emphasize the 'modernism' in the Eichler environment, he used some specific arrangements of the *Knoll* and *Hermann Miller* furniture that were 1950s' modern interior design brands. For these arrangements besides Braun, Stanford Art Professor Matt Kahn also worked to create modern compositions. He made a strong statement in these photographs (Adamson & Arbunich, 2002).

Figure 3.8: Terra Linda Eichler Homes by Ernest Braun, 1957. Credit: Photograph by Ernest Braun.

Braun tried to show the design quality, materials used, layout, landscape, and how to use these modern spaces in his shoots with capturing family members in an Eichler House. These photographs were used for advertisements and sales catalogs. Joseph Eichler also worked with professional advertising agencies such as *Oglivy & Mather* and *Honig &Cooper* to design Eichler marketing publications to reach out to more families (Adamson & Arbunich, 2002). The compositions in the photoshoots were very similar to early European modernists' house shoots such as Walter Gropius's compositions for Master houses in Dessau.

When it comes to the public visibility of the homes in architectural journals and magazines, an editorial support was needed to get a public visibility in mass-media. Since modern architecture was quite popular in California in the mid-century, most of the home and lifestyle magazines were promoting the new designs. The founder, Joe Eichler knew how to be a part of new design community and he made the Eichler Homes published in *House and Home, American Institute of Architects Sunset Magazine, Better Homes & Gardens.* These magazines also appreciated Eichler Design Awards (Ditto et. al., 1995). All the effort made them more visible in the public.

Social and Cultural Value

Besides being registered as a heritage by the legal authorities; social and cultural value of a residential architecture depends on how dwellers and other people perceive, behave and what they think about them. Although Levent Houses and Eichler Homes are protected by some regulations in various levels today, their image on the dwellers and public are different.

The neighborhood in which Levent Houses are located, has changed with the urban development. Although the area had a suburban characteristic in the 1950s, today it has become a part of the city center like how garden cities in London were intermingled with the city naturally (Creese, 1992).

By time, the area has turned into a financial and business district from a residential neighborhood which caused function changes on Levent Houses (Bilgin, 1996; Sadıkoglu & Özsoy, 2016). The area became popular among businesses so as to rent a single-family house to use as an office. This function change caused some tensions between the dwellers and the renters. With the increasing commercial use in the neighborhood, the community feeling has been harmed. When the function of the houses changed, the original design of the houses became widely damaged by the new business renters (Sadıkoglu & Özsoy, 2016). Fortunately, as a result of the efforts carried out by the Non-Government Organizations (NGO) and some individual initiatives, Levent neighborhood was registered as a heritage site in 2008.

The leading NGO of Levent Houses is 'Çagdas Levent Dernegi' (ÇLD) which was founded by the Levent Houses owners and dwellers. The main aim of the organization was to preserve and sustain the physical, social and cultural characteristics of the area. Like Eichler Network, ÇLD also organized events and publications about Levent Houses. With the volunteers and dwellers' effort, the neighborhood was registered as a cultural heritage site which expresses the earlier examples of Turkish modern architecture and urban planning.

There was no specialized architectural design firm or builder to renovate these houses, at any rate only a few of the owners or renters tended to preserve the original design of the houses. The sales and the rent of the houses were not centrally controlled by specialized real estate agencies that helped to support and educate the potential or target dwellers.

Since their foundation, Eichler Homes tried to create a community feeling and an identity as an 'Eichler Dweller' or 'Eichler Owner' by the company. Living in an Eichler is still prestigious among Californian families today. It became a symbol of the mid-century lifestyle. There are Eichler fans who organize events such as Home-Tours to show the details of the designs in different neighborhoods (Eichler Home Tours, 2021). Although Eichler Company went out of business in the1970s, a number of volunteers are still working to sustain the network between Eichler dwellers and lovers. Since 1993, a network called '*Eichler Network*' has been actively working to support Eichler homeowners. This NGO also supports a home-maintenance referral service for architectural renovations to preserve Eichler Homes. Moreover, Eichler Network publishes quarterly journals on California Modernism to send them to Eichler Owners (Eichler Network, 2021). These volunteer initiatives helped to sustain the social and cultural value of Eichler Homes, and it supported the public awareness.

There are some architectural design agencies that are specialized in Eichler renovation and there are real estate agencies that are authorized to sell or rent Eichler Homes in various locations. This specialization also helped to educate the dwellers or target dwellers about their value (Swartz, 2018).

Unlike Levent Houses, most of the Eichler Homes are still in use with their original function as dwelling, and settlements that they were built in are still 'residential' neighborhoods that helps to remain their original functions.

Conclusion & Discussion

In the beginning of this chapter, it is asked that, what does help to protect the ethos in modern single-family houses, how can we make modern single-family houses and settlements more secure in order to sustain their value? European modernism influenced the other parts of the world by the 1920s. But the theory and the practice have been evolved in non-European countries. As part of a modernism and modern life- style propaganda agent in the1950s, single-family houses were examined in this chapter to understand how different countries re-shaped modern housing architecture which was developed by the European Modernists. The first part of the research helped us to explain how different modernism values emerged in Istanbul and San Francisco, Bay Area in the design process of the projects. In the second part we focused on the 'modernism ethos' by Eichler Homes and Levent Houses. Both of the projects were in the same direction in order to create a modern lifestyle inspired by earlier examples of modern single-family houses within a garden city concept. Their target audience was middle income families who wanted to live in a modern place. Today, the changes in and around these houses affected their recent value.

It was proposed to define the total ethos/value of these modern settlements with the help of their architectural and socio-cultural values. In the study, to compare the examples, archival materials such as architectural projects, sales flyers, newspaper advertisements were collected. All these materials helped us to reveal how these single-family housing projects were valued by the dwellers or other individuals and groups.

According to the findings, to create and sustain a modernism ethos/value, it is important to develop strategies from the beginning of the ideas/design. Having a modernist vision, hiring well-known and successful modernist architects, and collaborating with other professionals such as artists and designers is important for the acceptability of the project.

For both marketing and documentation (as a heritage), visibility is another important factor for the single-family houses. Working with a professional photographer and publishing these photos of the project in journals and newspapers can support the architectural value.

The community feeling is another point for this value, the Eichler has a great network with its dwellers and Eichler followers/fans, and this helped to support the public awareness. But in Levent Houses, the changing user profile (office users) negatively affected the awareness of the social and cultural value of the houses.

When it comes to talking about the economic value, while Eichler Homes protect their value as modern single-family houses, Levent Houses have had major changes in their prices because of the change in the area caused by the recent urban transformation and the change in the functions of the houses.

According to the findings, in order to create and sustain the value of a modern single-family house, the initiatives should start with the design process in the early stages of the project development with the help of the design and development professionals. Moreover, it is crucial to make effort on publishing the images in mass-media to help increasing public visibility and awareness on the architectural value. As the most important actors, dwellers of these houses, should be trained to be able to manage and sustain the value. Besides, their participation to non-governmental preservation and conservation organizations can be a helpful collaboration to increase the public awareness and to protect the value. While all important individual and small group initiatives are listed above, we can say that governments and legal offices, of course, have more power to preserve and sustain these buildings with the help of strict and well-defined regulations.

References

Adams, A. (1995). The Eichler Home: Intention and Experience in Postwar Suburbia. *Perspectives in Vernacular Architecture*, 5(1), 164–178. http://www.jstor.org/stable/3514253

Adamson, P., & Arbunich, M. (2002). *Eichler: Modernism Rebuilds the American Dream*. Gibbs Smith Publisher.

Akcan, E. (2012). *Architecture in Translation: Germany, Turkey and Modern House*. Duke.

Anon, (2009). *Berlin Modernism Housing Estates, Inscription on the UNESCO World Heritage List*, 2nd Edition, Verlagshaus Braun.

Aru, K. A. (1956). 4. Levend Mahallesi. *Arkitekt*, 1956–03 (285), 140–153.

Aru, K. A., & Gorbon, R. (1952). Levend Mahallesi. *Arkitekt*, 1952–09-10 (253–254), 174–181.

Bahr, E. (2007). *Weimar on the Pacific: German Exile Culture in Los Angeles and the Crisis of Modernism*. University of California Press.

Bilgin, I. (1996). Anadolu'da Modernleşme Sürecinde Konut ve Yerleşme. In Y. Sey (Ed.), *Tarihten Günümüze Anadolu'da Konut ve Yerleşme* (pp. 472–490). Tarih Vakfi Yayinlari.

Bozdoğan, S. (2002). *Modernism and Nation Building: Turkish Architectural Culture in the Early Republic*. University of Washington Press.

Creese, W. L. (1992). *The Search for Environment: The Garden City: Before and After*. Baltimore: John Hopkins University Press.

Di Guilio (Ed.). (2012). *Suburbanscapes*. Cost Action TU0701 Improving the Quality of Suburban Building Stocks. Alinea Editrice.

Ditto, J., Stern, L., & Wax, M. (1995). *Eichler Homes: Design for Living*. Chronicle Books.

Durth, W. (2014). International Architecture. In F. Gschwind and K. Groke (Eds.), *Weissenhof Museum in the Le Corbusier House* (p. 6–9). Zurich: Kraemerverlag.

Eichler Greenmeadow Community Map. (2021, September 10). Retrieved on September 10 from https://greenmeadow.org/about/#history

Eichler Home Tour (2021, January 21). *Eichler Home Tour.* Eichler. http://eichlerhometour.org

Eichler Network (2021, January 23). *Eichler Network*. https://www.eichlernetwork.com

Gönlügür, E. (2015). Exhibiting American Domestic Modernity at the Izmir International Fair. In M. O. Gurel (Ed.), *Mid-Century Modernism in*

Turkey: Architecture Across Cultures in the 1950s and 1960s (pp. 85–112). Routledge.

Güvenç, M., & Isık, O. (1999). *Emlak Bankasi 1926–1998.* Tarih Vakfi Yurt Yayınları.

Heynen, H. (1999). *Architecture and Modernity.* MIT Press.

Jacobs, J. (1961). *The Death and Life of Great American Cities.* Random House.

Lane, B. M. (2007). *Housing and Dwelling, Perspectives on Modern Domestic Architecture.* Routledge.

Le Corbusier. (1927). *Towards a New Architecture* (F. Etchells, Trans.) The Architectural Press. (Original work published 1923).

Mumford, L. (1989). *The City in History: Its Origins, Its Transformations, and Its Prospects.* Harcourt, Brace & Co.

Sadıkoglu, H., & Özsoy, A. (2016). A Study on Examining the Spatial Quality of the Modern Period Housing Stock. *Megaron Journal, 12*(2), 203–212.

Serraino, P. (2006). *Icons of Northern California Modernism.* Chronicle Books LLC.

Serraino, P. (2018). *Julius Shulman, Modernism Rediscovered.* Taschen.

Smiley, D. (2007). Making the Modified Modern. In B. Miller Lane (Ed.), *Housing and Dwelling: Perspectives on Modern Domestic Architecture* (pp. 285–296). Routledge.

Smith, E. A. T. (2019). *Case Study Houses* (P. Goessel, Ed.). Taschen.

Swartz, K. (2018, October 5). Interview with the Eichler Home Real Estate Agent, California.

Yıldız, D., & Özsoy, A. (2016). Modern Konutu Yeniden Okumak: Avrupa'dan ve Türkiye'den Sıra Ev Örneklerine Karşılaştırmalı Bir Bakış. In Y. Dulgeroglu Yuksel, E. Gur, D. Yildiz (Eds.), *İstanbul'da Konut [binbir çeşit]* (pp. 127–145). İTÜ Vakfı Yayınları.

Hande Tulum Okur

Efsun Ekenyazıcı Güney

4 Documenting the Evolutionary Process of Apartments in Kadıköy, Moda between 1960 and 1980

Introduction

Located on the Anatolian side of Istanbul, Kadıköy region is one of the heart beats of the city and it is a special case in terms of its dwelling culture since it represents a variety of the dwelling units of different eras (Figure 4.1). It is still possible to follow even the oldest dwelling patterns of this region dating back to nineteenth century, as well as the modernist examples of the apartments of early twentieth century. But, unfortunately the historical dwelling pattern of Kadıköy is being ruined and it is getting harder to observe the representatives of different periods because of the ongoing urban transformation process. While this transformation is hardly effecting the historical mansions or detached houses because some of them are being preserved, apartment buildings of the twentieth century are being effected mostly, there is no specific preservation law even for the iconic representatives of the apartment buildings. These building are mostly dated back from the late 1950s to the late 1980s and they are the ones that are under the risk of demolishment due to their plot sizes, low number of stories.[1]

1 Therefore, it is possible to construct new apartments with more stories. Additionally, these big sites sometimes allow more than one apartment blocks.

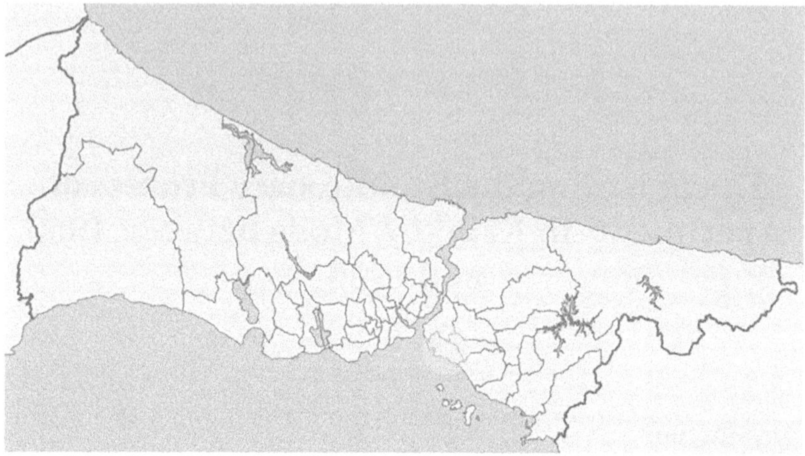

Figure 4.1: Istanbul municipality map highlighting Kadıköy region. Source: Created by the authors.

In terms of modernist architectural practice in the twentieth century, this era could be considered as a critical period for dwelling culture because of the fact that it has a special and distinguished architectural language that manifests itself in the aesthetical details on the façade and plan organizations.

Among the regions of Kadıköy, Moda is one of the critical ones that a specific apartment pattern from the 1960s to 1980s is observed. That's why this study focuses on Moda which also comes to the fore as a suitable sample area for an examination of architectural practices of different eras in terms of dwelling culture with its significant examples. Some of the showcases of the1960s–1980s are being demolished due to the ongoing urban transformation, and it is getting harder to observe these noteworthy apartments even here. When a literature research is conducted, it is understood that the dwelling culture of Moda in this era had not been emphasized sufficiently yet as well. The aim of this chapter is to contribute to the historiography of dwelling culture of Moda, Kadıköy by documenting the showcases of the specific era. Documenting these examples might help with the apartments' preservation and conservation and might shed light on potential future studies.

In the context of this chapter, firstly evolutionary process of the dwelling culture of Kadıköy is investigated in a chronological way. Secondly, Moda region is emphasized in terms of its dwelling culture. Finally, the dwelling culture of the specific era of 1960–1980 in Moda is analyzed through selected apartments' spatial organizations.

Evolutionary Process of the Dwelling Culture of Kadıköy

In the nineteenth century, the housing typology of Kadıköy was composed of wooden and masonry mansions (*konak*) and summer resorts (*köşk*) with two-stories within big gardens far from each other (Kütükçü, 2014, p. 2). In the early twentieth century, there was a shift that affected the dwelling phenomenon of Istanbul since Ankara was announced as the new capital. Istanbul has lost its critical impact and the government paid attention on the new capital's urbanization for a while. In the 1930s, the rent houses/apartments[2] with three or four[3] stories for the middle and upper classes, and modern dwelling units (villas) which were mostly rational concrete houses within gardens that were designed by prominent Turkish architects for the upper class had come to the fore (Bozdoğan, 2002). In the 1940s, the architects focused on an architectural language which aims to add a national flavor to modernist architecture through detached houses in gardens (Bozdoğan, 2010). Also, apartment buildings reflecting the architectural phenomenon of the traditional style nourished by the archetype of Turkish house (Acciai, 2017) were constructed (Tulum & Ekenyazıcı Güney, 2018).

In the 1950s, there was a paradigm shift due to the transformation of the national and international policies of the country. The internal migration to Istanbul created a breaking point for apartmentization in this era as well. Since there was an increase in the population, both apartmentization for the middle-income classes and informal dwellings *(gecekondu)* for the low-income classes attempted to accommodate the residential demand (Tulum & Ekenyazıcı Güney, 2018). Here, some apartment blocks were constructed on the plots of the demolished mansions and detached houses *(villas)* (Cantürk & Paker Kahvecioğlu, 2016) where the others were built on empty plots. The internal migration also effected the housing development of Kadıköy in the same way. In fact it became a site of attraction in the1950s (Hür, 1993). In this era, some

---

2 Rent house (kira evi) is a kind of apartment block that started to appear in the 1930s. In rent houses, each of the units of the floors were rented to different families by the owner of the rent house (Cantürk & Paker Kahvecioğlu, 2016). In this way the rent houses of the 1930s is different than the apartments of the 1960s in terms of the fact that, the apartments in the 1960s may have different owners for each unit.

3 There are also exceptional cases such as Tüten Apartment and Üçler Apartment (1935) which are composed of five stories.

apartment projects reflected the modern aesthetical canons of the period in terms of plan and façade organizations (Bozdoğan, 2010). The interior organizations of these apartments were mostly different than previous dwelling unit organizations. This new organization (living spaces next to the entrance of the unit and specialized bedrooms aligning through a new spatial route; corridor space with a service zone) was welcomed by many countries in a short period with no distinction made based on cultural or historical architectural references (Turangil, 2010). Another important issue in this era is the increase of the number of stories of the apartments by the effects of the urban planning regulations, due to the increase in the population and the housing demand (Gök et al., 2018).

The development plans and laws of 1964 and 1965 (property ownership law) led to a new transformation process and many previous dwelling units were turned into apartment blocks with four to five stories (Görgülü, 2016). These developments not only effected the housing density and the population of the region, they also created a new dwelling pattern (Yazıcıoğlu Halu, 2001), with a particular emphasis on the design of the façade as an extension of the plan organizations and modernist architectural experiments with the help of several architects; Emin Onat, Demirtaş Kamçıl, Rahmi Bediz, Melih Koray, Nişan Yaubyan, Muammer Gerekli (Tulum & Ekenyazıcı Güney, 2019) (Figure 4.2). In the meantime, there was also an overriding typology of apartments; standard apartment blocks that were constructed according to the build-sell process *(yap-sat)* with a general architectural approach that consists of a similarity in both plan & façade organizations (Tekeli, 2010; Altan et al., 2015).

Figure 4.2: Apartment examples; Dilman Apartment (Architect: Melih Koray), Gerekli Apartment (Muammer Gerekli), Erenköy Palas Apartment (Melih Koray), Di-Ka Apartment (Nişan Yaubyan). Source: Photos by authors.

The most drastic change in the city in terms of urbanization was observed in the1970s, first by the effects of the Bostancı-Erenköy master plan in 1972, and then by the construction of the Bosphorus Bridge in 1973. Thenceforth, Anatolian side of the city, especially Kadıköy started to urbanize. Afterwards, newly constructed roads and the dense industrial and dwelling zone of European side had started to move towards Kadıköy. So, the urban pattern of Kadıköy was redesigned in an intense way (Görgülü, 2016) and as a consequence, population was doubled soon. But, the 1980 military coup slowed down the urbanization process until the urban regulations of 1985 that increased the density and height of the dwelling units (Arıkan & Gökmen, 2016). While some of the wooden mansions, detached houses and the precursor showcases of apartments continued to exist, others were demolished and left their turns to new buildings (Tulum & Ekenyazıcı Güney, 2019). In the meantime, there was an attempt to block the pervasion of informal settlements and transform them to apartments through the Mass Housing Law of 1984 (Arıkan & Gökmen, 2016). These regulations did not mostly affect Kadıköy region in the 1980s but later it started to change the informal settlement areas.

It should be underlined that urbanization process had accelerated rapidly and public interventions could not answer all of the different aspects of housing problems in 1950–1980 period in Istanbul. The attempts to regularize the informal housing by the help of reconstruction peace arrangements (zoning amnesty) in 1965–1980 were not sufficient enough that the concept of social housing started to pop up as a new solution for housing construction in the late 1960s. For this reason, the state's Mass Housing Administration (TOKİ- *Toplu Konut İdaresi*) was established in the 1980s in order to support the housing issues.

By the end of the 1980s due to the changes in social, cultural, economic aspects and the desire to live in a safe environment, people urged to settle in gated communities as a new dwelling form by the improvements of the transportation system (Akalın, 2016). These gated communities that started to emerge in the late 1980s needed large and empty spaces because of their multi-functional program. Thus, some were built in the outskirts of the city but some were located in the empty zones within the city such as Alkent Etiler (1989), Altunizade *(Konaklar)* Mansions (1988–1993), Göztepe Soyak (1985–1992). There were also exceptional cases that had relatively smaller scales in Kadıköy dated back to the late 1980s and early 1990s such as Sümko *(Sitesi)* Housing Complex, Dilkum Housing Complex, Eston Housing Complex, Koru Housing Complex, Yasemin Housing Complex. Since these settlements were located at the central zones, they were composed of limited number of residential blocks and a few facilities such as parking, playground, recreation areas, pool etc.

After the 1999 earthquake and the 2001 economic crisis, there was again a search for a new dwelling type, which resulted in residences through singular blocks that are located in the city center (Yüksel & Akbulut, 2009). Some of these residences were somehow similar to the gated communities in the context of a multi-functional program such as Ataşehir Varyap Meridian. In the meantime, there were also residences providing safety to its users which were constructed in the places of the demolished apartments.

Meanwhile, it is also important to underline the radical changes in the urban administration of Istanbul in the 2000s. Especially Law no.6306, for the Regeneration of Areas Under Disaster Risk became a major tool that defines new bureaucratic regulations to retransform the unhealthy building stock. But these regulations did not offer a holistic perspective, it continued with singular implementations and it started to effect each region with vast demolishment, especially in Kadıköy.

To sum up, the construction of the gated communities in Kadıköy area specifically was visible in the late 1980s and 1990s. The regeneration of the informal settlements is dated back to the twenty-first century. For example, Yeni Sahra and Fikirtepe regions, which were once housing informal settlements, are now full of newly constructed gated communities and residences. It is important to stress that only some parts of Kadıköy were influenced by these typologies. Principally, newly constructed singular apartment buildings started to be an important part of Kadıköy's housing pattern. For example, in Moda region, when an apartment building is demolished because of the urban transformation process, a singular apartment building is constructed instead. Since the land is very limited here, no other facilities are observed unlike the gated communities and the residences.

As a result of the urban transformation process, the existing housing pattern of Kadıköy is being transformed, so most of the noteworthy representatives of the former periods could not be observed. Some of the old mansions within big gardens are still being preserved but the dwelling function of the mansions are mostly transformed[4] (Cantürk & Paker Kahvecioğlu, 2016) to banks, educational buildings, restaurants, etc. Their gardens on the other hand, are generally hosting new apartments and residences as the neighboring units of the mansions. Since the number of the demolished buildings of the previous eras are increasing, the existing housing pattern is being transformed into one dominated by apartments.

4 The mansion of Kuriş family in Erenköy and Reşat Paşa Mansion in Kozyatağı are some of the showcases.

Dwelling Culture of Moda

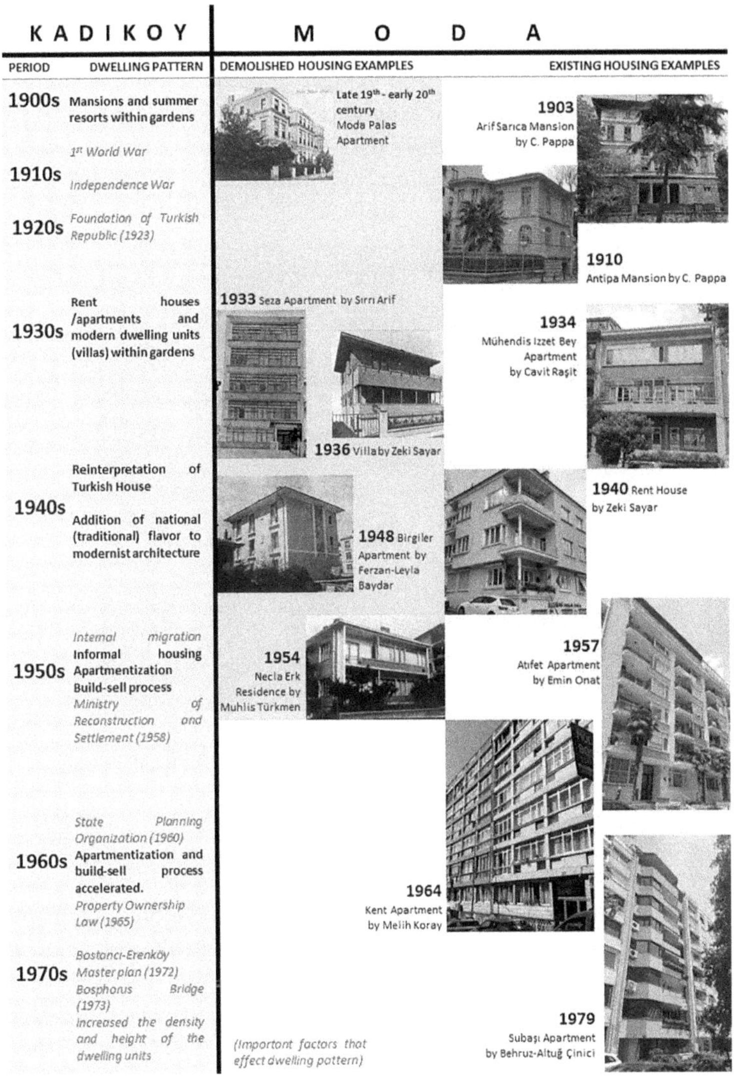

Figure 4.3: Evaluation process of Kadıköy, Moda in terms of dwelling culture. Source: Designed by the authors.

Moda, which was a natural peninsula with meadows and gardens on the Anatolian side of the city, is one of the regions where mostly the Armenian, Greek, Italian and British families inhabited since the late eighteenth century (Ekdal, 2005; Sezginalp, 2017). An important urbanization process started and the area became more accessible and popular in the nineteenth century (Aşar, 2019). From that time on it became an important residential and social part of the city (Kömürcüyan, 1952, pp. 301–303). Moda (Figure 4.3) is still a very popular center in terms of its socio-cultural opportunities and residential speciality.

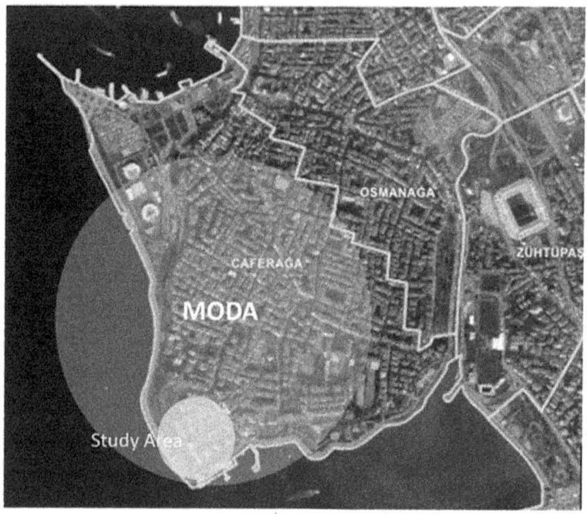

Figure 4.4: Partial Kadıköy map highlighting Moda region & study area.
Source: Designed by the authors.

When the residential culture of the twentieth century in the area is studied, (Figure 4.4) a transformation is observed after the foundation of the Republic. Especially in the1930s, architectural practice started to flourish and lots of 'modern' residential examples with volumetric and geometric compositions, asymmetrical organizations, rounded corners, flat roofs, wide balconies/terraces (Bozdoğan, 2010) for nuclear families appeared (Sezginalp, 2017). When a literature review in Arkitekt Journal is employed, many showcases of the era that are mostly designed by famous architects such as Zeki Sayar, Abidin Mortaş, Rebii Refik Gorbon, Cavit Raşit are realized. The prominent cases which are both modern villas and rent houses (apartments) are Villa Sani Yaver by Zeki Selah (Selah, 1932), Röntgen Apartment by Zeki Selah (Selah, 1933), Mühendis İzzet

Bey Apartment (Raşit, 1934), Dr. Ziya and Dr. Zeki Rent Houses (Mortaş, 1935), Rent House by Zeki (Selah) Sayar (Sayar, 1940) (Figure 4.5).

Figure 4.5: Old (Raşit, 1934; Sayar, 1940) (open source) and current photos of Mühendis İzzet Bey Apartment by Cavit Raşit and Rent house by Zeki (Selah) Sayar (Photos by authors).

On the other hand, when the common residential architectural language of the 1940s is analyzed, a transformation in the design language is noticed. Here, a design approach with nationalist influence with a reflection of Turkish/Ottoman residential culture through wide eaves, sloped roof, hipped roof, cantilevered projections or projections with bracings is seen. A villa in Boğaziçi (1946) by Sedad Hakkı Eldem (Eldem, 1946), a residential unit in Büyükada (1946) by Emin Necip Uzman (Uzman, 1946) and Elagöz House in Ortaköy (1947) by Halit Femir (Femir, 1947) may be considered as the prominent cases in Istanbul. So, a clear difference in the residential culture had been detected, especially in the second half of the 1940s; the modernist, rationalist architectural approach of the 1930s was not fully observed. But when a similar research is conducted in Moda, Kadıköy, it is observed that there is only one single case found in Arkitekt journal with a traditional, national architectural approach; Birgiler Apartment (1948) (Baydar and Baydar, 1950) by Ferzan and Leyla Baydar (Sezginalp, 2017). Also, there are other residential cases; rent houses dated back to the 1940s that may be found in the Arkitekt journal, but these followed a modernist architectural language without a nationalist influence.

After the dominant architectural trend of the 1940s, a new modernist approach in architecture, 'International Style' was identified in the 1950s. Especially, Americanization started to reflect on the culture in Turkey, it affected the life style, social-cultural activities, art and architecture (Akcan, 2001). So, formal concepts that refer to the International Style of the 1930's became popular in architecture with slight differences. Sibel Bozdoğan calls this era in Turkey as a turning point for Turkish modernity (Bozdoğan 2006, pp. 62– 70).

The 1950s modernist architectural language was also reflected in the residential culture through the designs of Emin Onat, Nevzat Erol, Abdurrahman Hancı, Haluk Baysal, and Melih Birsel. In this era, it is possible to mention the traces of that language in both single family residences (villas) (Necla Erk Residence) (Sezginalp, 2017) and mostly concrete apartment buildings with 4–6 stories, which were replaced by the 1930s rent houses and old mansions. For example, in the plot of Moda Palace, a new apartment block Marmara Apartment was built in 1957, and later in the 1970s, Manzara Apartment was constructed on the same plot (Civelekoğlu, 2020).

Moda is such a region that some representatives of the residential pattern of the 1950s may still be observed in. For example, Marmara and Atıfet Apartments by Emin Onat (both 1956–57) (Figure 4.6) are two showcases of the period that reflect the dominant design approach of the time such as transparency with the help of big glass openings/windows, big balconies with stilized railings, etc.

Figure 4.6: Marmara and Atıfet Apartments. Source: Photos by authors.

There are some major features that effect the housing phenomenon in the1960s. Establishment of the Ministry of Reconstruction and Settlement to regulate and organize all activities related with housing in 1958 is one of them. Also, in order to design and organize a planned growth The State Planning Organization was established in 1960 and this organization prepared five-year development plans and annual programs (Bozdoğan & Akcan, 2012, p. 141). These caused a rise in the quantity of the apartment construction, a transformation process of the built environment in the region. The residential texture of the area, especially between the 1960s and 1980s, was mostly protected until the twenty-first century. But due to the last urban transformation process, this texture and buildings are in danger. Therefore, it is important to document and preserve these buildings with a distinguished architectural language that is shown through their plan organizations, rhythmic volumetric expressions, solid-void relationship balance, the variety and combination of different materials and techniques, aesthetical details, and different typography. Therefore, the era between the 1960s and 1980s will be highlighted in the next part of this chapter.

Deciphering the Era of 1960–1980 of Moda's Residential Culture

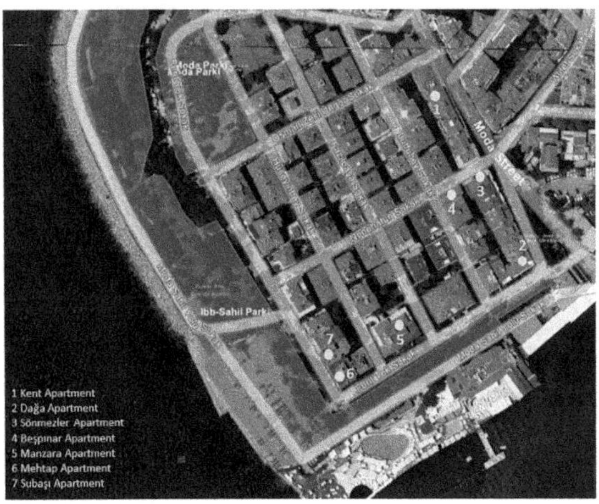

Figure 4.7: Partial Moda map showing the research cases. Source: Designed by the authors.

In order to decipher the dwelling culture of Moda in 1960–1980 period, the authors conducted several site visits and prepared a list of the noteworthy apartments of this era. Then, an archival research is employed at the Kadıköy Municipality in order to find the architects and additional information about these buildings and consequently, the list which shows us some of the representatives of the era that still exist in Moda is elaborated (Table 4.1).

Table 4.1: The list of noteworthy apartments of 1960–1980 in Moda. Source: Prepared by authors

YEAR	ARCHITECT	APARTMENT NAME	LOCATION (BLOCK NO-PARCEL NO)
1960	BEKIR IHSAN UNAL	AKGÜN APARTMENT	MODA 1240-75
196?	MELİH KORAY	RÜYAM APARTMENT	MODA 1198-34
196?	MELİH KORAY	AYLİN APARTMENT	MODA 123-1
196?	MELİH KORAY	UZUNAL APARTMENT	MODA 131-19
1960-65	UNKNOWN	IHLAMUR APARTMENT	MODA 1288-19
1961	MEHMET ALİ HANDAN	CİMCOZ APARTMENT	MODA 127-3
1961	HAMIT DURU	LEYLAK APARTMENT	MODA 151/14
1962	MELİH KORAY	MODA PALAS APARTMENT	MODA 123-15
1963	GAYYUR TEZCANLI	UFUK APARTMENT	MODA 79-1
1964	MELİH KORAY	KENT APARTMENT	MODA 123-14
1964	MELİH KORAY	ZAFER APARTMENT	MODA 123-7
1964	ZEKİ SAYAR	ÖZ APARTMENT	MODA 12-74
1965	MELİH KORAY	ÖZOĞUZ APARTMENT	MODA 111-38
1965	MELİH KORAY	ÇINAR APARTMENT	MODA 123-2
1965-68	EMİN ONAT	ESİT APARTMENT	MODA 1165-17
1966	UNKNOWN CONTRACTER	GÜNAYDIN APARTMENT	MODA 109-43
1966	MELİH KORAY	SELAHATTİN BEY APARTMENT	MODA 117-5
1966	MELİH KORAY	YONCA APARTMENT	MODA 131-18
1967	FÜRUZAN GAMSIZ	TEVFİK TAŞÇI APARTMENT	MODA 76-2
1967	LÜTFİ ZEREN	TANAY APARTMENT	MODA 111-40
1967	MELİH KORAY	ÇINAR APARTMENT	MODA 123-2
1967	UNKNOWN	MURAD APARTMENT	MODA 1233-9
1967	ÜNVER BOZBAY	DAĞA APARTMENT	MODA 76-1
1967	HAYRİ AYBAR	SÖNMEZLER APARTMENT	MODA 76-9
1967	MELİH KORAY	SÖNMEZ APARTMENT	MODA 76-9
1967-69	ATAY ALİYAZICIOĞLU	EBRU APARTMENT	MODA 1273-40
1968	MELİH KORAY	GEZİ APARTMENT	MODA 1288-59
1968	MELİH KORAY	BORA APARTMENT	MODA 139-2
1968	YÜKSEL UMUTER	SABİR SAMİ BEY APARTMENT	MODA 79-10
1969	MELİH KORAY	BULGURLU APARTMENT	MODA 123-5
1970	KAMER ŞAHBAZ	CİHAN APARTMENT	MODA 140-38
1970	ERGÜN GÜNAYDIN	BEŞPINAR APARTMENT	MODA 76-8
1970	MELİH KORAY	HUZUR APARTMENT	MODA 1165-46
1970	ERGİN GÖMÜÇ	MANZARA APARTMENT	MODA 78-1
197?	İBRAHİM PAŞALIOĞLU	YILMAZ APARTMENT	MODA 1288-89
1971	UNKNOWN	EDİZ APARTMENT	MODA 110-28
1972	YAVUZ ÜNAL/ÖNAL	KAMAY APARTMENT	MODA 76-7
1974	NURHAN KALPAKÇIOĞLU	KURT APARTMENT	MODA 76-3
1974	NURHAN KALPAKÇIOĞLU	GÜL APARTMENT	MODA 76-6
1974	İBRAHİM PAŞALIOĞLU	NİL APARTMENT	MODA 1288-68
1975	NİZAMETTİN ÖZBEK	BİNBİR APARTMENT	MODA 77-4
1978	MELİH KORAY	MEHTAP APARTMENT	MODA 79-2
1979	ŞADİ ADIGÜZEL	BABADAN APARTMENT	MODA 1288-97
1979	BEHRUZ&ALTUĞ ÇİNİCİ	SUBAŞI APARTMENT	MODA 79-3

Here, in order to analyze this specific era, selected representatives (Figure 4.7) will be highlighted from the list above. Before doing that, it is important to understand the general architectural approach of the era. The apartmentization process of Moda accelerated due to the regulations related with property ownership law. This caused a change in the population of Moda due to the families who agreed with contractors to construct new apartments instead of their houses. So, newcomers both from upper class families and middle class families bought flats in these apartments, and that led to both a change in the number and the demographic composition of the population of Moda. These new apartments presented many modernist features in architectural language such as material use, heating facilities, elevator, sanitary elements, maid's room, storage and cellar (Sezginalp, 2017). On the other hand, these apartments in Turkey could not completely compete with their international peers especially due to the lack of interior qualities such as the unique modernist furniture design (İnce Güney, 2005). This led a change in the profile of the apartments of Moda, the old dwelling units; mostly mansions started to vanish after the 1960s (Sezginalp, 2017) and attached houses started to be constructed next to each other in the plots of the region (Oskay, 2021). But, it is still possible to observe rare existing mansions such as Arif Sarıca Mansion.

A master plan which is still valid for the region was prepared in 1972 (Atun Atlı, 2019). That master plan reorganized the gardens of old big mansions of the region and these gardens were split into smaller parcels of the new apartments (Kadıköy Kaymakamlığı, 2021). Another important issue that speeded the urbanization process up was the opening of Bosphorus Bridge in 1973. By the help of this bridge, Kadıköy region had become more assessable. In the meantime, Kurtköy, Pendik, Kartal districts were announced as industrial zones (Arkitera, 2013). All of these improvements had led Kadıköy to be an attractive point. Moda, as a part of Kadıköy had also been influenced by these improvements.

In the 1980s, as the boundaries of Istanbul expanded, many of the existing dwelling units were demolished and replaced with new ones (Görücü, 2018). This process has had little impact on the Moda region because the boundaries of Moda stayed still during this era. Therefore, it is possible to see the representatives of 1960–1980 era because of the fact that the urban pattern of Moda was mostly preserved until the recent urban transformation process.

Figure 4.8: Façades of the selected apartments; (first row) Kent, Dağa, Sönmezler Apartments, (second row) Beşpınar, Manzara, Mehtap, Subaşı Apartments.
Source: Photos by authors.

Within this context, it is possible to assert that some representatives of the era present façade organizations that include a consistent grammar and a proclivity to provide dynamism. (Figure 4.8). In this chapter, some showcases that reflect the exceptional architectural design language of the era through dynamic approaches (exceptional ones) and some showcases that demonstrate the common, unpretentious design language of the era (regular, common ones) are selected according –especially- to their façade languages and locations among the prepared list (Table 4.1). In this way, gaining a broader perspective is aimed. Subaşı Apartment is selected because its designer is one of the most famous architects of the country, Behruz Çinici. This apartment is among the limited number of the buildings he designed in Istanbul. Mehtap Apartment is selected due to its organic design approach in terms of its façade organization which was a rare approach earlier. Sönmezler Apartment, located on a corner is composed of two blocks and also contains breeze block elements on the façade. This dominant façade element was mostly used in public buildings in that era. Kent and Manzara Apartments are selected due to their framed system façade organization which was one of the common features of the façade design in that era. Also the designers of these two buildings Melih Koray and Ergin Gömüç were partners for a while, that partnership may have influenced their architectural language. Dağa and Beşpınar Apartments were selected because they are representing the frequently observed and unpretentious façade design language of the era which is visible through the use of concrete construction technique, linear metal railing design and neutral color palette. These two cases which do not have particularly distinguishable façade designs are evaluated as the common, regular apartments of the era.

With the help of these cases, the variety of interior organizations are analyzed and the differences are examined. So, here floor plans of these apartments are emphasized to understand the variety of the spatial organizations (Figures 4.9 and 4.10).

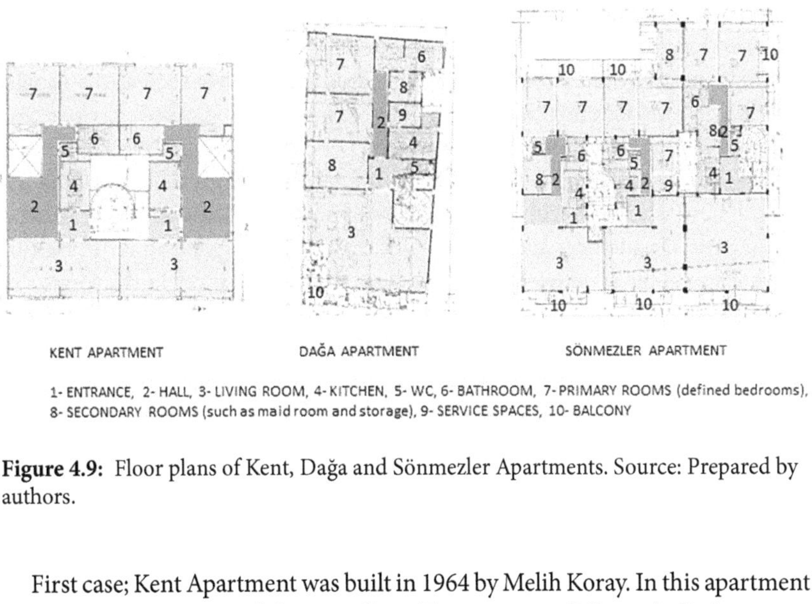

Figure 4.9: Floor plans of Kent, Dağa and Sönmezler Apartments. Source: Prepared by authors.

First case; Kent Apartment was built in 1964 by Melih Koray. In this apartment there are two symmetrical flats in a floor. There are two different halls (entrance, hall) in these flats. In this plan type there is a welcoming entrance area; attached to the kitchen, living room and also a big hall. This big hall is in between a living room and the small hall that separates the private zones and the public zones.

Second case; Dağa Apartment was designed by Ünver Bozbay in 1967. In this apartment, each floor has one flat and when these flats are analyzed a different interior organization is realized. Therefore, that interior organization is evaluated in a more detailed way than the others. Here, the entrance hall of the flats leads to the living area, WC, kitchen and the cellar while the corridor of the private core welcomes the residents to three bedrooms including a child bedroom and a shared bathroom with a dressing zone. While the biggest bedroom which is closest to the bathroom and the dressing zone is the master bedroom, the smallest bedroom is designated for the child. There is no closet drawing in the master bedroom, the designer probably assumed that the dressing zone will be sufficient for that function. Additionally, there is a seating area in the master bedroom on the ground floor, but on the upper floors there are also additional desks in these rooms. It is possible to claim that the master bedrooms were starting to be designed more elaborately. This shows that these bedrooms were more than just sleeping zones. When the upper floor flats' living rooms are analyzed it is seen that they are much bigger. These big living rooms are designed for gathering, seating, and dining functions; the furnishing design idea of the designer points out different zones for these functions. Another important change is the L-shaped balcony of the upper floors. There is a variety in the flooring materials, the designer proposed a differentiation regarding the zones such as the rooms, wet spaces, corridor and the entrance hall.

The following case Sönmezler Apartment, which was designed by Hayri Aybar in 1967, has two different entrances from different directions so the building has two different staircases with similar design approaches. There are three flats on a floor, two of which are alike in terms of their spatial organization. These two flats are somehow symmetrical but there are slight differences in the context of the dimensions and forms. Here, the entrance directly opens to the living room and the kitchen, and also the private hall is accessed from the living room to the private zones. Another difference between these two flats is an additional working area with an access from the master bedroom. Third flat, on the other hand is bigger than the other ones due to its orientation within the site. Here the entrance hall is in between the living room, kitchen and WC, it separates these zones and the private zones.

The first case which dates back to the 1970s to be analyzed in this chapter is Beşpınar Apartment which was designed by Ergün Günaydın in 1970. Here, a specific entrance area is not defined, instead there is a long hall from the entrance in between the living area, kitchen and the private zones. This plan type had become overly popular in the 1970s and 1980s.

The next case; Manzara Apartment was designed by Ergin Gömüç in 1970. In this case there is a welcoming entrance area that connects living room, kitchen, WC and cellar. This entrance area is integrated with a private hall through which the bedrooms and bathroom are accessed.

Third case of the 1970s apartment examples is Mehtap Apartment, designed by Melih Koray in 1978. This apartment has a unique organic interior organization, therefore it is analyzed particularly. There is variety in the number of the flats of each floor; three floors have one big flat, the others have two flats and one of these is a duplex unit. Also, a big entrance area that leads to the living room and the kitchen is defined. This area narrows down to a L-shape hall that is connected to the primary and secondary rooms, WC, bathroom and cellar. The biggest private room with a balcony is the master bedroom and this room includes a private bathroom. There is a service window in the kitchen connecting it to the living room as a specific design idea. The organic approach of Koray, continues with the curved corner walls of the hall and the living room walls. Here, a focus on circulation spaces and wet spaces is observed through the floorings and the furnishing.

Fourth case; Subaşı Apartment is designed by Behruz and Altuğ Çinici in 1979. Here, there are two light wells and a private hall separates the entrance area, living room and kitchen from bedrooms and the wet spaces. Similar to Mehtap Apartment, there is a service door from the kitchen to the living room and also a master bedroom with a bathroom is observed. Therefore, it might be considered that at the end of the 1970s the master bedroom idea had started to be used.

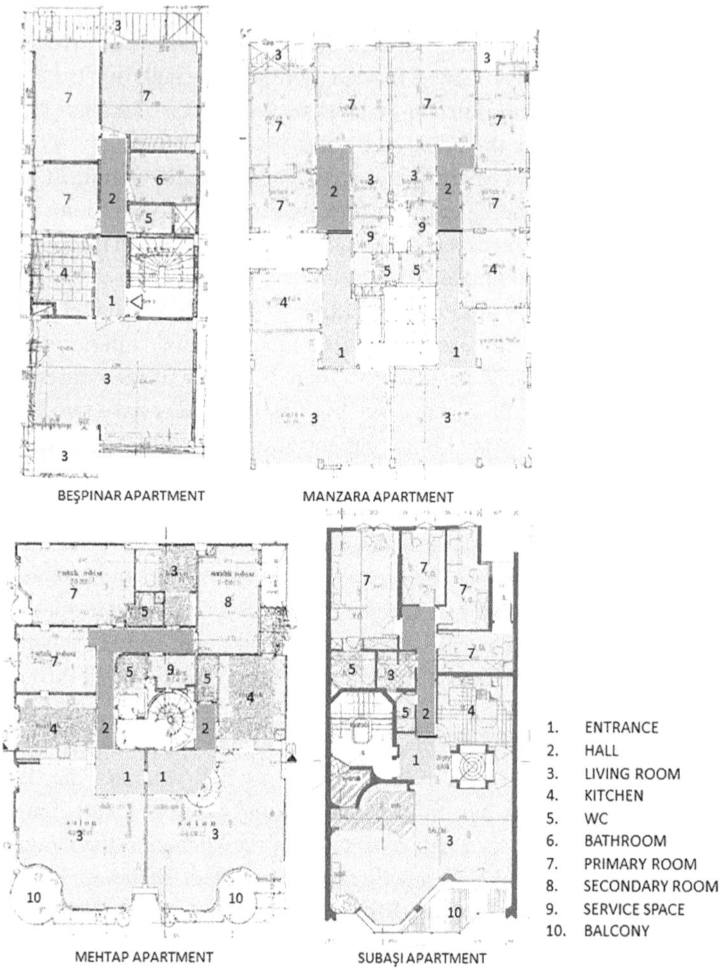

Figure 4.10: Floor plans of Beşpınar, Manzara, Mehtap and Subaşı Apartments. Source: Prepared by authors.

When these examples (Figures 4.9 and 4.10) are analyzed in a comparative way, a symmetrical design approach in the plans of the apartments which contains two flats in a floor is mostly observed. This approach which dates back to the first half of the twentieth century (Mutdoğan, 2014) is also observed in apartments of the 1960s and 1970s as well.

The analyzed examples show that the entrance areas of the interiors designed in 1960s are usually separated from the halls with a door privatizing the rooms and bathroom. These entrance spaces are sometimes integrated with the living areas. So, in such examples, from the entrance door, the interior of the living area is observed. But, in the 1970s it is possible to realize a change in the organization of the entrance area. In some cases, such as Beşpınar Apartment, the entrance area and the hall are combined into a narrow corridor providing access to both living areas and the private rooms. Also in some other cases, such as Manzara and Subaşı Apartments, the entrance area is designed as a connection module to the living area and the kitchen. A corridor space that is separated by a door leads the users to the other spaces such as the primary rooms and secondary rooms. So, as Pınar Sezginalp (2017) underlines these corridors/halls separate the public from the private. Also İhsan Bilgin claims that, these new corridors/halls integrated to the plans also offered rooms with different functions and wet space zones (Erten Bilgiç, 2008).

In this chapter, the rooms are considered as two different groups; primary and secondary rooms. Primary rooms are the bedrooms and the secondary rooms are the ones for the maid, storage etc. Only the defined bedrooms are named as primary rooms in the plan schemes. The cellar, called service space here, is designed in relation with domestic units such as kitchen. But, the need for a maid is transformed into a day-laborer in time and the functions related with the maid such as maid's room, cellar and the storage had started to be smaller and these functions became a part of the kitchen. So, it is possible to say that many functions had started to transform in the 1970s, for example the service spaces and secondary rooms had started to lose their functions and eventually got lost. According to Sezginalp (2017), the new daily life routine was mostly based on an individual life style so that the bedrooms started to be larger in time. Because instead of spending time in the living room, people started to spend most of their times in their bedrooms. Among the analyzed examples, this approach is realized by the furnishing of the bedrooms with desks, armchairs, and master bathrooms. So, it is possible to see the foot prints of the master bathrooms in the 1970s which would become common and popular later.

Concluding Remarks

There are different studies that focus on the dwelling culture of Istanbul, Kadıköy which analyze the eras and architectural figures through housing typologies. Among these eras, 1960–1980 period was not underlined in the literature regarding the dwelling units, specifically the apartments until recent studies that mostly focus on some designers such as Maruf Önal, Nişan Yaubyan, Melih Koray[5] and their designs. Due to the recent urban transformation process, this era in Kadıköy is also important since its representatives are being demolished day by day.

Moda, which represents many layers of the dwelling culture covering the apartments has not been emphasized sufficiently in the architectural literature except for a few studies such as the publications of Pınar Sezginalp and Tanla Atun Atlı.

Moda has survived from the urban transformation process until recently. Because, here the regulations pay attention to the height of the buildings and do not mostly allow to build higher buildings than the previous ones unlike many other parts of Kadıköy. That's why Moda could survive from the process for a long while since it was not very profitable for the constructors. But, since Moda became so popular for the last few years, the prices of the apartment units accelerated. Therefore, new apartments started to get the places of the old ones slowly. Due to the fact that Moda has not been affected by the urban transformation process harshly yet, it is still possible to observe the representatives of the dwelling culture of the different eras, specifically apartments. But it should be underlined that many apartments dated back to the twentieth century, mostly to 1960s–1980s are in danger in terms of the urban transformation process. So, the documentation and analysis of these cases are critical for contributing to modernist architectural literature in Turkey. That's why, here, a selection of apartments dated back to this specific era are analyzed in order to represent the variety of the interior organizations through plans. It is realized that there were many attempts to create different atmospheres in the interiors even if some of the façade organizations were not assertive. It is understood from the examples that there was a slow transition of the interior organizations from the 1960s to the late 1970s. In the meantime, it should be underlined that there was a standardization process which ended up with alike plans and façades. As a result, the attempts examined in this chapter are critical in terms of demonstrating the variety. Lately, the representatives of these exceptional cases have disappeared due to the recent urban transformation process, and the newly constructed ones within the process seem to (re)produce the sameness in terms of plans and facade organizations. It could be argued that the experimental architectural approach of the demolished apartments could serve as a model for newcomers, allowing for differentiation and creation of a unique interior atmosphere for each

5 For more information, Ekenyazıcı Güney, E. and Tulum, H. (2021).

apartment through plan and façade organizations. Investigating the sameness issue in future studies might be useful for understanding the current status of the dwelling culture of Moda[6].

Due to the urban transformation process, unfortunately the apartments that survived until now are also in danger, so it is very important to document and preserve these apartments. For future studies, it is also recommended that focusing on more apartment buildings and more architectural figures would help to enlighten the era of 1960—1980, which still has too many mysteries to be unearthed.

References

Acciai, S. (2017). The Ottoman-Turkish House according to Sedad Hakkı Eldem, a refined domestic culture suspended between Europe and Asia, *ABE Journal*, 11, 2–3.

Akalın, M. (2016). Mekânsal ayrışmanın bir yeni biçimi olarak kapalı kapılı siteler Akkent Konutları örneği, *Hitit Üniversitesi Sosyal Bilimler Enstitüsü Dergisi*, 9(2), 923–956.

Akcan, E. (2001). Americanization and anxiety: Istanbul Hilton Hotel by SOM and Eldem. *Proceedings of the Oriental-Occidental Geography, Identity, Space.* Turkey. 38–44.

Altan, E., Akpınar, İ., & Akay, A. (2015). Architecture in İstanbul in the republican period. From antiquity to the 21st century, *History of Istanbul*, 9.

https://istanbultarihi.ist/716-architecture-in-istanbul-in-the-republican-period

Arıkan, B., & Gökmen, G. P. (2016). Kentsel mekânın fiziksel katmanları, konut dokusunun oluşumu ve Feneryolu Mahallesi'nin "risk" li dönüşümü, *Idealkent*, *7*(20), 966–998.

Arkitera (5 March 2013). *Geçmişin Modern Mimarisi-1: Kadıköy*. https://www.arkitera.com/haber/gecmisin-modern-mimarisi-1-kadikoy/

Aşar, K. K. (2019). *Struggle, and back home: Gentrification of Moda* [Unpublished doctoral thesis]. CEU.

Atun Atlı, T. (2019). Kadiköy Moda semtinin tarihi ve kentsel sit olarak tanımlanmasi ve korunmasi için öneriler [Unpublished M.A. Thesis]. Istanbul Technical University.

6 For example, Bahar Yayla and Nilay Ünsal Gülmez made an investigation on the newly erected apartments of Bağdat Street of Kadıköy in terms of their façade organization experiments. According to this investigation they made a classification such as double-skin or rhythmic façades (Yayla & Ünsal Gülmez, 2016).

Baydar, F., & Baydar, L. (1950). Birgiler Apartmanı, *Arkitekt, 07*(222), 153–155.

Bozdoğan, S. (2002). *Modernizm ve ulusun inşası, erken cumhuriyet Türkiyesi'nde mimari kültür.* Metis Yayınları.

Bozdoğan, S. (2006). A lost icon of Turkish modernism: Expo '58 pavilion in Brussels, *DOCOMOMO Journal, 35*, 62–70.

Bozdoğan, S. (2010). From 'cubic houses' to suburban villas: Residential architecture and the elites in Turkey. In C. Kerslake, K. Öktem & P. Robins (Eds.), *Turkey's engagement with modernity: Conflict and change in the twentieth century* (pp. 405–424). Palgrave Macmillan.

Bozdoğan, S., & Akcan, E. (2012). *Turkey: Modern architectures in history.* Reaktion Publications.

Cantürk, E., & Paker Kahvecioğlu, N. (2016). An alternative dwelling history narrative: The story of the 'apartment', *ITU A Z, 13*(3), 93–107.

Civelekoğlu, L. (2020). Bir yangın yerinin FOtopsisi. https://lcivelekoglu.blogspot.com/2020/10/bir-yangn-yerinin-fotopsisi-fotografl.html

Ekdal, M. (2005). *Kapalı hayat kutusu Kadıköy Konakları*, Yapı Kredi Publications.

Ekenyazıcı Güney, E., & Tulum, H. (2021). 1960–1980 Yılları Arasının Üretken Figürlerinden Melih Koray'ın Apartman Tasarımlarındaki Cephe Dili, *Megaron, 16*(3), 454–467.

Eldem, S. (1946). Boğaziçi'nde bir villa, *Arkitekt, 05*(06), 99–103.

Erten Bilgiç, D. (2008). Kentleşme sürecinde konut olgusunun geçirdiği değişimler çerçevesinde Yukarı Değirmendere-Çarşıiçi Mahallesi örneği, *Megaron, 3*(1), 1–15.

Femir, H. (1947). Ortaköy'de E. Elagöz Evi, *Arkitekt, 07*(08), 153–156.

Gök, S., Çıtak, C., & Apaydın, T. (2018). Türkiye'de konut politikaları ve dönüşen Kadıköy. *Proceedings of the İstanbul I. Konut Kurultayı.* Turkey, 760–805.

Görgülü, T. (2016). Apartman tipolojisinde geçmişten bugüne; kira apartmanından "rezidans'a" geçiş, *Tüba-Ked, 14*, 165–178.

Görücü, Y. (2018). 1960'dan Günümüze kadarki apartman tipi konutlarda mekânsal dönüşümün incelenmesi: Gaziantep Örneği, *Süleyman Demirel Üniversitesi Mimarlık Bilimleri ve Uygulamaları Dergisi, 3*(2), 21–51.

Hür, A. (1993) "Erenköy". In N. Akbayar et al. (Ed.), *Dünden Bugüne İstanbul Ansiklopedisi*, Turkey and the Economic Social History Foundation Publishing.

İnce Güney, Y. (2005). *Appropriated 'a la Franga': An examination of Turkish modernization through the lens of domestic culture* [Unpublished doctoral thesis]. Michigan University.

Kadıköy Kaymakamlığı. (2021, May 30). *Geçmişin modern mimarisi Kadıköy.* http://www.kadikoy.gov.tr/gecmisin-modern-mimarisi-kadikoy-ilcemiz

Kömürcüyan, E. Ç. (1952). History of İstanbul: 17th century İstanbul, Istanbul University Press.

Kütükçü, T. (2014). *Geçmiş zamanların, mekanların ve hatırlamaların rafında Kadıköy'ün kitabı.* Ötüken Neşriyat.

Mortaş, A. (1935). Dr. Ziya ve Dr. Zeki Kira Evleri, *Arkitekt, 10*(58), 281–284.

Mutdoğan, S. (2014). Türkiye'de çok katlı konut oluşum sürecinin İstanbul örneği üzerinden incelenmesi. *Hacettepe Üniversitesi Sosyolojik Araştırmalar*, 1–24.

Oskay, B. (2021). Bir Moda Caddesi anlatısı, *Arredamento mimarlık, 345*, 102–107.

Raşit, C. (1934). Mühendis İzzet Bey Apartmanı, *Arkitekt, 03*(39), 69–70.

Sayar, Z. (1940). Bir kira evi, *Arkitekt, 11–12*, 241–244.

Selah, Z. (1932). Dr. Sani Yaver Villâsı, *Arkitekt, 05*(17), 131–136.

Selah, Z. (1933). Röntgen Apartmanı, *Arkitekt, 08*(32), 231–236.

Sezginalp, P. (2017). *Transformation of residential interiors in the Moda district of İstanbul* [Unpublished doctoral thesis]. Middle East Technical University.

Tekeli, İ. (2010). *Konut sorununu konut sunum biçimleriyle düşünmek*, Tarih Vakfı Yurt Yayınları.

Tulum, H., & Ekenyazıcı Güney, E. (2018). Kentsel bellekte mimarlık ve sanat ilişkisinin rolü. *Proceedings of the İstanbul National Design Days Symposium.* Turkey. 104–113.

Tulum, H., & Ekenyazıcı Güney, E. (2019). Cephede estetik vurgu; Türkiye modern mimarlığında Muammer Gerekli apartmanları, *Yapı, 451*, 46–49.

Turangil, K. (2010). Türkiye Mimarlığı: Türkiye'de Konut Kültürünün Değişimi. https://www.bisav.org.tr/Bulten/38/702/turkiye_mimarligi_turkiye_de_konut_kulturunun_degisimi

Uzman, E. (1946). Büyükada'da bir ev, *Arkitekt, 07*(08), 153–155.

Yayla, B., & Ünsal Gülmez, N. (2016). Cephe hikayeleri ile Bağdat Caddesi'nde kentsel dönüşüm, *Konsept Projeler, 52*, 58–67. http://www.nadaaa.com/blog/wp-content/uploads/2017/01/KonseptProjeler-KP52-CepheHikayeleri.pdf

Yazıcıoğlu Halu, Z. (2001). *1950–1970'lerde İstanbul'da konut mimarisi: Bağdat Caddesi örneği* [Unpublished M.A. Thesis]. Istanbul Technical University.

Yüksel, U., & Akbulut, M. T. (2009). Tüketim odaklı mimarlığın son yıllardaki yeni ürünleri: Rezidanslar, *Megaron, 4*(2), 110–118.

Part II
Mega Projects and Urban Transformation

Ali Devrim Işıkkaya

5
Eternal Now of Urban Metastasis in Istanbul

"The public sphere is the container of politics."

Oscar Negt & Alexander Kluge (1993)

Introduction

Today's global urban region Istanbul as a developing (alive) metabolism is still a dynamic open system, where complex and multiple economic, social, and physical conditions are overlapped. This mentioned social and physical changing aura/structure is being expanded particularly since the first quarter of the twentieth century until today over six different periods (fragmented city of Istanbul as the Ottoman capital between 1453 and 1923, socialist/militarist republic city Istanbul between 1923 and 1950, capitalist city under construction between 1950 and 1983, big city of transformation between 1983 and 2002, the third world/ developing country metropolis Istanbul between 2002 and 2021) and their thresholds (Bilgin, 2010) according to the Istanbul 19:10-2010 Exhibition. This enormous fragmented, oil strain, or patchwork kind enlarging morphology is manipulated, managed, or triggered through the governmental contemporary urban interventions particularly over the last hundred years. Each government as the representative and amalgamate of new regional, national, and international idealisms re-designed, re-produced, or re-mapped the "palimpsest" Istanbul, instead of focusing on how to realize spatial justice (Soja, 2010) in other words just-city morphology (Fainstein, 2010).

Today's patchwork morphology composed of many social and physical dichotomies of the city has enlarged eighty times especially during the last fifty years (Korkmaz, 2010) within the socio-cultural polarization between the populations, segregations, evaporation of the urban poor and forced evictions, gentrification politics, and urban transformation scenarios, accordingly dominated the contemporary city culture.

The governmental urban "mainlandization" scenarios are shaped through processes of "deterritorialization" and "reterritorialization" (Bontje, 2019) implementations of largely disconnected archipelagoes, or discrete spaces which cannot be attached to a sustainable urban system. Moreover, these settlements are often problematized as "generic cities" (city in city format) as a part of the concept of splintering urbanism[1] (Graham & Marvin, 2001) where there might include new interstitial spaces[2] as nightmares instead of "hope city" Istanbul expanded through segmentations.

Therefore this phantasmagoria or giganto-mania (Bora, 2011) in other words over – scaled, spontaneous, additive, aggressive urban transformation process can also be described as an endless space permutation (re – locations), kind of an "*urban metastasis*[3]" including many discreteness in new contingences, divisibility in indivisibilities, endless translocations of new settlements like lesions in body demolishing the original tissue/urban morphology transmitted by transportation lines, capitalistic arteries, mega projects, gated communities – housing projects, shopping malls as urban cancerious cells (Ungers, 1997), and etc. (as cells, tissues, neural system, organs etc. in body) in terms of governmental investments since the 50s.

So the term "*Urban Metastasis – Metamorphosis*[4]" as a metaphor based on medical – architectural analogy here argues that time is indivisible into smaller parts but places are all divisible, and by extension all measurements, space/ time coordination. This situation does evolve to an illusion in terms of many changings and distorted augmentations – augmented distortions. Contextually

1 **Splintering urbanism**: Massive archipelagoes loosely laced together by huge new infrastructure networks. In such places, position and centrality are configured less by geographical location with respect to "downtown" than by the conditions of buildings and places with respect to global-local networked infrastructures (Graham and Marvin, 2001).

2 **Interstitial space**: Marginalized spaces largely ignored by the sub-centers and disconnected from the networked infrastructures (Graham and Marvin, 2001).

3 **Metastasis**: Greek original word (**metastasis, μετά, meta "next, nextly", στάσις, stasis, "translocation, permutation"**, also the meaning of the indivisibility of time including linear time, a moment of linear time as an eternity of cyclical time. The orientation of linear time as an illusion. The eternal now of the development of secondary malignant growths at a distance from a primary site of cancer (Oxford Commission, 2019). The illusion of discreteness, measurement, and momentum. Metastasis argues that time is indivisible into smaller parts and all divisibility, and by extension all measurement, is an illusion. Metastasis asserts that each moment contingent upon being divided would itself become an eternity. Metastasis declares that space emerges from time and is isomorphic indivisible as well (Cevizci, 2014).

4 **Metamorphosis**: The process of transformation from an immature form to an adult form in two or more distinct stages, transfiguration, transmutation, differentiation (Oxford Commission, 2019).

urban space as a lesion let us experience a kind of an eternal now out of control as Istanbul does live in permanently.

This chapter focuses on the endless altering urban expansive typology in terms of urban articulations or lesions, mainlandization scenarios, splintering urbanism by highlighting/analyzing the metastasis/metamorphosis process in the eternal now of the urban region Istanbul as a metabolic organism. The discussion is based on analogies, through the public and private urban investments, urban transformation projects, mega-scaled projects, new transportation networks, and housing projects as the settlements – tools – reasons of mentioned urban metastasis – metamorphosis between the thresholds over the six main periods underlined in the Istanbul 1910–2010 Exhibition including governmental urban scenarios and implementations, erase and re-write policies within their possible impacts on the urban mind and identity. This chapter makes also a projection to the future of the city in terms of changing the urban metastasis (the enlarging geography of hard capitalism) context into a kind of *urban tropism*[5] (land of justice, sustainability, peaceful and valuable sharing, dialectic, sensitive, architectural and urban improvement) concept over all the city.

Urban Transformation Process Through Thresholds and Scales

The process of the transformation of Istanbul from a traditional fragmented empire capital into a multi-faceted metropolitan region and the history of the governmental policies and their impacts on the city can be described in six different thresholds sections – periods (Bilgin, Güvenç; Korkmaz, 2010) when also the quantitative and qualitative scale is changing according to the political, social and cultural interventions in the urban region as follows:

---

5 **Tropism**: A **tropism** (from Greek τρόπος, tropos, "a turning") is a biological phenomenon, indicating growth or turning movement of a biological organism, usually a plant, in response to an environmental stimulus. Tropisms are typically associated with plants (although not necessarily restricted to them). **Tropism**, response or orientation of a plant or certain lower animals to a stimulus that acts with greater intensity from one direction than another. It may be achieved by active movement or by structural alteration. Forms of tropism include phototropism (response to light), geotropism (response to gravity), chemotropism (response to particular substances), hydrotropism (response to water), thigmotropism (response to mechanical stimulation), traumatotropism (response to wound lesion), and galvanotropism, or electrotropism (response to electric current). Most tropic movements are orthotropic; i.e., they are directed toward the source of the stimulus. Plagiotropic movements are oblique to the direction of stimulus. Diatropic movements are at right angles to the direction of stimulus (Goetz, 1987).

Body as organ, organ as body (330–1453); **Constantinople as introverted, compact medieval capital of Byzantium Empire:**

- public and private buildings (organs) constitute the unique medieval compact and introverted, humble but monumental morphology of urban pattern (body),
- architecturally strong dialectic between unit and manageable whole.

Organs without (instead of) body; fragmented settlements of Istanbul as the Ottoman capital (1453–1923):

- first urban sprawl, disintegration period, simplex relation between the city and the palace/palatial organization as city in city morphology constructed on Byzantium medieval urban compactness (body as organ, organ as body), authoritarian regime,
- local urban interventions especially during the eighteenth to nineteenth century, fragmented collage city,
- no urban providence or policy, no planning, and applications for the future of the mega – city,
- weak dialectic relationship between urban regions due to the lack of total urban planning scenarios and architectural design concepts,
- lack of advanced transportation facilities, no pre-described zones and arteries of urbanization, introverted – disconnected rural accommodational allocations remaining from medieval times including palatial domestic life style imitations, distantly situated settlements as detached colonies, development without any masterplan and zoning strategies.

Constructing the body; socialist/militarist/administrative/republic city Istanbul (1923–1950/first erasing and rewriting policies):

- creation of the modern citizen and compacting the secularist, early modern morphology of the city of Mustafa Kemal Atatürk's administration (Bilgin, 2010),
- sewing the slits by local masterplan implementations, filling the gaps between the detached settlements, connecting the allocations through transportation arteries, public zones – buildings, first urbanization period,
- giving way to the republican project of re-making the city into the big stage of modern life, creation of modern citizen, the eclipse of Istanbul's cosmopolitan vitality,
- new roads, new public spaces, and urban landscapes, new regime's strategic interventions for connecting and re-ordering the urban fragments inherited from the Ottoman Empire,

- shaping Istanbul as a homogeneous, coherent, clean city, constructing the master-planned entity – contemporary body on traditional urban layout (organs), unification of fragmented city.

Start of metamorphosis; capitalist city under construction (1950–1983/first global wave, second erasing and rewriting policies):

- second erasing and rewriting period, oil engaged capitalistic scenarios of governmental rightist Democrat Party (the government in the fifties) and development operations of the governments on the city of industry, quantitative explosion, ushering in an era of irreversible growth, expansion, and multiplication (Korkmaz, 2010),
- expansion parallel to highways and Marmara shoreline to the north, new global commercial arteries, second urban sprawl,
- start of social, cultural, physical, urban, and architectural metamorphosis,
- beginning of urban transmutation, architectural transfiguration, and differentiations according to the global populist, industrialization politics, and implementations,
- expunging/annihilating the traditional morphology – original identity particularly on the historic peninsula of the city,
- transformation from middle scaled pedestrian city of articulations into vehicle oriented big scale urbanity of global modern,
- occupation of the urban land by the capitalist land lords (physically and socially metamorphosed public space seized by the capitalist investors).
- first encounters with the anonymous face of modernity, mass culture, mass movements, and mass migrations, populist politics into informal urbanization,
- new urban landscapes of apartment blocks (expanse of metastasis through housing projects and informal squatter settlements as investments of land and property developers), transforming the old "shore city" into a vast "hinterland city" (Güvenç, 2010), vehicle oriented city of interferences.

The capitalist enterprises of the Democrat Party caused to the "urban implosion" which points to how import – substitution macroeconomic policies and domestic – market oriented industrialization affected the shape of urban space and the production forms and mechanisms of the built environment (Bilgin, 2010).

Between urban metamorphosis and metastasis; capitalist big city of transformation (1983–2002/second global wave, third erasing and rewriting policies):

Starting from the beginning of the 80s according to the global economic rivalry between the world cities (Sennett, 2005) and the third world cities in progress, Istanbul expanded accordingly in the east – west, and north direction in episodes.

The patchwork morphology constituted of many social and physical dichotomies of the city. The socio-cultural polarization between the populations, segregations, evaporation of the urban poor and forced evictions, gentrification policies and urban transformation scenarios dominated the contemporary city culture accordingly. Istanbul transformed from an industrial city into a borderless urban region.

- third erasing and rewriting period, gentrification and governmental urban transformation implementations, facing the tragedy of common space,
- expansion parallel to highways and Marmara shoreline to the north, new global commercial arteries, third urban sprawl as urban metastasis through commercial/national, and international commercial spaces, shopping malls, plazas, and gated communities to the north, east, and west,
- continuity of social, cultural, physical, urban, and architectural metamorphosis, beginning of urban transmutation, transfiguration, and differentiations,
- international and financial development of the city, de-industrialization and real estate applications process.

Istanbul as one of the global, capitalist edge city of the world according to the urban management and urban transformation scenarios of the capital oriented rightist governmental ANAP (Motherland Party) Party as representative of second generation of Islamic- rightist governmental "troika" (Bora, 2011), has been dominated by the full liberalization policies and urban interventions of service industry and administration.

Urban metastasis – architectural metamorphosis of the metropolitan Istanbul (2002–2019/third global wave, fourth erasing and rewriting policies):

With the momentum gathered from the restructuring process following the earthquake of 1999 and the financial crisis of 2001, the metropolitan area became a more attractive place for real estate investment than ever before. Reconstruction/re-allocation process of public space between new bourgeoisie and proletarian had been managed by the capital oriented rightist government AKP [The Justice and Development Party (JDP)], as the last generation of the rightist "troika" in Turkey, (Bora, 2011). Istanbul, according to the impacts of the third global wave around the world has been transformed into today's developing country's metropolis and can be evaluated as a permanent and independent, dynamic, open, renovated system of anarchic, archaic indicators, and symbols (Lefebvre, 1973). Istanbul, city of Janus-faced polarizations transformed from an industrial city into a borderless urban region as the most expanded, dense, economically powerful (capitalist), socially multi-layered metropolis in Turkey including many contradictory situations, and their in-betweens.

In this case Istanbul does still share typical characteristics with the other developing country metropolises such as Mexico City in Mexico, Rio de Janeiro in Brazil, Cairo in Egypt, Johannesburg in the Republic of South Africa, Mumbai in India or Shanghai in China (Drakakis, 2000). This city can now be defined as the city of infinite layers (charged with the vitality) and pluralities full of oxymoronic elements.

Istanbul (always under construction) has been transformed into a multi-economical urban region, a global finance city/capital of culture, education, entertainment, and tourism etc. as a locomotive for the country's development and undertook a strategic position for the country. Contextually the city has been evolved to a strategic region of prestige, and a political case study particularly for the contemporary neo-Islamic, neo-liberalist, and post-modern government since 2002.

Fourth erase and rewriting policies through urban interventions and implementations of the last government tend to change Istanbul both physically and socially. The last government and its municipality tried to rewrite the "new" post-modern, neo-liberalist, conservative urban mind, and identity by re-mapping/designing, and applying the sacred/agreed "new" urban morphology of the metropolis (encouraging the continuity of urban metastasis). Istanbul urban region expanded once again to east-west and north parallel to the highways episodically. The last governmental policies reinforced the urban metastasis by enhancing the endless masterplan modifications, mega-scaled transportation projects, over-scaled housing projects through the environmental handicapped macro decisions and implementations without enough scientific support.

These mentioned expunge and rewrite policies on Istanbul caused both the urban metamorphosis and metastasis particularly through transportation lines and fragmented housing projects as seen in the Figure 5.1. The governmental implementation methodologies have been materialized by the previous municipality in order to complete the re-conquest of the self-shaped city Istanbul through making city policies. In this context, the ruling party has deliberately fed the construction industry as a meaning and representative of development, reconstruction, and redistribution of social, cultural, and physical life. Groups of engineers, contractors, and media linked to the government are also responsible for the seizure and redistribution of non-commoditized places under a compulsory construction culture in the overall country and particularly in Istanbul.

Figure 5.1: Urban metastasis through housing agglomerations from south to north.
Source: [Authors' archive].

AKP (JDP) as the inventor of feudal democracy which is also known in most of the developing countries, took over the Istanbul Metropolitan Municipality Administration in 1995, and the Government of the Republic of Turkey in 2002. During the process, the city was seized and reconfigured primarily in administrative, social, and finally in physical aspects. This triple-headed period beginning from 1995, adorned with its actual form after 2002, and reaching present may sequentially be detailed in terms of triggering process of the urban metastasis and architectural metamorphosis as follows:

Administrative implementations of policies (organizational – social metamorphosis):

- o building a strong and effective operational network, kind of an amalgamate among all governmental units, metropolis, districts and all local municipalities, (non)governmental organizations, domestic and foreign sponsors, investors, entrepreneurs, planners, project designer groups, undertakers, media organizations and other parties,
- o managing the mentioned units through the government's extensions, party supporters, followers, and other allies,

- o bringing up a young population with higher education in international scale as white-collar specialists and experts, who share the party's view, policy, and ideology as members or followers of the party; placing them at the government, municipalities, and various strategic offices and organizations with power on urban management and practices,
- o re-arranging the relations (allocation of fields of autonomy) between local governments and central government with the top down regulations foreseen under the title "Public Governance Fundamental Act,"
- o extension of the duties, powers, and fields of responsibility of local governments – municipalities in terms of re-definition of the effectiveness of local politics,
- o creating its own entrepreneur – contractor – performer holding companies – groups which are loyal and able to work in coordination with the party in the context of common vision and mission/policy with respect to urban and architectural production policies,
- o triggering the social, political, economic, cultural, and political polarization in the city by supporting the cooperation, collaboration and corporation in the conservative, traditional, and endocentric majority with origins from the provinces,
- o absorbing the republican, secular, and high profile educated citizens (the former owners of the city); modern minority or "the other" was literally localized along the Bosphorus and Marmara sea shorelines; sorting out the other; decentralization of the other's behaviors and memories, whether related or not with the city; changing the DNA, possession and mission of the Governmental Mass Housing Administration (TOKI) established in the 80s during the last two decays, using the organization as a governmental urban design tool, as an urban, and housing investor/representative and profit earner implementer, an alternative source of income for the party. As a result of those regulations, TOKI as the "latest goddess of the construction myth" (Çavuşoğlu, 2011) became the only authorized organization in the field of housing and land production.

Urban and architectural implementations of governmental ideology (morphological metamorphosis and metastasis):

- o making (dominating) the city, re-conquering the city by many political occupations or penetrations, re-shaping the urban region, designing the daily private, and public life and its spaces, privatization of the public sphere for liberal (neo-liberal) market order (Zizek, 2013),

- changing the demography of the city qualitatively and quantitatively according to the aim of manipulation of the social and physical crisis particularly at slum quarters and changing it into a political advantage and opportunity, encouraging the immigration to the city,
- designing the social and economic polarization between secular, modern, republican and conservative inhabitants of Istanbul and let the rich population rule the city,
- shrinking the secular public space by encouraging private space of the rich (new bourgeoisie) and also by enlarging the religious public spaces (predefined preferred and limited common area),
- application of urban transformation projects; liberalized (deregulated) planning and zoning regulations in order to carry out quick and hassle-free investments in the fields such as construction, real estate, and tourism (Balaban, 2011),
- allocation of the lands and plots of the public to various urban projects mainly through their sale to urban transformation projects; damaging the autonomous morphological structure of the city,
- encouraging the vehicle oriented urban region by adding new arteries, highways, motor roads; neglecting and demolishing the natural geography and environment; decreasing the greenery zones and under–ground water sources city does benefit,
- emphasizing the oil strain like expansiveness (metastasis) of the artificial urban region to the east, west, and especially to the north in terms of extensions and additions of the motorways, third bridge crossing the Bosporus and the newly located over–scaled airport; transformation of the city into a giant special property knitted by motor roads,
- damaging the unique, autonomous morphological structure of the city by emphasizing the mega-scaled projects (Canal Istanbul, Istanbul Airport, new highways, Çamlıca Mosque and etc.), and encouraging the city enlargement and urban metastasis,
- "Dubaization" of the Istanbul silhouette by placing either religious or commercial over-scaled constructions to strategic regions of the city (urban metastasis and architectural metamorphosis of the Istanbul horizon),
- perpetual housing projects (closed–loop housing areas–gated communities) designate the eternal now and endless enlargement of the city, and cause mainly urban metastasis and architectural metamorphosis.

- o rejecting or ignoring the early modern architectural heritage, disabling, misusing, delaying, or neglecting the restoration of indoor and outdoor early modern and secular spaces,
- o sorting out, disabling or neglecting early modern parks, urban landscapes, squares, and outdoor spaces that are presentative and complementary to the modern, contemporary, secular, early modern period republic image.

Conclusion

"Could space be made a peaceful instrument of social transformation, a means of changing the relationship between individual and society by generating a new lifestyle?"

Bernard Tschumi (1996)

As a result of the current urban policies, designs, projects, and implementations drafted on Istanbul, the city on two continents separated with a strait, on a 30 km-wide and 100 km-long area between the Marmara Sea and the Black Sea has been partly damaged in terms of its authentic urban/architectural properties. Polarization in economic and social senses has been amalgamated in the overall urban region. The city loses its urban physical and social identity, unique morphology, and memory by a large extent. In the nearest future Istanbul's metropolitan region's natural resources, reserves will critically be reduced; its geographical properties, topography, and morphology will probably be metamorphosed with weak concentrations in terms of quality and quantity.

Istanbul, designed as a kind of new – brand is now the premises of the founder government which is passivated on the one hand and activated on the other hand through containment/commoditization/commercialization policies. During this kind of construction, re-construction and de-construction process (Koolhaas, 1994) the city as an endless urban region, an uncontrolled developing macro-organism in an urban metastasis, and architectural metamorphosis under penetration of giganto-manic projects has been transformed into a post-modern, pornographic artificial structure including overlapped events, places, and communities. The city Istanbul as a metropolitan metastasis can be considered both as a geography of loop prone to social and physical disasters and as an oxymoronic semantic cohesion with its continuously–erased and re–written memories in a kind of an eternal now.

The capitalist – neoliberal development process caused the urban metastasis, allowing the geography to own or create by capitalism, which also victimized the city to the never-ending propagation of urban growth while ignoring the social, environmental, and political consequences. In this sense, especially the modern city and metropolises are the subjects and objects of the reproduction and consumption of capitalism. The urban sphere/metropolis that generates its own economics as a reflection of multilayered political mediations (Harvey, 2012) signifies something beyond the total of a land or lands at certain sizes as an object of the construction works, or an integral of the capitalist system.

The preceding process is also the process of continuous pillage of the public sphere/the public's sphere by the propertied class that considers the city/metropolis as a vast reservoir of prosperity by means of police, gendarmerie, military, and state (government) as Marx (Harvey, 2012) also expressed. In addition, the government of the capital as the power that determines the final order manages to plunder not only the proletarian but also the earth, public space by exploiting inexhaustibly the symbiosis created by others to acquire prosperity (Harvey, 2012). So the public space is easily given to the Bourgeoisie.

The political criticism of the Republic of Turkey indicates that almost all political parties or formations that have come to power since 1950 acted as the representatives of the capitalist – investor class or the money with the characteristics similar to those afore-listed; and they shaped big cities such as Istanbul, Ankara, and Izmir in a rightist approach mostly in accordance with their own "isotopia" (the rational space order realized by capitalism and the state) for all "heterotopia" (all urban practices) as Lefebvre described (1973). Accordingly, as the container of politics, the public sphere (Negt & Kluge, 1993) is manipulated, modified, and has been made eligible for the global relations for the contemporary "over-qualified" inhabitants.

In this context, the social and physical transformation/metamorphosis experienced in Istanbul – the mega urban region that this chapter focuses on – especially during the last sixty years which conceptualized and applied by the political governments complement each other in a periodical order as the new creators of the urban memory and identity. In the present economic and social climate created by the last government accordingly, a giant *architectural* and *urban transformation has itself been metamorphosed into an urban metastasis* particularly for the last twenty years with the motivation of exhibiting the city's competitive superiorities. However, trying to create an Istanbul vision without considering the entire vision of Turkey, putting the city into a competition with the world's cities as if it was a separate country by ignoring the integrity and balances of Turkey and allocating all available resources to this field only was just a tendency for the interests of big capital groups. In this context, economic, social, cultural and physical polarization has seriously increased and will continue to increase in all greater cities of the country. The neo-liberalist and also authoritarian (conscious schizophrenia), capitalist government and its hit men – the municipalities – who act like technocrats or technicians considered the entire Istanbul as a land and source of profit, who approach the citizens as if they were customers. They produced the exact climate and geography foreseen and needed by the capitalist system again and again, and changed the DNA of Istanbul into a continuously expanding social and physical metastasis, a kind of oxymoron morphology including both high modern and indigenous dichotomies.

With its various manifestations and over – scaled dimensions Istanbul city is also promoted as future engines of growth in national policies (Gülhan, 2011). The metropolitan area today is still a kind of hope city (Van Leynseele & Bontje, 2019) which may also be seen as "space of exception and expectation" (Ong, 2007) in terms of its history, multi – layered morphology, strategic location, and development process. This thematic and dramatic urbanization developments of competing geo – economic regions represent all-inclusive city, managed in public – private – partnerships dealing within speculative urbanism/ urban metastasis. On the other hand, the hegemonic governmental urban implementations providing the continuity of the synchronous metastasis and metamorphosis transform the planning regime itself into an informal entity, one unable to carry out this speculative, territorialized urban renewal, and regeneration process (Bhan, 2013) including many social and physical contradictions.

As a world – class city to be a part of a major cities league in the globalized neo–capitalistic aura, Istanbul is presented as an urban imaginary (Gülhan, 2011), urban policy rhetoric. Roy (2011) calls it "a 'phantasmagoria' which does include a unique 'aesthetic mode'" of semi planned-ness of timeless morphological metastasis. Moreover, it is often problematized as "generic city" as a part of the concept of splintering urbanism (Graham & Marvin, 2001) in the twenty-first-century urban development where there might include new interstitial spaces as nightmares instead of hope.

This endless growing city of national and global expectations, but at the same time an urban village for the local inhabitants, is a good place to demonstrate this "mainlandization attempt" as one of the remarkable presence of marginalized speculative Janus-faced morphology (Murray, 2015) presenting experiments of promulgation of urban inequalities today (Van Leynseele & Bontje, 2019).

This mentioned urban metastasis including neo-capitalist "deterritorialization and reterritorialization generic policies," have been written by the previous national and international land lords (stakeholders, government, and local administrations), re–shapes the perpetual "archipelago city" (Bhan, 2013) Istanbul, the city of uncertainty.

Today's municipality (representative of CHP, Republican People's Party) should consider a dialectic, fruitful urban development for the whole geography. Today's administration should mainly and firstly focus on how to realize "spatial justice" (Soja, 2010) in other word a "justcity" (Fainstein, 2010) and should conceptualize an urban tropism (peaceful, sustainable, re-creative, and positive development) based on equity, diversity, and democracy instead of urban metastasis. Otherwise this expanding city as a giant urban metabolism will probably transform into a sponge settlement and urban sprawl, which will absorb and annihilate itself, and its environment in the nearest future.

References

Balaban, O. (2011). What for is construction sector a locomotive?. *Birikim*, Birikim Publishers, Istanbul, Turkey, Vol. 270, 19–27.

Bhan, G. (2013). The Real Lives of Urban Fantasies, Environment and Urbanization. *Environment and Organization*, 26, 232–235.

Bilgin, I. (2010). The Great Implosion, 1950–1980, *Istanbul 1910–2010 Exhibition Book*, Bilgi University Publishers, Istanbul.

Bontje, M. (2019). Towards Large – Scale City Reconstruction from Satellites, Shenzhen: satellite city or city of satellites?, *International Planning Studies*, 24– (Issue 3–4), 255–271.

Bora, T. (2011). Turkish conservation and construction desire. *Birikim*, Birikim Publishers, Istanbul, Turkey, Vol. 270, 15–19.

Cevizci, A. (2014). Philosophy Dictionary (Felsefe Sözlüğü), Say Publishers, Istanbul.

Çavusoglu, E. (2011). Property and construction fetish in Islamic neo-liberalism. *Birikim*, Birikim Publishers, Istanbul, Turkey, Vol. 270, 40–52.

Fainstein, S. (2010). *The Just City*, Cornell University Press, Ithaca, NY.

Goetz, W. P. (1987). *Encyclopedia Britannica*, Encyclopedia Britannica Publisher, London.

Graham, S., & Marvin, S. (2001). *Splintering Urbanism Networked Infrastructures, Technological Mobilities and the New Urban Condition*, Routledge, London/New York.

Gülhan, S. (2011). Urban income in Turkey: From government contractor to the real estate developer. *Birikim*, Birikim Publishers, Istanbul, Turkey, Vol. 270, 27–34.

Güvenç, M. (2010). The Republican Intervention, 1950–1980, *Istanbul 1910–2010 Exhibition Book*, Bilgi University Publishers, Istanbul.

Harvey, D. (2012). *Rebel Cities, from the Right to the City to the Urban Revolution*, Metis Publishers, Istanbul.

Koolhaas, R. (1994). *The City: Construction, re-Construction, de-Construction, city of risc*. Junius Publishers, 94–98.

Korkmaz, T. (2010). Pressure of global between 1980s - 2000s, *Istanbul 1910–2010 Exhibition Book*, Bilgi University Publishers, Istanbul.

Lefebvre, H. (1973). *Writings on Cities*, Blackwell Publishers, London, 5–108.

Murray, M. (2015). City Doubles: Re-Urbanism in Africa, edited by F. Miraftab, D. Wilson, and K. Salo, In *Cities and Inequalities in a Global and Neoliberal World* (pp. 92–109). Routledge, New York.

Negt, O., & Kluge, A. (1993). *Public Sphere and Experience Towards an Analysis of the Bourgeois and Proletarian Public Sphere*, University of Minnesota Press, London.

Ong, A. (2007). *Neoliberalism as Exception, Mutations in Citizenship and Sovereignty*, Duke University Press, Durham, NC.

Oxford Commission (2019). *Oxford Dictionary*, Oxford University Press, London.

Roy, A. (2011). *Worlding Cities: Asian Experiments and the Art of Being Global*, Wiley-Blackwell, Chichester, 279–306.

Sennett, R. (2005). Capitalism and the City, edited by S. Read et al. (Eds.), In *Future City*. Spon Press, Vol. 4, 178–194, New York

Smith, Drakakis, D. (2000). *Third World Cities*, Routledge, pp. 86–113, New York

Soja, E. (2010). *Seeking Spatial Justice*, University of Minnesota Press, Minneapolis, MN.

Tschumi, B. (1996). *Architecture and Disjunction*, MIT Press, London.

Ungers, O. M. (1997). *The Dialectic City*, Thames and Hudson LTD., London.

Van Leynseele, Y., & Bontje, M. (2019). Visionary cities or spaces of uncertainty? Satellite cities and new towns in emerging economies. *International Planning Studies*, Abingdon 24 (3–4), 207–217.

Zizek, S. (2013). Trouble in Heaven. Thinking of The Resistance: Gezi Case 2013, Monokl Publishers, 65–75, Istanbul.

Ahmet Sezgin

Nilay Ünsal Gülmez

6
From Infrastructural Developmentalism to Mega-Projects: "The Istanbul Canal"

"We believe that we will crown the works and services we have brought to Turkey for 19 years with the Istanbul Canal, a worldwide project." (Recep Tayyip Erdoğan, 2021a).

"While we build the Istanbul Canal, we will build 2 smart cities around it" (Recep Tayyip Erdoğan, 2019).

Introduction

In his social media accounts in 2020, Recep Tayyip Erdoğan, president of Turkey and head of the Justice and Development Party (JDP), declared his pet project Istanbul Canal to be "a crown for the works and services achieved in the 19 years long period" (Erdoğan, 2021a). Erdoğan's choice of words and attempt locate Istanbul Canal, a mega-project of an artificial channel roughly parallel to Bosporus, in the context of what he frequently described as "work" (eser) and "service" (hizmet) in his speeches[1]. In his speeches, "politics of service" meant focusing not on the politics of identity but rather serving the nation by constructing infrastructure, public works, and providing services (Bayraktar, 2018, p. 112; Joppien, 2019, p. 166). Emphasis on "work" located him within the lineage of the right-wing leaders who fashioned themselves as champions of infrastructure projects in Turkey. Indeed, he directly referred to these leaders in his speeches at the occasion of groundbreaking ceremonies of the infrastructures related to the Istanbul Canal (Halktv, 2021). This promotion of the Istanbul Canal Project is at the new crossroads of the politicization of infrastructure

1 Through this chapter, the Istanbul Canal refers to the water channel whereas the Istanbul Canal Project is meant to cover the real estate development and infrastructure construction related to the Canal.

projects in Turkey and the rhetoric and vocabulary of neoliberal urban regeneration. This chapter aims to concisely summarize the enduring politicization of infrastructure projects in Turkey and then scrutinize how Istanbul Canal is refashioned with a new vocabulary of neoliberal policies in its promotion. The project and the discourse about it span multiple layers and situate itself within a larger context of real estate gigantism and the new city building trend that has been popular in the developing world for the past two decades, as well as developmentalism based on infrastructure projects.

This chapter first offers a brief overview of the politicization of Istanbul bridges over the Bosphorus as pet infrastructure projects of right-wing leaders. Then, it unfolds a neo-liberal way of instrumentalizing infrastructure projects through the Istanbul Canal case as part of a new city building trend. For this purpose, the chapter reveals the continuities and ruptures with the past and conducts a discourse analysis to decipher the implicit and explicit motives in the promotion of the Istanbul Canal.

The Politicization of Bridges on Bosphorus

In 1974, the cover of the speech booklet of the 7th party congress of the Justice Party in Turkey featured its leader Süleyman Demirel just in between the illustration of the 15 July Martyrs Bridge (formerly named the Bosphorus Bridge) and the Keban Dam (Figure 6.1). These two water infrastructure projects were pet projects of Demirel who was nicknamed the king of the dams. The poster aptly captured the politicization of the mega infrastructure projects in multiparty politics in Turkey since the 1950s (Kaçmazoğlu, 2012, pp. 187–8). The left-wing and right-wing antagonism was the fault line of the politicized debates over infrastructure projects. The construction of a series of automobile bridges on Bosphorus since the 1970s constitutes an exemplary case of the persistent nature of politicization. Bridges on Bosphorus were very prominent structures crossing the minimum width of 750 meters of the natural strait that divides the main city of Turkey into two. They were instrumental in the transformation of Istanbul into a vehicle-oriented metropolitan area.

Figure 6.1: Süleyman Demirel with 15 July Martyrs Bridge and the Keban Dam. Source: The cover of the speech booklet of the 7th party congress of the Justice Party, 1974. [Authors' archive].

Beginning with Demirel's tenure, a series of bridges became a trademark of successive right-wing leaders in Turkey. Demirel championed the 15 July Martyrs Bridge (1970–73) against the mostly left-wing dissidence to the project on the grounds of efficient transportation, urban aesthetics, and economic independence (Aslan, 2011, pp. 111–4). The second bridge on Bosphorus, Fatih Sultan Mehmet Bridge (1980–86), was also built by a right-wing party, the Motherland Party, headed by Turgut Özal. Recalling the debates over the 15 July Martyrs Bridge, Fatih Sultan Mehmet Bridge received sharp criticism from the left as the pet project of Özal and another step in introducing rampant capitalism and automobilization to the city (Figure 6.2). Indeed, the bridges on Bosphorus triggered the urban sprawl of the city and the emergence of new residential areas. Forests of the city were opened up for controversial residential projects for high-income families (Aslan, 2011, pp. 117–8). Therefore, the bridges were perceived as tools of real estate speculation as well as projects serving the transportation infrastructure of the city. So, when Erdoğan announced and then started the construction of Yavuz Sultan Selim

Köprü şov

Başbakan, Fatih Sultan Mehmet Köprüsü'nü yürüyerek geçti...

Özal'dan, 1557 mutlu adım

- Başbakan Özal, Asya ile Avrupa'yı ikinci kez birbirine bağlayan 1090 metre uzunluğundaki Fatih Sultan Mehmet Köprüsü'nü yürüyerek ve her adımda mutluluğu yüzünden okunarak tam 1557 adımla geçti
- **Avrupa yakasındaki kurdeleyi kesen Başbakan Özal'la, Asya yakasındaki kurdeleyi kesen Japon Büyükelçisi Wachi, köprünün tam ortasında buluşarak birbirlerini kutladılar.**

● 19. sayfada

"ZAFER" YÜRÜYÜŞÜ Başbakan Turgut Özal, Fatih Sultan Mehmet Köprüsü'nden, peşinde bir "ordu", zafer kazanmış kumandan edasıyla geçti. Başbakan, bu ilginç yürüyüş sırasında, gazetecilerin ısrarları karşısında, sık sık korkulukların yanına gidip eliyle köprüyü veya Boğaz'ı göstererek pozlar verdi. Bu arada, zaman zaman sesini yükselterek, kendisine eşlik edenlere, köprüyle ilgili teknik bilgiler verdi. (Fotoğraf: Hürriyet Murat ÇETİN)

Figure 6.2: Özal crossing Fatih Sultan Mehmet Bridge Under Construction for Inspection on Foot. Source: 'Bridge Show. 1557 Happy Steps from Özal' Hürriyet News. 17 November 2021 (First published in Hürriyet on 17 November 1987).

Bridge, it began to be seen in the politicized history of the bridges on the Bosphorus in Turkey[2]. Since the beginning of multi-party politics and the tenure of the revered leader Adnan Menderes in the 1950s, there was an emphasis on the "service" and creating "works". Özal drew on the term "government of service" in describing the mission of his government. Similarly, Erdoğan drew on the concept of "politics of service" (Türk, 2014). As well as creating a major transportation artery, Yavuz Sultan Selim bridge caused real estate speculation. From its announcement until its completion in 2016, real estate values in many nearby districts of Istanbul increased dramatically (Şahin, 2021a). The pace of housing development increased in the northern districts like Sarıyer and Zekeriyaköy, as the mega-projects began to be publicized and constructed (Menteş & Töre, 2020, p. 402).

2 For right-wing leaders and their promotion of "service" see Cengiz (2021).

The construction and inauguration story of the Yavuz Sultan Selim Bridge was full of symbolism reflecting the conservative politics of the ruling party. It was launched on the anniversary of the Ottoman conquest of Istanbul (Karakaş, 2013) and named after the sultan who obtained the title of caliph for the Ottomans (Gürkan, 2013). With this bridge, JDP clearly positioned itself in the line of conservative politics and their mega-projects. Yavuz Sultan Selim Bridge is part of a set of mega-projects in the northern part of the city. It constitutes the main traffic artery for the Istanbul Airport, completed in 2018, and is close to the spot where the Istanbul Canal will meet the Black Sea.

While connecting the Black Sea to the Marmara Sea with two new cities on both sides, Istanbul Canal would be a new chapter in the long history of the politicized projects of Turkey that the story of the Bosphorus bridges succinctly exemplifies (Figure 6.3). From the outset, it was associated with the personal vision of Erdoğan, head of the ruling JDP. Erdoğan publicized the Istanbul Canal as his "crazy project" just before the 2011 elections (TRT Haber, 2011). Examination of the promotion and debate surrounding the Istanbul Canal reveals how it becomes a forerunner of a new approach to mega-projects in Istanbul in terms of its political/ideological and economic goals, as well as its scale, in tandem with the recent Global trend in the World that pushes the limits of neoliberalism by boosting real-estate markets.

Figure 6.3: The Istanbul Canal's Route. Source: Randam. Own work. Adjusted from Kanal İstanbul.svg. (Open Source) https://en.wikipedia.org/wiki/Istanbul_Canal#/media/File:Istanbul_canal_map.svg.

The Shifting Context of Mega-Projects: Real Estate Meets Gigantism

The Istanbul Canal clearly pursues the rhetoric about infrastructure projects by Turkish right-wing politicians in power since the 1950s. Nonetheless, the official narrative about the Istanbul Canal also bears striking similarities to the world's ongoing "urban image making" or "city branding" strategies. A discourse analysis deciphering the narrative's codes has the potential to reveal the coinciding contexts of mega-projects from a global perspective.

With the rise of entrepreneurialism as a mode of urban administration and governance, city marketing with a focus on promotion yielded to city branding, and global competitiveness began to dominate the concept (Kavaratzis, 2004; Eraydın 2014). Mega-projects act as the catalyst of urban entrepreneurship and growth; they are assumed to have a (positive) impact on the image of the cities (Batuman, 2018, p. 153). The scale of such projects is extending from signature buildings to urban renewal projects, islands, city fragments, or new cities created mostly on reclaimed land.

New cities represent the utmost scale in mega-projects proliferating in number since the 1990s. Moser and Côté-Roy (2021, p. 2) treat them as "ideological and discursive constructions […] based on the aspirations of their builders", "built from scratch on a tabula rasa that is designed to be both geographically and administratively separate from established cities", and "projecting a distinct brand, architectural identity, and vision of the future"[3]. Among the main motives behind this proliferation take part the "financialization of real estate and infrastructure and the emergence of housing as a key investment vehicle" in addition

3 New city construction is not new. Many new towns/cities have been constructed following the Second World War in response to the scarcity of housing and following the independence of former colonies such as Chandigarh (India), Brasil (Brasilia), Islamabad (Pakistan) (Moser and Côté-Roy, 2021, p. 2). The new city building trend has spread all over the Global South. Songdo (South Korea) and Masdar City (UAE) are among the most well-known and early samples close to completion. However, there are numerous projects promoted in developing countries of the Global South such as Silk City, Bubiyan Island (Kuwait), DUQM (Oman) Hope City (Ghana), Dholera Smart City, Levasa (India), Yachay (Ecuador), Waterfall City (South Africa), KAEC, NEOM (Saudi Arabia), Naypyidaw (Myanmar), Putrajaya, Cyberjaya, Forest City, Penang (Malaysia), Dompak Eco-City (Indonesia) Foum el Qued, Bouregreg Valley Development Project (Morocco), Nur-Sultan (Astana) Turkmenistan, Modderfontein New City (South Africa), Konza Technology City (Kenya), Eko-Atlantic City (Nigeria), Yinchuan (China) and many others.

to the growing role of technology companies that incites smart housing and smart urban development. Two major themes that come forward in the legitimization of new cities are the "smart technology-driven urbanism" and "green urbanism" aiming to create sustainable, efficient, and low-impact ecological environments (Moser & Côté-Roy, 2021, p. 4). Federico Cugurullo (2018) manifests "the gaps between ideas and realities" in these two models, after a thorough analysis of the case studies of the Masdar City of UAE and Hong Kong, exposing approaches to sustainability from different perspectives. He proposes the term "Frankenstein Urbanism" to describe the fragmented nature of such urban experiments, which most of the time result in a "forced union of different, incongruous parts", (Cugurullo, 2018, pp. 74–5) instead of deploying holistic, harmonious and innovative city planning methods (Cugurullo, 2018, p. 87).

The keywords selected to define the Istanbul Canal resonate with these popular themes of "smart" and "eco" used for marketing cities and regions worldwide. Indeed, the Istanbul Canal represents a significant shift in this regard in the history of mega-projects in Turkey since the 1950s. Until the 2000s, mega-projects were mostly infrastructural in nature, such as highways, bridges, and water projects (dams, ports), as in other developing countries in the region. With its powerful and visible component of real estate speculation, the Istanbul Canal deviates significantly from traditional developmentalist rhetoric in Turkey[4]. On the project's website, it is presented as an infrastructure and a large water project in comparison to world-famous canals built in the late nineteenth century. The justification of the project was based on the potential dangers experienced in the Bosphorus due to increased seaway traffic. Nonetheless, the project calls for the construction of two new cities on either side of the Canal. From this vantage point, the Istanbul Canal, which is charged with city branding strategies, is consistent with the global narrative, as it seeks its place in the competitive neoliberal market.

---

4 Ayşe Buğra discusses two lives/phases of developmentalism in Turkey. According to her, in the first period, between the Second World War and the 1980s, the political parties sustained protectionist policies aiming to prevent "creative destruction." Policies were oriented towards the "protection of domestic economy with trade barriers and financial controls as well as a series of agricultural subsidies, wage and, price controls, and different instruments of demand management …Labour, land, and money were indeed not commodities." In the second period, starting with the late-century globalization in 1980s such protectionist measures have been renounced in the context of market-oriented development strategies for the sake of full-financial liberalization (Buğra, 2017, 5).

Criticization of mega-projects in developed and developing countries shed light on the characteristics of the Istanbul Canal. Pierre-Arnaud Barthel (2010) addresses similarities and dissimilarities between the mega-projects of the West and Arab Countries in the 2000s. Major similarities are the unprecedented scale of the investments, targeting wealthier classes for the return of investments despite the declarations focused on the public good, and use of natural amenities (river, oceans, lagoon, and overlooking lands) which leads to the expropriation of the land and relocation of the settlers. Nevertheless, mega-projects in Arab countries entail informalization of the decision-making processes, lack of participatory approach, and social mobilization related to authoritarian state power. Díaz Orueta and Fainstain (2008, pp. 764–5) draw attention to some common features of mega-projects in the last decades. Their completion time is long, hence political-economic changes may occur during their development and the completed projects hardly are compatible with the initial proposals. Sometimes realizing the project might not be the ultimate goal as claimed by Harris-Brandts and Gogishvili (2018). They argue that "the agency of outlandish design proposals to promote urban boosterism and regime security can be preferable to that of realizing such high-cost, technically complex, and rapidly obsolete projects" (p. 90) as in the case of Zira Island and Khazar Island Projects in Baku Azerbaijan.

The scrutiny of the promotion of the Istanbul Canal reveals that the vision of the project resonates with these characteristics in relation to scale, target populations, relocations of populations, conversion of natural resources, decision-making process, and role in political agendas. After a decade since the announcement, there has been the approval of the environmental plan and zoning plans, the announcement of several housing projects, and the organization of the groundbreaking ceremony of Sazlıdere Bridge, one of the bridges that cross the canal, as the inauguration of the construction of the overall project on June 26, 2021. Criticism of the project has been resting upon the rather incomplete sketch of it drawn by these steps and promotional visions of the project. Uzunçarşılı Baysal (2021) criticized the Istanbul Airport and the Istanbul Canal for their potential risks of displacement and deterritorialization. Indeed, the largest and first private housing project as part of the Istanbul Canal was to take place close to the Istanbul Airport, namely in Arnavutköy district, particularly for the employees of the airport (Güneş, 2018; Şahin, 2021b; Yeniçağ, 2021). This criticism of the Istanbul Canal can be located within the burgeoning investigation of the Islamic-conservative communities fervor for public works and construction. As Bora remarks, Istanbul Canal takes this attitude to an unprecedented scale while evoking iconic images of global metropolises (Bora, 2021).

A Discourse Analysis on Istanbul Canal

Since the initial announcement of the Istanbul Canal as the "crazy project" of Erdoğan, there hasn't been a detailed description of the overall project, for instance, the planning and specifications of the settlement that will be built alongside the canal. Nevertheless, investigation of the available info derived from the official website of the project, Erdoğan's and bureaucrats' speeches, and official releases reveal an outline of the scope, key concepts, and initiatives.

In his first public announcement of the project in April 2011, Erdoğan mentioned the safety of transportation between Marmara and the Black Sea as the main aim of the Istanbul Canal. Nevertheless, he also depicted it as a project of "urbanism", "family", "tourism and culture", as well as "transportation". He further underlined that it was an "environmental project" as it "safeguards green, animal, and plant lives". For Istanbul, the construction of the canal meant becoming "a city through which two seas pass". (TRT Haber, 2011). Indeed, part of Istanbul would become an island after the completion of the project. In line with Erdoğan's inauguration speech, the official website of Istanbul Canal referred to safeguarding the passage between the Black Sea and the Marmara Sea as the main purpose. "To protect the historical and cultural fabric of Bosphorus" and "to increase its security by avoiding the accelerating amount of sea-way traffic" were among the objectives that were related to the creation of a safe passage. The official website of the project adds "forming a modern settlement with horizontal architecture in the case of the Istanbul earthquake" to the list as the last objective (Kanalistanbul.gov.tr). While the official rhetoric legitimized the necessity of such an alternative sea-way on safety grounds, the vision of creating new cities on both sides of the Canal has been part of the official promotion of the project since its first publicization.

Shortly after the announcement of the project, there has been questioning of the necessity and objectives of the project. Dissection of the criticism of the project and the government's subsequent response is beyond the scope of this chapter. Yet, two main tracks of criticism will be addressed about the government's discourse on the topic. Firstly, critics underlined the environmental and ecological risks that will be created by the new water channel. It is claimed that the Istanbul Canal will wipe out invaluable freshwater resources and cause substantial destruction of the northern forests and agricultural lands of Istanbul. Secondly, critics underlined the fact that the Istanbul Canal contradicted the Istanbul Metropolitan Municipality's Environmental Plan of 2009, which recommended a linear macroform for the city along the East-West axis and a development model comprising compact sub-regions (Kılıç, 2020).

According to the project's detractors, the government's enthusiasm for the project despite all the criticisms revealed the project's true motivation, namely real estate speculation.They claimed that the Istanbul Canal is a new tool to trigger the construction-driven economy in Istanbul (Kılıç, 2020, 48). Changes in the zoning plans of the project strengthened these suspicions about the main motivation of the project. For instance, the total ratio allocated for housing and commercial facilities has been increased from 38.79 % to 47.97 % and the passive green zone has been narrowed from 100 meters to 80 meters (Habertürk, 2020).

In fact, the Istanbul Canal is not the only waterway project that has been brought to the agenda since the 2011 elections. On the European side of Istanbul, there is another Canal Project, the Riva Canal, which was announced to the public in 2012. The process halted in 2014 has been activated in 2020[5].There are other smaller canal projects in Anatolia, like Ephesus Antique Canal Project (Yeşil gazete, 2020) or Çeşme Canal (Pehlivan, 2020). Anatolia's smaller canal projects are being considered as part of tourism development plans. Despite being the focus of attention, it appears that the Istanbul Canal is not the only example of infrastructure projects, specifically canals, being used to boost real estate and attract foreign investment.

While responding to these criticisms of the project, Erdoğan, JDP politicians, and bureaucrats situated the debate in the context of the politicization of the infrastructure projects in Turkey. Erdoğan invoked the "us" and "them" dichotomy, echoing Turkey's long history of polarization over infrastructure projects (Erdoğan, 2018). Beginning with the announcement of the project in 2011, Erdoğan repeatedly referred to the project in his speeches on the occasion of various inauguration ceremonies and political meetings. In the recurring "us" and "them" dichotomy, Erdoğan disapproved of "them" for not "being able to comprehend" the project (Cihan Haber Ajansı, 2013). In this context, Erdoğan directly linked the Istanbul Canal to the series of right-wing government projects, namely, as all "completed despite this mentality" (Erdoğan, July 2021b). Furthermore, Erdoğan assured his audience about the success of these projects as "we" have achieved "forming great civilizations" in history (Erdoğan, November 18, 2014). Despite this potent response, criticism of the Istanbul Canal could be still delegitimizing the project as the attractiveness of such mega-projects is on a knife-edge. As underlined by Doğan and Stupar (2017, 287) as "environmental awareness and social cohesion" are promoted widely by competing cities in the

5 Please see http://megaprojeleristanbul.com/#kanal-riva for the timeline of the project (access 04.04.2021).

world, this ground for the criticism of the project jeopardizes its global attractiveness. In this respect, proponents of the Istanbul Canal were eager to portray the urban schemes of the project in a positive light regarding the above-mentioned terms.

Several concepts of urbanism had key roles in the depiction and popularization of the Project by the government. Keywords of "horizontal architecture", "smart city", "low-dense housing" were in the description of the project on the official website (Kanalistanbul.gov.tr b).

> "With the 'Kanal Istanbul Project', two exemplary smart cities will be built based on horizontal architecture, which will make Istanbul breathe with traffic, social facilities, and green areas. The maximum projected population in the region is 500,000 people.
>
> In these new settlement areas, low-density housing areas dominated by low-rise (maximum 4–5 floors) horizontal architecture in the neighborhood concept and commercial, official institutions, coastal facilities, urban regional social reinforcement areas, urban regional green, and sports areas, university area, technology development zone, tourism area, eco-tourism area, health tourism area, congress, and fair area and logistics zone areas that serves for the residential areas will take place." (Kanalistanbul.gov.tr b)

"Eco" and "smart" visions of the project match with the popular themes used to brand cities since the second half of the 1990s. In Turkey, the proliferation of the concept of "smart city" can be traced back to the 2010s shortly before the announcement of the Istanbul Canal. It first entered the vocabulary through the field of informatics in Turkey (Bilişim Dergisi, 2010). In 2011, Menderes Türel, one of the youngest metropolitan mayors of Turkey from JDP, referred to the concept in his address to the Grand National Assembly of Turkey on the occasion of the foundation of the Ministry of Environment and Urbanism. His speech endorsed the municipal works of the JDP in the field of infrastructure and advocated a new period of "municipal works" that will base on the new concepts of "smart city" and "ecological city" (TBMM, 2011, 70–71). This was also the time of the EU's call for proposals for smart cities and communities being reverberated in the Turkish media (TÜBİTAK, 2011, 123). The concept of "smart city" started appearing as a topic in the activity reports of municipalities in Turkey while describing their future visions or technological applications that serve towards this end. For instance, the Department of Information Technologies of Kayseri Metropolitan Municipality had the aim of increasing the use of technology in the services in line with the municipality's slogan "Smart City Kayseri" (Kayseri Büyükşehir Belediyesi, 2016, 36 and 362).

In 2016, the concept made its way into the speeches of Erdoğan and the Minister of Environment and Urbanism at "the Convention of Urban Renewal and Smart Cities" organized by the state and private sector. In his speech, Erdoğan promptly recognized the changing expectations of the inhabitants of the city as the level of economic welfare increases. He referred to the concept of "smart city" in the context of the Istanbul Canal and defined it as the "integration of the city and technology". He encouraged the adaptation of "smart city applications" as a modern remedy for "urban sprawl", "noise", and "environmental pollution". Furthermore, Erdoğan brought his vision of urban architecture and smart city together. He stated that "smart city does not mean vertical architecture" and "vertical architecture shall not be allowed in the vicinity of the Istanbul Canal" (Türkiye Cumhuriyeti Çevre ve Şehircilik Bakanlığı, 2016).

In the same year, Istanbul Metropolitan Municipality hosted the annual and International Smart City Expo that specifically focused on bringing together technology firms and cities from around the world (YTÜ Yıldız Teknopark). At the Expo, Kadir Topbaş, the mayor of Istanbul Metropolitan Municipality, emphasized the cooperation of "local governments", "housing industry", and "firms generating technology". He expected a mayor to act like a CEO (İSTTELKOM AŞ). Topbaş's statement exemplified the government's eagerness to be part of the global trend towards rebranding cities through technological innovation. As Haarstad and Wathne demonstrate "hegemonic policy discourse" presents technological solutions as the way forward for cities across the world as a blueprint for their future. Within this discourse, local actors drew on the "smart agenda" to reframe their initiatives (Haarstad & Wathne, 2019). The increasing inclusion of the concept "smart cities" in the rhetoric of the "municipal works" was within this context and alongside neoliberal economic policies.

The governmental interest in the topic subsequently culminated in the Presidential Circular on the National Smart Cities Strategy and Action Plan (2020–2023) published in the Official Gazette in December 2019 (Resmi Gazete, 2019). Within a month, Murat Kurum, Minister of Urbanism and Environment, declared at the opening ceremony of the Smart Cities and Municipalities Congress and Exhibition that Istanbul Canal will be the first project to adopt "all of the smart city products and services" at once. These would include smart buildings, innovative environment and infrastructure systems, and transportation technologies. Echoing Erdoğan, Kurum also touched on the topic of "horizontal architecture". He foresaw a "new period" of urbanization in which horizontal architecture would be the basis (Türkiye Cumhuriyeti Çevre ve Şehircilik Bakanlığı, 2020).

Indeed, Erdoğan's and Kurum's emphasis on "horizontal architecture" can be traced back to the beginning of the 2010s concurrent with the publication of the Istanbul Canal. In the government program of 2014, prime minister Ahmet

Davutoğlu shortly touched on the topic and announced that "horizontal not vertical urban development" would be the case in the coming period. Afterward, he reaffirmed that "our cities would be liveable" and "brand cities" (Resmi Gazete, 2014). At "the Convention of Urban Renewal and Smart Cities" in 2016, Erdoğan elaborated on the topic. He praised the Housing Development Administration of Turkey (TOKİ) and expected it to advance "horizontal architecture", "neighborhood culture", and "vernacular architecture" in their projects (Erdoğan, 2016a). He expected the interpretations of the "Seljuk" and "Ottoman" architectural styles to dominate the urbanization (Erdoğan, 2016b). At the urbanism council meeting, Erdoğan elaborated the contrast between horizontal and vertical architecture, the first enables inhabitants to live "close to the earth" the latter was a real estate speculation to "make much money from less land" (Erdoğan, 2017). At the beginning of 2017, news agencies reported a new zoning ordinance after Erdoğan's statements over "horizontal architecture" (Sputniknews, 2017). In its "new direction", TOKİ claimed to adopt "horizontal architecture" alongside vernacular architecture and neighborhood-oriented projects towards accomplishing sustainable settlements (Turan, 2018).

At the beginning of 2019, the upcoming local elections in March vitalized the concept of "horizontal architecture" as part of the election manifesto of JDP. Alongside smart cities and cities respecting the environment, "horizontal architecture" was one of the 11 articles of the manifesto (Cumhuriyet, 2019). Erdoğan reiterated his government's commitment to "horizontal architecture" in a live program broadcasted by several national channels (Türkiye Cumhuriyeti Cumhurbaşkanlığı, 2019). It seemed to kickstart a new promotion cycle of the concept. A short video by JDP titled "Horizontal Urbanism" portrayed it as an architectural approach that will strengthen the old neighborhood culture and earth in the cities. Horizontal Urbanism would be implemented especially in the areas that are recently opened to urban development (AK Parti, 2019). Shortly afterward, the start of the projects of in total 50.000 units of social housing in 67 cities was announced (TOKİ Haber, 2019). As a new and sensational urbanism project, Istanbul Canal became a fertile ground to implement the widely promoted albeit vague vision of "horizontal urbanism". As well as ensuring harmony with "human scale" and "ancient values", (Gündoğmuş, 2018), horizontal architecture would provide safe residential areas in a major earthquake zone and substitute "damaged" buildings in Istanbul. The government's vision of the Istanbul Canal as a smart city and case of horizontal urbanism seemed to resonate. Sinan Genim, a JDP-leaning architect, praised the new city alongside the Istanbul Canal as "an alternative to the Bosporus" as the urbanization there will be "horizontal rather than by skyscrapers". (Elmacıoğlu, 2019).

Nevertheless, uses of the keywords smart and horizontal only offer a sketchy picture, and a concrete presentation of the urbanism and architecture of the planned "cities" alongside the Istanbul Canal is mostly lacking. Horizontal architecture does not appear to be a comprehensive perspective on urbanism but more of a limit on the height of the buildings, as Kurum declared that the maximum number of stories in the Istanbul Canal will be four (Başakşehir Belediyesi, 2018). In this regard, Turkish intellectuals' perspectives of urbanism have yet not made their way to enhance and reinforce the government's concepts of smart city and horizontal architecture. Indeed, there is an exploration of the humanistic values of the city based on "horizontality" and Ottoman urbanization is a topic of academic interest. Turgut Cansever, a respected Turkish architect and city planner in conservative circles, has been an inspiration for this purpose (Düzenli, 2016). Such academic examination of the topic is yet to be fulfilled by the proponents to create a substantial direction in urbanism from the keyword "horizontal architecture".

Conclusive Remarks

The rhetoric about the Istanbul Canal Project in the official website and Erdoğan's and bureaucrats' speeches echo the vocabulary of right-wing leaders', namely Menderes, Özal, and Demirel. On the other hand, this rhetoric is also refashioned by new terms like "smart city" and "horizontal architecture" in line with the recent global popularity of mega-projects and their gigantic scale. The Istanbul Canal Project represents the most speculative and "crazy" touchstone of the recent global approach to mega-projects in Turkey, which aims to open Istanbul to a competitive neo-liberal market by policy-makers with trendy concepts. Replicating the emphasis on the "smart" and "eco" in global city branding, JDP has intertwined the concept of "smart city" with the vision of the Istanbul Canal Project since the early 2010s. The use of the term "eco" appears to be more restrained reflecting the selective use of city branding concepts as they diverge in generating international support and market value. In the context of "service" to and "works" for the nation, the emphasis placed on the project's infrastructural value and the related agenda to pursue the track laid out by right-wing leaders of the past comes together with the contemporary city branding rhetoric and popular themes used to propagate the project.

Large-scale real-estate oriented unfinished mega-projects such as human-made archipelagos in Dubai, ghost cities in China, and incomplete, halted, decelerated, or deserted new city building attempts in the Global South (Asia, Africa, Latin America and Oceania) as a result of global/local economic crises demonstrate the risks and importance of planning, particularly when engaged in urban entrepreneurship, and display lessons to be learned from. In the case of the Istanbul Canal, there is a plausible possibility that it will remain sketchy as an urbanization idea while being an effective economic model of real estate development. The current urban renewal and conservation movement in Turkey, particularly in Istanbul, raises questions about the scope and scale of real-estate generating mega-projects. Because the economic bottleneck that Turkey has been experiencing since 2016 has slowed the pace of urban renewal and the production of gated communities and large-scale housing projects.

The future of Istanbul is inextricably linked to the investment value imposed on housing in Turkey by all actors of the built environment; not only policymakers and implementers but also people of all income levels who are primarily interested in individual gain as a result of the current conjuncture. Investment-oriented perception of housing helped boost the sector and had a major role in the growth of the Turkish economy. One major aim of the Canal seems to invigorate the new housing production and promote it as a natural byproduct of Istanbul's biggest mega-project. From here many questions arise: What will be the lasting legacy of the construction of globally branded new cities in the lineage of "works" by the right-wing leaders? Who will demand these houses? Istanbulites, the new rich classes known as Anatolian tigers (Anadolu kaplanları), or wealthy classes from the Global South, primarily the Middle East, looking to invest or gain Turkish citizenship? What will be the impact of the two cities on both sides of the Istanbul Canal and residential projects on the residential preferences of West Istanbul Island Istanbulites? What effect will the new gated communities and brand projects of the Istanbul Canal have on the real estate sector in different parts of Istanbul? Right now, all of these critical questions are up in the air while the detailed project is yet to be crystallized. Nevertheless, information and the subsequent research about the planning and implementation processes, as well as the demographic-social-economic-environmental impacts of the project have the potential to open up fresh perspectives. Adaptation of global strategies in local contexts of mega housing projects is also an open and crucial question. If the Istanbul Canal Project is completed, it will be a fertile ground to explore these questions.

References

Ak Parti (February 27, 2019). Yatay Şehirleşme. https://www.youtube.com/watch?v=Ns5pJ7yyMWA

Aslan, Ş. (2011). Birleştiren ve ayrıştıran işlevleriyle İstanbul'da boğaz köprülerinin toplumsal dili [Social discourse of Bosphorus Bridges in Istanbul with their connecting and segregating roles]. *İstanbul Üniversitesi Siyasal Bilgiler Fakültesi Dergisi [Journal of Istanbul University Faculty of Political Sciences]*, 0(44). https://dergipark.org.tr/tr/pub/iusiyasal/issue/594/5981

Barthel, P.-A. (2010). Arab mega-projects: Between the Dubai effect, global crisis, social mobilization and a sustainable shift. *Built Environment* (1978-) Vol. 36, Issue. 2, pp. 132–145. https://www.jstor.org/stable/23290061.

Başakşehir Belediyesi (2018, August 13). Kanal İstanbul'da yapılar 4 katı geçmeyecek [Buildings will not exceed 4 floors in the Istanbul Canal]. https://www.basaksehir.bel.tr/kanal-istanbul-da-yapilar-4-kati-gecmeyecek

Batuman, B. (2018). *Milletin mimarisi. Yeni İslamcı ulus inşasının kent ve mekan siyaseti. (The architecture of the people. Urban and spatial politics of the new Islamist nation building).* Metis Yayınları [Metis Publishing].

Bayraktar, U. (2018). Policy-making at local level: An analysis of Turkish municipalities. In C. Bakır & G. Ertan (Eds.), *Policy Analysis in Turkey* (pp. 105–120). Policy Press.

Bilişim Dergisi (2010). Kamu, yerel yönetimler ve iş dünyası, "Bilişim Kentleri" nde buluştu [Public, local administration and the business world met at "Communication Cities"], Vol. 38, Issue. 127, pp. 31–32.

Bora, T. (2021). Türk muhafazakarlığı ve inşaat şehveti [Turkish conservatism and construction lust]. In T. Bora (Ed.), *İnşaat ya Resulallah [Construction ya Resulallah]* (pp. 9–15). İletişim Yayınları (İletişim Publishing).

Buğra, A. (2017). Two lives of developmentalism: A Polanyian view from Turkey. *International Development Policy | Revue internationale de politique de développement* [Online]. URL: http://journals.openedition.org/poldev/2306 8. Accessed 14 March 2021). DOI: https://doi.org/10.4000/poldev.2306

Cengiz, F. Ç. (2021). Türkiye'deki merkez sağda devlet, siyaset ve hizmet ilişkisi [State, politics, and service relationship in the center-right in Turkey]. *Marmara Üniversitesi Siyasal Bilimler Dergisi [Marmara University Journal of Political Science]*, Vol. 9/1, pp. 156–174. DOI: https://doi.org/10.14782/marmarasbd.767419

Cihan Haber Ajansı [Cihan News Agency] (2013, October 12). Erdoğan: Boğaz güzel, ama Kanal İstanbul daha güzel olacak [Erdoğan: The Bosphorus is beautiful, but the Istanbul Canal will be more beautiful]. https://www.youtube.com/watch?v=9e6rxS4V-f4

Cugurullo, F. (2018). Exposing smart cities and eco-cities: Frankenstein urbanism and the sustainability challenges of the experimental city. *Environment and Planning A: Economy and Space*, Vol. 50, Issue 1, pp. 73–92. https://doi.org/10.1177/0308518X17738535

Cumhuriyet (2019, January 31). Erdoğan açıkladı: İşte AKP'nin 11 maddelik seçim manifestosu [Erdogan explained: Here is the 11-point election manifesto of the JDP]. https://www.cumhuriyet.com.tr/haber/erdogan-acikladi-iste-akpnin-11-maddelik-secim-manifestosu-1225277

Díaz Orueta, F. and Fainstain, S. S. (2008). The new mega-projects: Genesis and impacts. *International Journal of Urban and Regional Research*, Vol. 32, Issue 4, pp. 759–767. DOI: https://doi.org/10.1111/j.1468-2427.2008.00829.x

Doğan, E. and Stupar, A. (2017). The limits of growth: A case study of three mega-projects in Istanbul. *Cities*, 60. http://dx.doi.org/10.1016/j.cities.2016.09.013.

Düzenli, H. İ. (ed.) (2016). *Ufkî şehir Turgut Cansever'in izinde [Horizontal city at the footsteps of Turgut Cansever]*. Klasik.

Elmacıoğlu, L. (2019, December 26). "Kanal İstanbul" tartışması büyüyor ["The Istanbul Canal" debate grows]. *Independent Türkçe*. https://www.indyturk.com/node/108891/haber/kanal-istanbul-tart%C4%B1%C5%9Fmas%C4%B1-b%C3%BCy%C3%BCyor

Eraydin, Z. (2014). *The global image of the city: Impacts of place branding on the image of Ankara*. [Unpublished thesis for the PhD Degree]. Ankara: Middle East Technical University.

Erdoğan, R. T. (2014, November 18). Bu nesil bilgi ve hikmeti beraber yüklenmelidir; O zaman gelecek daha farklı olacaktır [This generation's knowledge and wisdom should be loaded together; Then the future will be different]. Türkiye Cumhuriyeti Cumhurbaşkanlığı. https://www.tccb.gov.tr/haberler/410/1502/bu-nesil-bilgi-ve-hikmeti-beraber-yuklenmelidir-o-zaman-gelecek-daha-farkli-olacaktir

Erdoğan, R. T. (2016a, April 16). Kentsel dönüşümü, bir hayal olmaktan çıkartıp gerçeğe dönüştürdük [We transformed urban transformation from being a dream to reality]. Türkiye Cumhuriyeti Cumhurbaşkanlığı. https://www.tccb.gov.tr/haberler/410/42488/kentsel-donusumu-bir-hayal-olmaktan-cikartip-gercege-donusturduk.html

Erdoğan, R. T. (2016b, May 30). Paris'te yaşanan olaylardan dolayı endişeliyim [I'm concerned about the events in Paris]. Türkiye Cumhuriyeti Cumhurbaşkanlığı. https://www.tccb.gov.tr/haberler/410/44182/pariste-yasanan-olaylardan-dolayi-endiseliyim

Erdoğan, R. T. (2017, January 27). Tarihimizden ibret alarak, şehircilik konusunda hatalarımızın tekrarını önlemeliyiz [We should prevent the repetition of our mistakes in urban planning by taking lessons from our history]. Türkiye Cumhuriyeti Cumhurbaşkanlığı [Presidency of the Republic of Turkey]. https://www.tccb.gov.tr/haberler/410/70852/tarihimizden-ibret-alarak-sehircilik-konusunda-hatalarimizin-tekrarini-onlemeliyiz

Erdoğan, R. T. (2018, November 17). Millet bahçeleri açılış töreninde yaptıkları konuşma [Speech at the national gardens opening ceremony]. Türkiye Cumhuriyeti Cumhurbaşkanlığı [Presidency of the Republic of Turkey]. https://www.tccb.gov.tr/konusmalar/353/99746/millet-bahceleri-acilis-toreninde-yaptiklari-konusma

Erdoğan, R. T. (2019, December 31). Kanal İstanbul'un yanına 2 akıllı şehir [2 smart cities next to the Istanbul Canal]. *Sözcü.* https://www.aksam.com.tr/siyaset/kanal-istanbulun-yanina-2-akilli-sehir/haber-1034102

Erdoğan, R. T. (2021a, June). Eserlerimizi Kanal İstanbul ile taçlandıracağız [We will crown our works with the Istanbul Canal]. [Video]. https://www.youtube.com/watch?v=xnf6-Mby4Es&t=49s

Erdoğan, R. T. (2021b, July 2). Sakarya toplu açılış töreni'nde yaptıkları konuşma [Speech delivered at the Sakarya collective opening ceremony]. Türkiye Cumhuriyeti Cumhurbaşkanlığı [Presidency of the Republic of Turkey]. https://www.tccb.gov.tr/konusmalar/353/128587/sakarya-toplu-acilis-toreni-nde-yaptiklari-konusma

Gündoğmuş, Y. N. (2018, November 21). Çevre ve Şehircilik Bakanı Kurum: Kanal İstanbul Projesi'nde yatay mimari esas alınacak [Minister of Environment and Urbanization Kurum: The Istanbul Canal project will be based on horizontal architecture]. https://www.aa.com.tr/tr/turkiye/cevre-ve-sehircilik-bakani-kurum-kanal-istanbul-projesinde-yatay-mimari-esas-alinacak/1317357

Güneş, H. (2018, May 28). THY ve Emlak Konut'tan dev gayrimenkul projesi [Giant real estate project by Turkish Airlines and Emlak Konut]. AA (Anadolu Ajansı) Şirket Haberleri [Anatolian Agency Company News]. https://www.aa.com.tr/tr/sirkethaberleri/ulasim/thy-ve-emlak-konuttan-dev-gayrimenkul-projesi/645007

Gürkan, Y. (2013, May 30). 3. köprüye onun adı verildi [3rd bridge is named after him]. *Arkitera.* https://www.arkitera.com/haber/3-kopruye-onun-adi-verildi/

Haarstad, H. and Wathne, M. W. (2019). Smart cities as strategic actors. In A. Karvonen, F. Cugurullo, & F. Caprotti (Eds.), *Inside Smart Cities: Place, Politics and Urban Innovation* (pp. 102–116). Routledge.

Habertürk (2020, March 7). İşte Kanal İstanbul'dan beklenen gelir [Here is the expected income from the Istanbul Canal]. https://www.haberturk.com/son-dakika-haberler-iste-kanal-istanbul-dan-beklenen-gelir-2606765-ekonomi

Halktv (2021, June). *Erdoğan kanal İstanbul'u Erbakan, Demirel, Özal ve Menderes'e bağladı [Erdogan connects the Istanbul Canal to Erbakan, Demirel, Özal and Menderes].* Accesed 21 July 2021. Source: AA *https://halktv.com.tr/gundem/erdogan-kanal-istanbulu-erbakan-demirel-ozal-ve-menderese-bagladi-462914h.*

Harris-Brandts, S. and Gogishvili, D. (2018). Architectural rumors: Unrealized mega-projects in Baku, Azerbaijan and their politico-economic uses. *Eurasian Geography and Economics*, Vol. 59, Issue 1, pp. 73–97, DOI: https://doi.org/10.1080/15387216.2018.1462725

İSTTELKOM AŞ (n.d.). İSTTELKOM AŞ telekomünikasyon çözümleri ile akıllı şehirlerin İstanbul zirvesinde yerini aldı [İSTTELKOM JC took its place at the Istanbul summit of smart cities with its telecommunication solutions]. https://www.google.com/url?q= https://isttelkom.istanbul/isttelkom-a-s-akilli-sehirlerin-istanbul-zirvesinde-yerini-aldi/&sa=D&source=editors&ust=1628238084117000&usg=AOvVaw2VnLK9BXaHVCoKSrp4oJEx

Joppien, C. (2019). *Municipal Politics in Turkey. Local Government and Party Organization*. Routledge.

Kaçmazoğlu, B. H. (2012). *Demokrat parti toplumsal tartışmaları [Democrat party social debates].* Doğu Kitap [Doğu Book].

Kanalistanbul.gov.tr. *Nüfus ve yeni yerleşim alanı [Population and new settlement area].* Accessed 23 July 2021. https://www.kanalistanbul.gov.tr/tr/hersey/nufus-ve-yeni-yerlesim-alani

Kanalistanbul.gov.tr. *Projenin amacı [The goal of the project].* Accessed 23 July 2021 https://www.kanalistanbul.gov.tr/tr/neden/projenin-amaci

Karakaş, G. (2013, May 30). 3. gerdanlık Yavuz Sultan Selim oldu [3rd necklace became Yavuz Sultan Selim]. *Milliyet.* https://www.milliyet.com.tr/ekonomi/3-gerdanlik-yavuz-sultan-selim-oldu-1715915

Kavaratzis, M. (2004). From city marketing to city branding: Towards a theoretical framework for developing city brands. *Place Branding*, Vol. 1, Issue 1, pp. 58–73. DOI: https://doi.org/10.1057/palgrave.pb.5990005

Kayseri Büyükşehir Belediyesi [Kayseri Metropolitan Municipality] (2016). *2015 Yılı Faaliyet Raporu [2015 Activity Report].*

Kılıç, A. (2020). *Kanal İstanbul çalıştayı [The Istanbul Canal workshop].* İstanbul Büyükşehir Belediyesi [Istanbul Metropolitan Municipality].

Menteş, E. and Töre, E. (2020). Rant etkisinde Zekeriyaköy: Çepere yönelen planlama ve kullanıcı tercihlerine dair bir araştırma [Zekeriyaköy in the effect of unearned income: A Study on peripheral planning and user preferences]. *Planlama [Planning]*, Vol. 30, Issue 3, pp. 389–403. DOI: https://doi.org/10.14744/planlama.2020.14622

Moser, S. and Côté-Roy, L. (2021). New cities: Power, profit and prestige. *Geography Compass*, Vol. 15, Issue 1, pp. 1–15. DOI: https://doi.org/10.1111/gec3.12549

Pehlivan (2020, September 30). Çeşme projesi, İzmir'in 'Kanal İstanbul'udur [Çeşme project is Izmir's the Istanbul Canal]. *Gazeteduvar.* https://www.gazeteduvar.com.tr/cesme-projesi-izmirin-kanal-istanbuludur-haber-1500304

Resmi Gazete (2014, September 7). Başbakan Sayın Ahmet Davutoğlu tarafından Türkiye Büyük Millet Meclis'ne sunulan 62. hükümet programı [The 62nd government program presented to the Turkish Grand National Assembly by Prime Minister Ahmet Davutoğlu]. No: 29112.

Resmi Gazete (2019, December 24). Ulusal akıllı şehirler stratejisi ve eylem planı [National smart cities strategy and action plan]. No: 3098.

Şahin, İ. (2021a, July 30). Üçüncü köprü ile yıldızı parlayan bölgeler [Regions that benefited from the third bridge]. *Sözcü gazetesi.* https://www.sozcu.com.tr/2016/emlak/ucuncu-kopru-ile-yildizi-parlayan-bolgeler-1371230/

Şahin, İ. (2021b, July 4). Kanal İstanbul'un ilk özel projesi belli oldu [First private project of the Istanbul Canal has been announced]. *Sözcü.* Accessed 17 July 2021. https://www.sozcu.com.tr/2021/ekonomi/kanal-istanbulun-ilk-ozel-projesi-belli-oldu-6520392/..

Sputniknews (2017, March 29). İstanbul için yatay imar planı [Horizontal zoning plan for Istanbul]. https://tr.sputniknews.com/cevre/201703291027846570-istanbul-yatay-plan/

TBMM (Türkiye Büyük Millet Meclisi) [Grand National Assembly of Turkey] (2011). 2012 yılı Merkezi yönetim bütçe kanunu tasarısı ile 2010 yılı merkezi yönetim kesin hesap kanunu tasarısı plan ve bütçe komisyonu görüşme tutanakları [2012 central government budget draft law and 2010 central government final accounts draft plan and budget committee meeting minutes].

Toki Haber (2019, March 6). Yatay şehirleşmeyle 50 bin yeni sosyal konut [50 thousand new social housing with horizontal urbanization]. https://www.tokihaber.com.tr/haberler/yatay-sehirlesmeyle-50-bin-yeni-sosyal-konut/

TRT Haber [TRT News] (2011, April 27). İstanbul'a çılgın proje [Crazy project for Istanbul].

M. E. Turan (2018, May). Tokipark'lar ile daha çok yeşil [More green with Tokiparks]. *Toki Haber*, No. 99, p. 5.

TÜBİTAK AB Çerçeve Programları Ulusal Koordinasyon Ofisi [TÜBİTAK EU Framework Programs National Coordination Office] (2011). AB 7. çerçeve programı enerji araştırmaları alanı [EU 7th framework program energy research area]. *Çerçeve*, Vol. 19, Issue 56, pp. 118–123.

Türk, B. H. (2014). *Muktedir. Türk sağ geleneği ve Recep Tayyip Erdoğan.* İletişim Yayınları.

Türkiye Cumhuriyeti Cumhurbaşkanlığı [Presidency of the Republic of Turkey] (2019, February 23). Cumhurbaşkanı Erdoğan, CNN TÜRK-Kanal D ortak yayınına katıldı [President Erdoğan attended the joint broadcast of CNN TÜRK-Kanal D]. https://www.tccb.gov.tr/haberler/410/102126/cumhurbaskani-erdogan-cnn-turk-kanal-d-ortak-yayinina-katildi

Türkiye Cumhuriyeti Çevre ve Şehircilik Bakanlığı [Republic of Turkey Ministry of Environment and Urbanization] (2016, April 11). Kentsel dönüşüm ve akıllı şehirler kurultayı gerçekleştirildi [Urban transformation and smart cities congress was held]. https://www.csb.gov.tr/kentsel-donusum-ve-akilli-sehirler-kurultayi-gerceklestirildi-bakanlik-faaliyetleri-1503

Türkiye Cumhuriyeti Çevre ve Şehircilik Bakanlığı [Republic of Turkey Ministry of Environment and Urbanization] (January 15, 2020). Akıllı şehir uygulamalarında ilk örnek Kanal İstanbul olacak [The Istanbul Canal will be the first example in smart city applications]. https://csb.gov.tr/akilli-sehir-uygulamalarinda-ilk-ornek-kanal-istanbul-olacak-bakanlik-faaliyetleri-29695

Uzunçarşılı Baysal, C. (2021, April 11). Kanal İstanbul yenişehir projesi: Nasıl bir yeni şehir? Kim/ler için bu yenişehir? [The Istanbul Canal new city project: What kind of a new city? Who/s is this new city for?]. *Birgün.* https://www.cumhuriyet.com.tr/haber/iste-kanal-istanbulun-ilk-konut-projesi-1172831

Yeniçağ (2021, July 4). Kanal İstanbul'un ilk özel projesi belli oldu. Bakın bu sefer kime gitmiş [The Istanbul Canal's first private project has been announced. Look whom it's gone to this time]. https://www.yenicaggazetesi.com.tr/kanal-istanbulun-ilk-ozel-projesi-belli-oldu-bakin-bu-sefer-kime-gitmis-hem-de-sefik-birkiye-tasarlamis-461111h.htm

Yeşilgazete (2020, June, 2). Dördüncü kanal, Efes antik kenti'ne: "ÇED gerekli değil" kararı çıktı [The fourth canal, to the ancient city of Ephesus: "EIA is not required" decision was made]. https://yesilgazete.org/dorduncu-kanal-efes-antik-kentine-ced-gerekli-degil-karari-cikti/

YTÜ Yıldız Teknopark (n.d.). Smart city EXPO İstanbul 2016 akıllı şehirler fuar ve kongresi gerçekleşti [Smart city EXPO Istanbul 2016 smart cities fair and congress took place]. https://www.yildizteknopark.com.tr/tr/duyuru/smart-city-expo-istanbul-2016-akilli-sehirler-fuar-ve-kongresi-gerceklesti-584.html

Pınar Şahin

7
Urban Development Processes and the Changing Housing Patterns in Istanbul: The Case of Fulya Neighborhood

Introduction

Urban space is a complex and dynamic system. It changes under the influence of political, social, economic, and even ideological factors as well as physical and environmental factors. This change in the urban space also has an impact on the living and housing styles of the societies and redefines the housing patterns. Throughout history, housing has been affected by the dynamics of the urbanization processes, and this has manifested itself as periodic layers in housing patterns. In Istanbul, which has been the center of social, cultural, and political developments in every period, housing patterns have changed and even been redefined in parallel with urbanization experiences. However, the rapid urbanization started with the industrialization movements in the 1950s has deeply affected the spatial characteristics and meaning of housing. In particular, due to the migrations to the big cities, there have been significant changes in the urban space and, therefore, in the understanding of housing. On the other hand, the new construction techniques, and the incorporation of the apartment into the urban space as a representation of modern life brought new experiences to the urban morphology of Istanbul. The changes in the urban space became more evident after the 1980s, when neoliberal policies began to be implemented. This period was followed by the globalization discourses, and in the 2000s, housing came onto the scene with different forms of presentation. As a result, urban space has become the place where capitalism manifests itself in its most concrete form, and housing has become a commodity structured with rent-oriented strategies for the reproduction of capital.

Considering the changes in the urban space of Istanbul and, therefore, in the residential areas, the housing development and heterogeneous structure of the Fulya neighborhood, which is subject to this study, is remarkable. Fulya is a relatively dense neighborhood in the district of Şişli, which is on the European side of Istanbul. Located on the old Fulya streambed, which descends from Mecidiyeköy with a steep slope to the south, it is surrounded by Teşvikiye, 19 Mayıs, Gayrettepe, Dikilitaş, Mecidiyeköy, Merkez and Gülbahar neighborhoods. The neighborhood is bordered by the densely used axes of the city in the north and south directions.

One of the city's main arteries, Büyükdere Avenue, is located on the north side. This road connects Beyoğlu and Maslak and is an important trade and finance axes of the Istanbul metropolitan area. Moreover, on the south side of the neighborhood, Hakkı Yeten Street is located in the intersection point of Fulya, Teşvikiye, and Dikilitaş neighborhoods (Figure 7.1). This area consists of business centers, health facilities, and residence-type buildings and creates a new urban focus in the city with its unique identity. In the east, Prof. Dr. Bülent Tarcan and Yeşilçimen streets, and in the west Aytekin Kotil and Fulya Bayırı streets, connect Büyükdere Avenue with Hakkı Yeten Street from two different sides. On the north-south axis, the neighborhood is divided into sub-zones with Mehmetçik Street, Ortaklar Street, and Sakızağacı Street. Ortaklar and Sakızağacı axis consists of relatively high-quality apartment buildings with a more planned layout. The fact that this area is directly related to Büyükdere and is more convenient in terms of topography than the inner parts of the neighborhood is quite an essential factor in this. On the other hand, the sloping old streambed area near Mehmetçik Street has a different texture with irregular and unqualified apartment buildings.

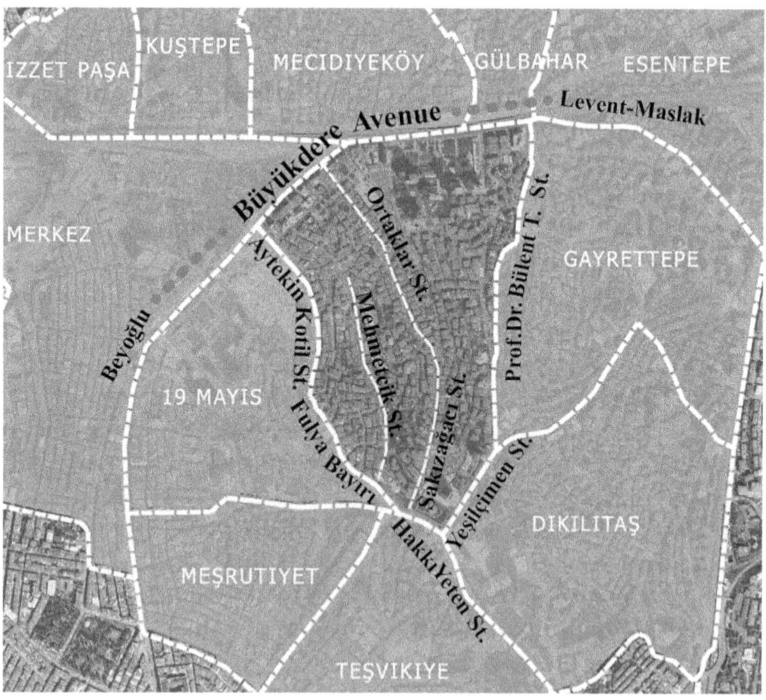

Figure 7.1: Fulya and Its Immediate Surroundings. Source: Map is Generated on Aerial Photo Accessed from Google Earth.

Today, different housing patterns can be seen in Fulya, from luxury apartments and residences to unqualified apartments. Also, the distinctions between the housing patterns at the boundaries of the neighborhood and in interior areas are dramatic. This creates diversity in the district, both spatially and socio-culturally. In this context, it is not possible to talk about a homogeneous spatial and social structure for the neighborhood. Nevertheless, the multi-layered structure of Fulya is also a result of the urban processes it has gone through from past to present. The neighborhood, which started to develop in parallel with the migrations after the 1950s, has been affected by the economic, political, and cultural changes of each period due to its central location. Thus, all these changes have also affected the housing patterns in the area. Accordingly, this chapter aims to examine the development of the housing patterns in the Fulya neighborhood due to historical dynamics and evaluate the current situation through this process. It is thought that the chapter will be useful in terms of assessing the existing housing stock in the neighborhood with an objective point of view and forming a base for future studies about the area.

The general structure of this chapter is organized as follows:

In the next section, the phenomenon of urbanization is emphasized, and housing patterns that develop in parallel with the urbanization of Istanbul are mentioned. The third part, which examines the transformation of the housing patterns in Fulya, is divided into sub-headings according to the thresholds, where significant changes are experienced in the political, socio-cultural, and spatial contexts in Turkey. The first part covers the period from the first years of the new republic, when modernization policies were effective, to the 1950s. The following section covers the period of 1950–1980 when the slum problems increased with the migration to the cities. In addition, apartment buildings are mentioned with examples as modern life representations of the period. This part continues with the 1980–2000 period when neoliberal policies prevailed, and housing presentation forms diversified. The following section covers the period from 2000 to the present, when globalization discourses were dominant, and housing became the focus of capital. The chapter ends with the conclusion part, which includes a general evaluation about the neighborhood.

Although there are many studies about Şişli and some of its neighborhoods, it was observed that there are not enough studies specific to the Fulya neighborhood in academic resources. Therefore, interviews were conducted with local administrations and neighborhood residents to obtain more detailed information about the region. The information obtained was supported by reports and photographs about the neighborhood and its immediate surroundings in the archives of old newspapers and magazines. In addition, through the old Istanbul aerial photographs, the periodic development of the region has been tried to be expressed on the urban scale.

Urbanization and Changing Housing Approaches in Istanbul

Housing is a concept that changes with economic, social, and cultural factors and can be evaluated in parallel with urbanization. In order to understand the changing housing context, it is necessary to examine the urbanization processes first. United Nations defines the urbanization process, or "*urban transition*", as a shift in a population from one that is dispersed across small rural settlements, in which agriculture is the dominant economic activity, towards one that is concentrated in larger and denser urban settlements characterized, in recent centuries, by a dominance of industrial and service activities (UN, 2018). However, it will be necessary to interpret urbanization as a more comprehensive change with social, economic, and cultural dimensions. Urbanization, in its broad sense, can be defined as a population accumulation process that results in the increase in the number of cities and the growth of today's cities in parallel with industrialization and economic development, creating an increase in organization, division of labor, and specialization in the social structure, and leading to urban-specific changes in people's behavior and relations (Keleş, 1995). Although the concept of urbanization has a long history, the industrialization that emerged in the West in the nineteenth century can be considered as the main factor in today's urban space understanding. Chaolin (2020) defines urbanization as a historical process initiated by the growth and development of industrialization, modernization, and globalization and accompanied by changes in population, society, economy, culture, politics, and ideology. According to Freyer (2014), industrialization affected almost every area of life during the nineteenth century. Working spaces, and therefore, job opportunities in cities have intensified, transportation and communication tools have developed, and as a result, cities have become the centers of attraction. Also, the population growth has progressed parallel with the increase in the means of production. In this context, urban society can be considered as a society born from industrialization (Lefebvre, 2003).

The urbanization experiences of the countries differ according to the economic development strategies they follow and the characteristics of their political regimes and administrations, and each period creates a unique city type (Sayar & Süer, 2004). In this context, the urbanization of Turkey has a different process than the West. In the first years of the Republic, a radical modernity project was pursued, and it was aimed to transform the country's lands into a nation-state space and the cities into places of modernity (Tekeli, 2015). According to this, this period can be evaluated in a different framework in the context of establishing a new state. In general, urbanization movements in Turkey gained momentum in the 1950s, after the Second World War. Political, economic, social facts and changes in production relations were decisive in terms of urban space in big cities, especially in Istanbul. In this period, migration from rural to urban areas was one of the most determining factors in urbanization and, accordingly, in housing developments. New industrialization policies, the decrease in the need for labor due to mechanization in agriculture, and attractive factors such as education, health, and social opportunities in major cities caused an increase in migration. However, unlike developed countries, urbanization and industrialization could not progress parallel in Turkey. Cities could not meet the large-scale migration and rapid population in terms of employment, housing, and infrastructure. As the housing problem reached dramatic levels, the immigrants started to build their own houses. These informal settlements, called slums, have caused the city to change and grow uncontrollably. In this context, slums can be considered as one of the main reasons for irregular urbanization after the 1950s. Erman (2012) states that slums as the "*informal*", "*unregulated*", "*unauthorized*", "*self-help*" housing of the urban poor characterize Turkey's irregular urbanization experience in this period. Slums were initially located parallel with the spatial distribution of working areas and industry in the urban space. However, over time, they expanded rapidly towards the city peripheries and led to the unplanned and rapid growth of the city. As a solution to the problem, these informal settlements were legalized with various laws and amnesties. Nevertheless, these efforts were generally the populist policies of the politicians of the period and could not prevent irregular urbanization. This was also a period in which slum dwellers' political power and organizational skills were evaluated within the opportunities provided by democracy (Akbulut, 1996). In the meantime, although apartment buildings were seen as a solution to the housing problem, they remained as structures that appealed to the upper-income group of the society for a long time since it was not possible to divide the land ownership. In this context, the condominium law enacted in 1965 was a significant development in terms of solving this problem which had a drastic influence on the morphologic transformation of the city. With the condominium law, the obligation to be the sole owner of a parcel has been removed. This was also the beginning of the build-and-sell strategy based on sharing.

After the mid-1980s, urbanization and unequal distribution of wealth reached unprecedented levels in Istanbul (Bozdoğan & Akcan, 2012). Also, with the impact of neoliberal policies, the urban space became a spatial expression of capitalist relations of production. In this context, urban space was no longer a passive geographical area but a valuable commodity that became effective in making a profit (Aslanoğlu, 1998). Economic and political transformations brought social and cultural shifts, and the emergence of new classes led to segregation in urban structure. Castells (2015) interprets the segregation in the urban structure as the reflection of the social structure on the space. When this argument is evaluated in the context of Istanbul after the 80s, it can be seen that the boundaries between the housing settlements were shaped according to social classes. This polarization in the social structure has led the upper and middle-upper income groups to create luxury housing areas isolated from other segments of the society. These areas have emerged as gated communities, which were generally on the peripheries of the city, or as housing blocks detached from their surroundings in the city centers.

At the beginning of the twenty-first century, multiple types of urban housing began to form the built environment of major cities. The forces of globalization on the big Turkish cities brought about the legalization of slum areas, the further proliferation of anonymous apartments, the emergence of gated communities, and the implementation of new administrative and design policies for mass housing (Bozdoğan & Akcan, 2012). In this period, urban space continued to be divided with new housing finance models and urban transformation policies. Through legal regulations and incentives, housing has been made an attractive investment object for national and international investors, which has triggered housing production. As a result, medium and large-scale real estate companies started to occupy central places in Istanbul with their investments. On the other hand, while informal settlements continued to exist as one of the city's main socio-cultural and spatial problems, urban space continued to be restructured throughout this process.

Development of Housing Areas in Fulya Neighborhood

Fulya and Its Immediate Surrounding Before 1950

In order to read the development processes of the housing areas in Fulya, it is necessary to mention the Şişli district first. Şişli is one of the oldest settlements in Istanbul with its rich background. The first settlement in the Şişli began with the Kurtuluş neighborhood, called "Tatavla" in the sixteenth century. The region gained importance with the settlement of a community made up of Greek sailors brought to work in the Golden Horn Shipyard and prisoners of war from Chios Island (Şişli Tarihçesi, n.d.). Although Şişli has a long history, the modernization movements within the framework of the Ottoman Westernization in the nineteenth century can be shown as the initial steps of today's urbanization. The first significant population increase in the region occurred with the masonry building demands of the wealthy foreign minorities affected by the great Beyoğlu fire in 1870. Increasing settlement in the area has led to the development of transportation and infrastructure. The extension of the horse-drawn tram and electric tram from Taksim to Pangaltı and Şişli, the laying of electricity and gas lines, made the region one of the attractive living spaces of Istanbul after a while (İşözen, 2003). In addition, Mecidiyeköy, which is in the north of Fulya and has a significant impact on its spatial development, started to develop with the settlement of immigrants in the region by Sultan Abdülmecid in 1854. This can be accepted as the first settlement date for the area (Tümer, 1969).

Fulya, in the south of Mecidiyeköy, was an area on the old Fulya streambed, consisting of fields, gardens, and mulberry groves until the 1950s. An aerial photograph from 1946 shows that the area developed in the northern direction, near today's Büyükdere Avenue. With the increase in population, the city started to grow in the direction of this axis. In addition, various public buildings were built in its immediate surroundings. The French La Paix Hospital built in 1858, and the Etfal Hospital built in 1899, were among the first important public buildings in this period. In 1912, the horse-drawn tram depot, one of the oldest garages of IETT (ETTO), was opened and started to serve as a bus and trolleybus garage. Another significant development on Büyükdere Avenue was the Ali Sami Yen Stadium which was started to be built in 1936 and opened in 1944. In addition, within the scope of the economic policies of the Republican period, industrial structures began to develop in this region. A liquor factory was established in 1930 on Büyükdere axis, next to Ali Sami Yen Stadium area (Figure 7.2). The factory, designed by the French Architect Robert Mallet-Stevens and built with more advanced techniques than its time, was the symbol of the new Republican approach. The building was one of the earliest examples of rational-modernist industrial architecture in Turkey, with its cubic forms, symmetrical flat roofs, and rectangular openings in the horizontal direction (Yılmaz, 2015).

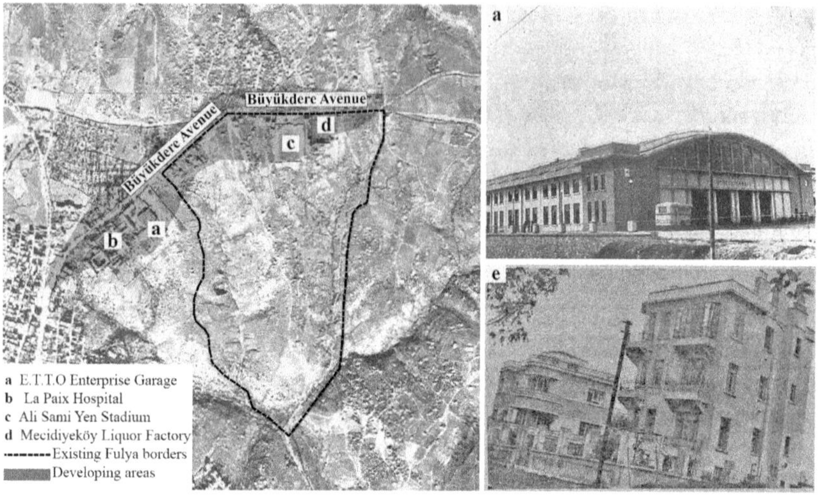

Figure 7.2: Aerial Photo of Fulya in 1946, E.T.T.O Enterprise Garage, Modern Houses. Source: Image A Adapted from "İstanbul Belediyesi E.T.T.O İşletmesi Garajı" by İ. İnan, 1949, Arkitekt, 11–12, p. 212., Image B adapted from "Zarf usulü ile ev yapılan köy" by Y.R. Önen, 1935, *Haber*, p.7, Map is Generated on Aerial Photo Accessed from https://sehirharitasi.ibb.gov.tr/.

During this period, housing areas have also developed in parallel with the urban development on the axis of Büyükdere Avenue and in its immediate vicinity. These buildings, which consist of low-rise apartments and detached houses, were designed with the modernist approaches of the period. The buildings had simple facades, cubic forms, and flat roofs, unlike traditional architecture. In the *Haber Newspaper* of 1935, the following words about the buildings draw attention: "Far away from old wooden houses, the wide field between these houses and the liquor factory built by the roadside, now is closed with masonry houses, cubic buildings. In fact, a four-story apartment was built on the road". It was also stated that some of these houses were not built legally and did not have title deeds (Önen, 1935). Similar statements about housing typologies in this area were also included in *Son Telegraf Newspaper* of 1938. In the article titled "*A perfect place with cute villas, country cafes, theater, everything… Mecidiye village*" the following sentences draw attention; "From the Şişli tram depot to Zincirlikuyu, where there was nothing but a few coffeehouses, now there are cubic houses, beautiful casinos, a great crowd of people" (Kayahan, 1938). These articles also included images of the new modern houses in this area (Figure 7.2).

1950–1980 Period: A New Neighborhood Shaped by Migrations

The political, social, and economic changes experienced after the 1950s caused significant transformations, especially in big cities. The main factor determining the morphology of Istanbul was the spatial distribution of the production facilities that emerged due to rapidly developing industrialization (Tekeli, 2015). The labor force in these facilities was met by the people who migrated from rural to the city. Along with the migrations, the population of the city also increased. In 1940, the population of the city was 991.237, while it increased to 3.019.032 in 1970 (Istanbul Büyükşehir Belediyesi, 2001). With the increase of migration, the construction of slums in the urban space had started to gain momentum. In the 1950s, when Turkey switched to multi-party life, the Demokrat Party came to power with the votes and support it received from the rural. The fact that this new administration avoided taking a hard and firm stance against the construction of slums also accelerated the spread of slums (Erman, 2004). The distribution of slum areas went parallel with the distribution of industry. In general, the slums, which were developed in Mecidiyeköy, Kuştepe, and Gültepe, were providing labor force to their immediate surroundings and Levent, Bomonti industrial areas (Tekeli, 2015). During this period, due to its location close to working areas, there were also many slum settlements located in the old streambed of Fulya. Especially the area between today's Aytekin Kotil Street and Ortaklar Street was a dense slum settlement (Figure 7.3). This area, which was developed entirely different from the northern part, was also subject to the newspapers of the period. In the newspaper reports, it can be generally seen that solutions to housing problems were sought by legalizing slums with laws and amnesties. However, legalization has not been a permanent solution to this. A newspaper report from 1970 stated that an area of 60 thousand square meters on the ridges of Fulya streambed started to slide due to heavy rainfall. About 40 slums were damaged, and some were emptied and sealed (Gönültaş, 1970). From these statements, it can be understood that instead of offering a systematic solution to the slum problem, only local and temporary interventions were provided.

On the other hand, the period after 1950 can be seen as the years in which the apartment buildings changed form in terms of production, ownership, and status. Apartments were no longer the buildings that the upper class of the Early Republican era rented out, but modern, relatively comfortable living spaces of middle-income groups (Görgülü, 2016). When the maps and photographs of the period are examined, it can be seen that apartment buildings started to be built on Ortaklar Street axis extending from Büyükdere Avenue to Sakızağacı Street (Figure 7.3). This axis developed with apartment-type buildings different from the slums in the inner parts of the neighborhood. Located at the end of Ortaklar Street, the Hilton Housing Blocks, built by Hilton Hotel employees in 1957, and the Mimarlar Apartment building, located just across, are among the oldest apartment buildings in this area. In other words, the region consisted of different socio-cultural classes and their housing patterns in this period.

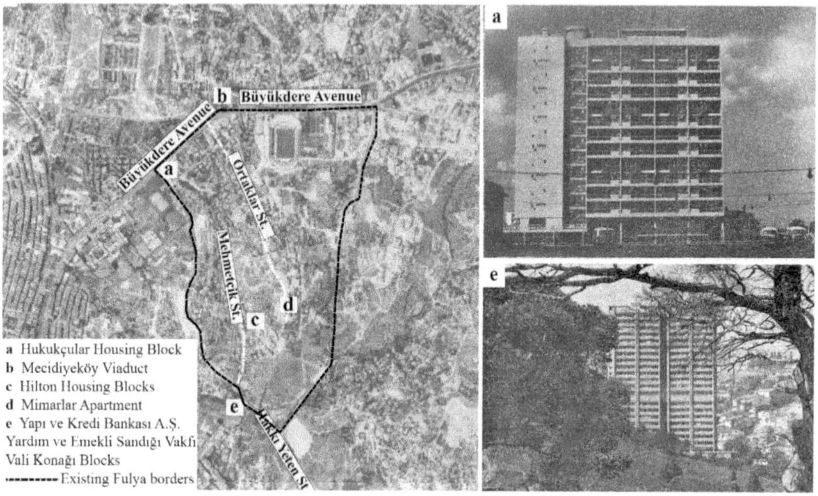

Figure 7.3: Aerial Photo of Fulya in 1970, Hukukçular Housing Block, Yapı ve Kredi Bankası A.Ş. Yardım ve Emekli Sandığı Vakfı Vali Konağı Blocks. Source: Image A Adapted from "Hukukçular Sitesi" by H. Baysal, M. Birsel, 1970, Arkitekt, 340, p. 157, Image B Adapted from "Yapı ve Kredi Bankası A.Ş. Yardım ve Emekli Sandığı Vakfı Vali Konağı Sitesi" by D. Tekeli, S. Sisa, 1978, Arkitekt, 371, p. 88, Map is Generated on Aerial Photo Accessed from https://sehirharitasi.ibb.gov.tr/.

In this period, the change in the architectural language, which was influenced by the Western modernism and generally seen in public buildings, was also reflected in the housing. The Hukukçular Housing block, designed by Melih Birsel and Haluk Baysal in 1960–1961, on the border of Büyükdere Avenue, can be interpreted as one of the representatives of the modernist architectural understanding of the period. The building, which was built by the Istanbul Lawyers Cooperative and had a quite different approach from the other housing structures in the neighborhood, became a striking example of a high-rise residence designed for the middle and upper-middle classes of the period (Tapan, 2005). Its design features were influenced by Le Corbusier's Unite d'Habitation in

Marseille, one of the best-known examples of the international modernist avant-garde. The building, which provided users a functional but not luxurious living space, demonstrated that modernism could be a quality, repeatable, and anonymous practice that could be attributed to middle-class users and their daily lives. However, today the building has become ordinary in the urban chaos of Istanbul, covered with giant billboards and almost indistinguishable (Bozdoğan, 2008). Also, Yapı ve Kredi Bankası A.Ş. Yardım ve Emekli Sandığı Vakfı Vali Konağı Blocks designed by Doğan Tekeli and Sami Sisa in 1972, was another important housing sample of the period. The building, which was located on the sloping land between Vali Konağı Street and Hakkı Yeten Street, was one of the modern architectural representations of its era. In a photo published in the Arkitekt Magazine of 1978, it is possible to see the contradiction between the building and the Fulya neighborhood behind it (Figure 7.3). This structure was influential in the development of Hakkı Yeten Street, with its general character and socio-cultural context.

In this period, one of the critical factors in the spatial development of Fulya was transportation. The Bosphorus Bridge, which was started to be built in 1970 and opened in 1973, and the subsequent connections to the ring roads, connected the two sides of the city and created a radical change in the accessibility relations. In the *Arkitekt Magazine* of the period, it was mentioned that a new road, which was planned to be opened between Şişli and Beşiktaş and to be completed in June 1974, would relieve traffic. The new road was started from Balçık Tarlası Street, opposite Şişli Mosque and after extending 1530 meters split into two at Fulya Bayırı. (Haberler ve olaylar, 1972). In addition, the Mecidiyeköy Viaduct, which was built in 1974 and opened in 1975, had been one of the developments that strengthened the region's transportation. These innovations in transportation made the area more attractive and diversified the functions in the urban space.

1980–2000 Period: Liberal Policies Era

After the 1980 military coup, Turkey entered a new era with the government's economic policies. During this period, neoliberal policies and rising globalization have led to the restructuring of urban space. Globalization can be defined as a process of interaction or integration of national economic systems through the growth in international trade, investment, and capital and the spread of modern technologies of industrial production and communication (Mohanty, 2020). With the effect of globalization, the increase in the flow of transnational capital, goods, people, information, and indicators has shaped the city's transformation (Keyder, 2013). Also, the actors in the city changed, and sectors such as informatics, communication, finance, banking, media, and advertising came to the fore (Ataman, 1999). Moreover, industrial functions were decentralized and often moved to suitable locations close to the main arteries outside the city. All these developments started to create a new architectural language in cities symbolizing prestige, status, and power within the scope of visualization of global capital in the 1990s (Akpınar & Kahvecioğlu, 2007).

On the other hand, a planned solution to the housing problem had not been achieved until this period. Residential buildings, which were usually produced by the build-and-sell method or through cooperatives, led to the formation of an unqualified urban environment. In addition, the establishment of metropolitan municipalities and the transfer of zoning planning and decision mechanisms from central administrations to municipalities brought a new building production process. Also, the ideology and function of planning had changed. While planning undertakes new functions such as removing the obstacles in front of the capital and attracting the capital to the city, the public interest, which was the main reason for its existence, had been pushed into the background (Öktem, 2011). This period was also remarkable in terms of the slum problem. The government's policies ignoring the construction of slum houses, and the support of the municipalities with their services, led to the inevitable increase of the slums. In the 1980s, due to facts such as continued urbanization, increasing building density in city centers, and developments in the service sector, the increasing demand for housing by the middle class led to the appreciation of slum areas. As a result, single-story houses with small gardens were demolished and became multi-story apartment slums (Adaman & Keyder, 2006). In this process, the amnesties, which were issued many times, had problematic consequences in terms of urban environment and social justice. The slums, which were started to be built due to desperation, gradually became a part of the rent-seeking order, and the rights given to the slum owners sparked several discussions in society. Those who turned the slums into ill-gotten gains, and politicians who did not prevent this looting system, became the focus of criticism.

The urbanization process of Fulya and the development of housing areas have progressed in parallel with the dynamics of the period. It is possible to reach the aerial photographs of the years 1982 and 2006 in the map archives of the Istanbul Metropolitan Municipality. In order to understand the development of the neighborhood in this period, it would be more accurate to make a comparative evaluation of the area through these two photographs (Figure 7.4). According to this, the development of the northern part, which is close to the Büyükdere Axis, is remarkable. Undoubtedly, the trade and business function of the region and the global discourses of the period also had a great impact on this. When the 1982 map is examined, it is seen that Ortaklar Street, which attracted attention with its apartment buildings in the previous period, developed more. In the 2006 map, this axis developed further in the direction of Sakızağacı and merged with Hakkı Yeten Street in the south. Hakkı Yeten Street, which created a buffer zone between Dikilitaş and Teşvikiye, was a fundamental factor determining the southern development of Fulya. In addition, Polat Tower, built in 1998 on this axis, was one of the first skyscrapers of the period. The building, which includes security, parking garage, fitness, swimming pool, sauna, reception, and concierge services, promised its users a privileged and prestigious life. This building had been a decisive step for the future development and identity of this area.

On the other hand, during this period, amnesties and permits to build up to four floors caused the slums to change in character and turn into apartments (Erman, 2004). As a result, the slums on and around Mehmetçik Street started to turn into apartments, and the area became even more crowded. However, unlike the apartment buildings under the influence of modern discourses, these buildings consisted of additional rooms, overhangs, and additional floors built onto the existing slum. Thus, today, this region, which consists of unqualified apartments with an unplanned and cramped urban layout, is inadequate in terms of urban services and the green areas.

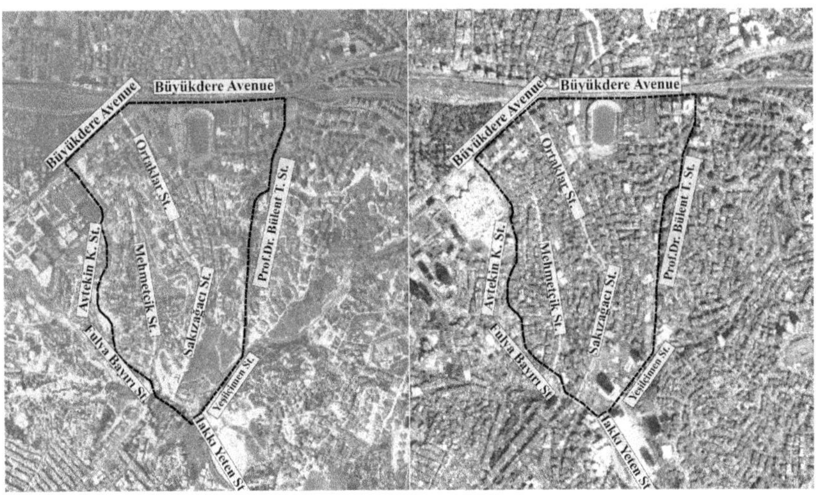

Figure 7.4: Aerial Photos of Fulya in 1982 and 2006. Source: Maps are Generated on Aerial Photos Accessed from https://sehirharitasi.ibb.gov.tr/.

Post-2000 Period: A Hybrid Neighborhood

The transformations in Istanbul's urban space and the developments in housing approaches continued in the 2000s. During this period, one of the most fundamental phenomena that drives the macro-form of Istanbul's urban space was globalization, which began to show its effects in the 1980s. With globalization, cities have changed economically, socially, and culturally by becoming the finance, informatics, and high-level service sector centers, rather than being industry-oriented places. In this process, the definition of the city has also changed, and big cities have begun to be described as metropolises with the values they represent and the new identities they have acquired. Furthermore, metropolises have become the focal point of capital as places of reproduction, and the value of urban lands increased.

In parallel with the global discourses, the urban morphology of Fulya continued to change after the 2000s. The neighborhood acquired a different character in the northern, southern, and eastern peripheries in line with the dynamics of the period. Although all these developments are remarkable, the development of Hakkı Yeten Street in the south has created a different spatial identity for the area. This street, where Fulya, Dikilitaş and Teşvikiye districts intersect, has become an intensely used axis with its multifunctional buildings and commercial functions after 2000. As stated before, Polat Tower, which is close to this axis and built in the late 90s, was one of the first important residential and office buildings of its period. After a while, in 2005, the Selenium 34 building was located to the next parcel with quite similar architectural character. In addition, the Selenium Towers in the Dikilitaş borders and Terrace Fulya Residences in the Teşvikiye borders are important multi-functional buildings in this region. In addition, the fact that some of the country's leading hospitals and health centers are settled in this area has caused the region to be identified with the health function. After a while, the office buildings around these hospitals started to be rented by the doctors, and eventually, the area has been named the health valley. These developments have also affected health tourism, and hotel buildings with different capacities were built in this area. In the northern part of the health valley, within the borders of the Fulya neighborhood, a hotel building was opened in 2020 with the concept of health tourism. The hotel usually serves guests from other cities or abroad for doctor visits. These developments have also affected the housing texture according to the function of the region and the segment it addresses.

On the north side of Fulya, which is adjacent to Büyükdere Street, there are several business centers, shopping areas, and social functions that have developed in parallel with the region's rapid urbanization. Cevahir Mall, which was opened in 2005 on the borders of the 19 Mayıs neighborhood, has become one of the attraction centers of the area. Moreover, after 2000, the existing building stock in the region has changed functionally. One of the most striking modernist housing structures of the 1960s, Hukukçular Housing Blocks, turned into a business center. Many of the apartments in this area have similarly transformed from residential functions to office functions, adapting to the general character of the region. Also, one of the critical developments after 2000, within the framework of the urban transformation agenda, was the expansion of the authorization of the Housing Development Administration of Turkey (TOKI) with the amendment made in the Mass Housing Law No. 2985 on 31.07.2003. TOKI, which has the authority to make or collaborate on profit-oriented projects to provide resources to the administration, has started constructing many luxury residences and commercial buildings in cooperation with the private sector (Özalp & Erkut, 2016). According to this, Torun Center and Quasar, built on Büyükdere Avenue, on the border of Fulya's connection to the Istanbul ring road, are two remarkable examples (Figure 7.5). These structures, which were built due to the privatization of Ali Sami Yen Stadium, have also brought about important discussions. These buildings create dramatic contrasts with the residential blocks around them regarding their architectural language and physical boundaries. In the continuation of this axis, Prof. Dr. Bülent Tarcan Street also feeds the commercial function of the region with hotels and business centers.

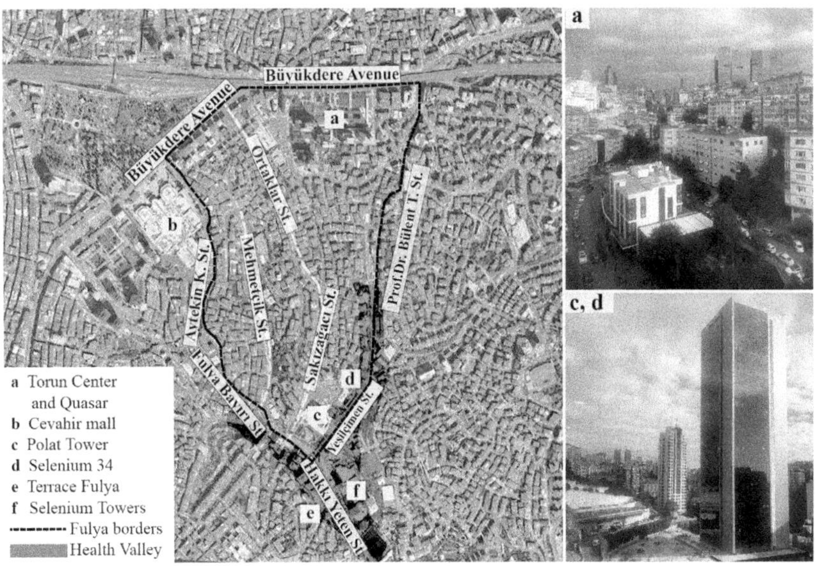

Figure 7.5: Aerial Photo of Fulya in 2021, Torun Center and Quasar from Mehmetçik St., Polat Tower and Selenium 34. Source: Author, map is Generated on Aerial Photo Accessed from Google Earth.

On the other hand, contrary to the changes and transformations in the peripheries, the inner parts of the neighborhood, which were generally slum areas in the past, continued to exist with apartment buildings in which the residential function was dominant. After the amnesties in the 1980s, the slums were converted into apartments, but the area was not developed in terms of urban space quality. Today, problems such as the difficulties experienced in public transportation due to the sloping topography of the neighborhood, the lack of children's playgrounds, green areas and parking lots continue to exist. Although the area is inadequate in terms of urban services and contains unqualified apartment examples, it is one of the preferred neighborhoods due to its central location.

Conclusion

Fulya is one of the multi-layered neighborhoods of Istanbul, where radical developments have been experienced in the production of space and, therefore, in housing patterns. However, the spatial development of the neighborhood differed in the inner areas and the borders, which led to a diversity in the housing patterns of the neighborhood. Undoubtedly, the strategic location of the district, the regions it interacts with, and the urban functions have a significant impact on this development scheme. The neighborhood, which started to develop with modern houses in the first years of the Republic, had entered a new urban development process due to industrial functions in its immediate vicinity. Especially after the 1950s, the neighborhood was subject to intense migration, which led to the emergence of slum areas on the former creek bed inland. However, these slums, built due to desperation initially, have turned into apartment buildings with the amnesties and created problematic settlements in terms of urban space quality. As a result, this region, where there is more fragmented and spontaneous development than a systematic urbanization, today has unqualified apartment buildings and inadequate urban facilities.

On the other hand, the neighborhood has gone through a different development process on the peripheries. In particular, the neighborhood's northern border, which is close to Büyükdere Avenue, has shown remarkable development in every period. Especially after the 1980s, the increasing value of urban land, decentralization of industry, dominance of global discourses, and capital-oriented approaches in the urban space have made Büyükdere an axis of attraction. In this context, there are various commercial, social, and cultural functions in the north of Fulya, which is close to Büyükdere Avenue. This multifunctional structure of the axis has also been decisive in the residential areas. After the 1990s, the transformation of the house from a living space to an object of prestige and investment has brought new forms of presentation to the agenda in housing production. Today, high-rise buildings located on the border of Büyükdere Street and presented with "luxury", "special" and "unique" discourses are at the center of discussions with their proportions and detached characters from their surroundings. Moreover, the south border of Fulya, which is adjacent to Dikilitaş, Teşvikiye, and Gayrettepe neighborhoods, has a similar housing texture due to its urban functions and socio-cultural segment. The commercial role of the region and the health function that attracted attention after the 2000s, resulted with the luxury apartments and high-rise residences, especially around Hakkı Yeten Street.

As a result, the Fulya neighborhood has been affected by each period's social, cultural, and political processes, and housing patterns have been shaped together with historical dynamics. In this context, today, the neighborhood has a hybrid structure that includes various housing patterns. The sharp differences between interiors and borders are undoubtedly a spatial manifestation of urbanization processes. Significantly, the old slum area where the apartments are located today has a problematic urban character. Although some apartments have been demolished and renovated with local interventions, a general solution covering the neighborhood and meeting all urban needs has still not been provided. The necessity of a comprehensive urban intervention also comes to the fore at neighborhood meetings, and the importance of facilities such as green spaces, parking lots, and children's playgrounds are emphasized. To sum up, a holistic spatial solution is urgently needed to eliminate the dramatic differences between the neighborhood's sub-districts and provide healthier and more balanced housing areas for the residents.

References

Adaman, F., & Keyder, Ç. (2006). *Türkiye'de büyük kentlerin gecekondu ve çöküntü mahallelerinde yaşanan yoksulluk ve sosyal dışlanma*. AB Komisyonu ve Çalışma Bakanlığı. https://ec.europa.eu/employment_social/social_inclusion/docs/2006/study_turkey_tr.pdf

Akbulut, M. R. (1996). Kaçak yapılaşmış alanların kentle bütünleştirilebilmesi için bireysel projeler yöntemi. In L. Akkal, Ö. Ertekin, & M. A. Yüzer (Eds.), *Habitat'a Doğru İstanbul 2020 Sempozyumu Bildiriler* (pp. 353–366). İTÜ Mimarlık Fakültesi Şehir ve Bölge Planlaması Bölümü.

Akpınar, İ. Y., & Kahvecioğlu, N. P. (2007). Küresel İstanbul'un mekansallaşması: kapalı özel siteler. In H. Yıldız & A. Eyüce (Eds.), *IAPS-CSBE Network Kültür ve Mekan Toplantıları Ulusal Sempozyum 1, Kent Kültür Konut Kitabı* (pp. 168–175). İstanbul: Bahçeşehir Üniversitesi.

Aslanoğlu, R. A. (1998). *Kent, kimlik ve küreselleşme.* Asa Kitabevi.

Ataman, O. (1999). 75 yılda kentleşme ve planlama. *Ege Mimarlık* 30, 31–33.

Bozdoğan, S. (2008). Haluk Baysal-Melih Birsel kitabı: Modern mimarlığımızın ustalarına gecikmiş bir ithaf. *Mimarlık* 340, 62–69.

Bozdoğan, S., & Akcan, E. (2012). *Turkey: Modern Architectures in History.* Reaktion Books.

Castells, M. (2015). *Kent, sınıf, iktidar* (A. Türkün, Trans.). Phoenix Yayınevi (Original work published 1978).

Chaolin, G. (2020). Urbanization. In A. Kobayashi (Ed.), *International Encyclopedia of Human Geography* (pp. 141–153). Elsevier.

Erman, T. (2004). Gecekondu çalışmalarında 'öteki' olarak gecekondulu kurguları. *European Journal of Turkish Studies (Thematic Issue).* https://doi.org/10.4000/ejts.85.

Erman, T. (2012). Urbanization and urbanism. In M. Heper & S. Sayari (Eds.), *The Routledge Handbook of Modern Turkey* (pp. 293–302). Routledge.

Freyer, H. (2014). *Sanayi çağı.* Doğu Batı Yayınları.

Gönültaş, G. (1970, April 20). Fulya bayırı kayıyor. *Milliyet.*

Görgülü, T. (2016). Apartman tipolojisinde geçmişten bugüne; kira apartmanından rezidansa geçiş. *Tüba-Ked* 14, 165–17.

Haberler ve Olaylar. (1972). 04(348), *Arkitekt,* 147. http://dergi.mo.org.tr/dergiler/2/273/3805.pdf

İstanbul Büyükşehir Belediyesi. (2001). *Sayım yıllarına göre istanbul nüfusu, sayımlar arası yıllık nüfus artış hızı ve yıl ortası nüfus tahmini.* http://www.ibb.gov.tr/tr-TR/BilgiHizmetleri/Istatistikler/Documents/demografi/t211.pdf Yılmaz

İşözen, E. (2003). *Şişli'de bir apartman.* Şişli Belediyesi Yayınevi.

Kayahan, M. (1938, July 9). Şirin villalar, kır kahveleri, tiyatrosu, her şeyi tamam bir yer. Mecidiye köyü. *Son Telgraf,* p. 5.

Keleş, R. (1995). Kentleşme ve Türkçe. *Dilbilim Araştırmaları Dergisi* 6, 1–5.

Keyder, Ç. (2013). Enformel konut piyasasından küresel konut piyasasına. In Ç. Keyder (Ed.), *İstanbul Küresel ile Yerel Arasında* (pp. 171–189). Metis Yayınları.

Lefebvre, H. (2003). *The Urban Revolution.* The University of Minnesota Press.

Mohanty, M. (2020). Globalization and cities. In W. Leal Filho, A. Marisa Azul, L. Brandli, P. Gökçin Özuyar, & T. Wall (Eds.), *Sustainable Cities and Communities. Encyclopedia of the UN Sustainable Development Goals.* Springer, Cham. https://doi.org/10.1007/978-3-319-95717-3_52

Öktem, B. (2011). İstanbul'da neoliberal kentleşme modelinin sosyo-mekansal izdüşümleri. *İstanbul Üniversitesi Siyasal Bilgiler Fakültesi Dergisi* 44, 23–40.

Önen, Y. R. (1935, November 28). Zarf usulü ile ev yapılan köy. *Haber*, p. 7.

Özalp, S., & Erkut, G. (2016). Kamu Yararı Perspektifinden İstanbul'da Kentsel Müdahaleler. *Planlama*, 26 (3), 234–250. doi: https://doi.org/10.14744/planlama.2016.92400

Sayar, Y., & Süer, D. (2004). Küreselleşme Sürecinde Konut Alanlarının Oluşumu ve Kentsel Mekâna Etkileri: İzmir-Çiğli Örneği. *Mimarlık*, 319,76–81. *Şişli* tarihçesi (n.d.). Şişli Belediyesi. https://www.sisli.bel.tr/icerik/sisli-tarihcesi

Tapan, M. (2005). International style: Liberalism in architecture. In R. Holod, A. Evin, & S. Özkan (Eds.), *Modern Turkish Architecture*. Chamber of Architects of Turkey.

Tekeli, I. (2015). İstanbul'un modernleşme öyküsü. In C. Yılmaz (Ed.), *Antik Çağ'dan XXI. Yüzyıla Büyük İstanbul Tarihi 1* (pp. 182–215). İstanbul Büyükşehir Belediyesi Kültür AŞ.

Tümer, S. (1969). *Mecidiyeköy'ün Beşeri ve İktisadi Etüdü,* [Final dissertation, İstanbul University]. http://nek.istanbul.edu.tr:4444/ekos/TEZ/06394.pdf

United Nations. (2018). *Sustainable cities, human mobility and international migration.* Report of the Secretary-General E/CN.9/2018/2. Version 2018-01-26. Commission on Population and Development (Fifty-first session). Economic & Social Council.

Yılmaz, C. (2015). Mecidiyeköy likör fabrikası. In C. Yılmaz (Ed.), *Antik Çağ'dan XXI. Yüzyıla Büyük İstanbul Tarihi 6* (p. 319). İstanbul Büyükşehir Belediyesi Kültür AŞ.

Naz Gümüşeli

8
A Comparative Study of Contemporary Strategies in High-Rise Housing Markets in Istanbul, Ankara and Izmir

Introduction

As in every field with the globalization process, changing individual/social needs and orientations led to transformations in the field of housing. Despite the fact that residential architecture differs in all societies, especially in recent years, the use of high-rise buildings as housing has grown in popularity. Although the search for different materials accelerated after the Great Chicago fire (1871), these structures began to become widespread in the early twentieth century, when the Art Deco style was active. From the beginning of the 1980s, the functions of these buildings began to take shape as living spaces. Today, these high-rise buildings are called skyscrapers, towers, or residences. Their common features are a number of excessive floors, technological structural systems, and integration of some services that differentiate them from apartment blocks and other housing types (Gifford, 2011). In this chapter, the high-rise residential building will be used as an inclusive term to refer to the buildings named tower, residence, or loft, whose common points are being high-rise structures. These buildings, which have different architectural features, are similar in terms of their functions and the socio-cultural context of users who prefers them.

High-rise buildings have been very popular in Turkey's metropolises as in other metropolises of the world. While there were only four commercial high-rise buildings in Istanbul in the last period of the twentieth century, today this number has reached almost one hundred and seventy. After the twenty-first century, radical changes took place in social and economic terms in Turkey (Çınar, 2014). With social segregation, class determining consumption objects have also changed and housing has begun to become one of these objects. The general promise of the new high-rise residential building types is to offer a new lifestyle. Although promises made in each of them are similar, the concepts emphasized in the marketing strategies are different. The aim of this study is to analyze Istanbul's high-rise residential marketing strategies and compare them with two other metropolitan areas, Izmir and Ankara in Turkey.

A Brief Overview of High-Rise Housing Concept

The history of high-rise buildings, which are often preferred as residences today, dates back to the past. After the Great Chicago fire in 1871, almost a third of the Chicago area was destroyed (Priwer and Phillips, 2009). Architects and engineers who needed to rebuild destroyed areas of the city sought to improve upon new materials, and existing technology. Although it is not clearly expressed as a high-rise building, the Leiter Building is the first structure designed with the new technology and the materials developed after the fire. William Le Baron Jenny, who is considered the father of the Chicago School, designed this building with a skeletal form and where glass is frequently used on the facades in 1879 (Sarkisian, 2016). The designers, who agreed on the design of structurally sound buildings, started to design taller buildings with the use of iron skeletal frames, terra cotta fireproofing materials, steel, and glass in this period. *The Home Insurance Company Building* (1885), *Chicago's Tacoma Building* (1887), and *New York World Building* (1890), are considered the first high-rise buildings designed with new technology (Priwer and Phillips, 2009). These buildings, which started to spread as a part of urban planning strategy, especially in the post-modern period, were designed as commercial buildings in the United States when the Art Deco style effect was dominant in the world during the 1930s and 1940s. *Shreve, Lamb & Harmon's The Empire State Building* (1931), *Allen's Chrysler Building* (1931), and *Hood's Rockefeller Center* (1939), are some of these commercial buildings in those years (Gümüşeli, 2016). At the same time, in Europe, in accordance with the definition of modernism before the Second World War, the West was dominated by housing for the working class and a new understanding of urban planning. CIAM (*Congress International d'Architecture Moderne*) congresses (1928), had pioneered the construction of high-rise architecture that would adopt this new modern trend (Turkington et al., 2004, p. 5). At one of these congresses, Le Corbusier presented the famous *Ville Radieuse* building as a modern residence and a new urban planning proposal. Although this design has not been implemented, it has revealed the existence of high-rise residences in Europe. After the Second World War, new urban planning approaches and new residential areas began to appear in both the United States and the Europe. The housing need that emerged after the war began to be met with high-rise residential building units with a mass housing approach. This was especially true in both the most northern and western countries, where high-rise residential buildings typified the 1960s mass housing construction era (Turkington et al., 2004, p. 6). Besides, there were several motivations for high-rise architecture such as the desire to build housing with new technologies, trust in modern architecture to create a more equitable society, plans to protect rural areas from mass development, improving living standards, and even using mass high-rise housing approach to solve the dwelling problems of societies (Turkington et al., 2004). *The Ronan Point in London* (1967) and the *Pruitt-Igoe* high-rise blocks in St. Louis (1955) are the first examples of high-rise residential buildings.

When the economic rise in Western societies began in the early 1990s, high-rise residential buildings started to emerge as a symbol of a different lifestyle. As the beginning of a new era of urban transformation, these buildings began to transform into living spaces preferred by the wealthy, particularly childless families. They were generally located close to the city center. At the end of the twentieth century, the position and function of high-rise residential buildings began to shift, especially in the United States and Europe. As globalization reached its apex in the 1990s, so did the approach to the housing sector. High-rise residential buildings have become increasingly important in the local housing market. Technological, socio-cultural, economic, and political trends, in addition to changing living standards, and increasing number of small households due to raising divorces and more people living alone, especially in Western countries led to this shift (Stapleton, 1980, p. 1107). As a result of these, the living space in those years was determined not only according to variables such as household type and income, but also according to variables such as desire, work, and leisure activities. Along with the United States and the Europe, high-rise housing has also exploded in the Middle East and South Asia since the twenty-first century. In the Middle East, it has been described as the emergence of a new housing concept. Since the millennium, people with high socioeconomic status started to prefer high-rise residential buildings as a house for many reasons such as security, location, and service in many parts of the world.

High-Rise Housing Concept in Istanbul

Turkey's high-rise housing development differs slightly from that of Europe and the United States. Especially in Istanbul, the build and sell housing culture of the 1950s has clashed with the neo-liberal and globalization policies of the 1980s. In the mid-1990s, many regulations were made that paved the way for private and foreign capital (Yüksel and Akbulut, 2009, p. 115). One of the noteworthy innovations of the new capitalism was to attract large capital groups directly to construction investments with the fluid capital, which had increased in weight during this period (Bilgin, 2006, p. 171). These new groups have made an effort to create new public spaces and have begun to design concept projects as business rather than residences. This approach has turned into a race to create living space under the control of the private sector with the changing socio-cultural structure since the twenty-first century.

In the 1990s, Maya Holding Company and Sabancı Holding Company, which had an important place in the Turkish economy, became the pioneers of the first high-rise structures in Istanbul. In these years, *Maya Tower* (1990), *Akbank Tower 1* (1992), *Akbank Tower 2* (1993), and *Sabancı Center* (1993) were the only commercial high-rise buildings in Istanbul/Turkey. The housing concept, which has been progressing horizontally, has begun to turn into a vertical form since the twenty-first century. Especially in Istanbul, vertical housing projects have started to increase rapidly despite the Bosporus Law that was enacted to protect the city's historical silhouette. After 2002, there was a boom in high-rise buildings designed not only for commercial use but also for residential use. Although most of these structures are commercial, there are also housing projects that cannot be underestimated. One of the main reasons that push investors to high-rise residential housing projects is the exorbitant price increases resulting from speculative land purchases and sales. Land cost, which had a share of 15 %–25 % in housing costs before the developments in recent years, has recently increased up to 50 % (Yüksel and Akbulut, 2009, p. 116). Most of high-rise buildings in Istanbul are built or have been built by investors who want to make use of the land they own (Yüksel and Akbulut, 2009, p. 115). On the other hand, the supply and demand issue is the other main reason for high-rise buildings being used as residences. The new upper-middle class that emerged in the twenty-first century is characterized as both the users, producers, and global capital of these places. This group prefers to live in high-rise residential buildings because they prefer the inclusion of services. Leaving aside the concept of changing social classes, the changing living conditions previously mentioned in the European example also play an important role in the preference of high-rise residences. Istanbul is one of the most crowded metropolises in the world today. Working conditions, changing family/household concepts, and the fact that individual life is at the forefront, as well as the approach of meeting needs quickly and easily, are among the major factors for living in a high-rise residence in Istanbul.

High-rise residences attract users by combining housing and mandatory/non-compulsory services on the vertical circulation axis and perceived as a time saver for the user. Most high-rise residences, especially in Istanbul, can provide the following services to their inhabitants today (Yüksel and Akbulut, 2009, p. 116):

- Reception
- Guest acceptance and guidance
- Phone forwarding

- Money exchange/ATM
- Wake-up service
- Emergency help
- Laundry/Dry Cleaning
- Repair
- Valet Service
- Restaurant
- Meeting/study room service

These are just a few, not all, but, of course, it is not possible to place these kinds of services in small areas. High-rise residences are a housing model that is expected to be located close to the financial center of the city, as a result of the decision made to attract the attention of the professional social group with high income. The selection of central locations and wide areas covered, combined with the contribution of high-rise character presented in the architecture of these structures, create a symbolism that shows that the urban struggle between the class strata resulted in favor of the elite (Erdinç and Gür, 2007, p. 76). High-rise residences also bear the appearance of a gated community because of its promise to offer a safe and isolated life. When evaluated structurally, the height is actually an architectural solution for vertical architecture in the face of the inadequate dimension of the parcels that can be built in the city center, but it also represents the elitist character that emphasizes the difference gained during the adaptation of the phenomenon to Istanbul in the physical context (Erdinç and Gür, 2007, p. 80). Erdinç and Gür explain their semantic and symbolic significance as such:

"In this context, the high and often gigantic physical structure constitutes an attention-grabbing physical entity affecting the silhouette; not only does it contain a symbolic expression of capital and the tendency of rising classes to be visible, but it also offers an elitist distinction and class representation that emphasizes power as a show of magnificence set out at the point of formalism to meet demands for differentiation, separation, luxury, and prestige" (Erdinç and Gür, 2007, p. 80).

Apart from a pure apartment building, these structures are designed in vertical relational integrity for both public spaces and houses. High-rise residential buildings are built with construction techniques suitable for high building quality in terms of load bearing structure, and material technology due to their proportions. Because of the expected earthquake in Istanbul, this situation is particularly effective at the consumer preference point. High-rise residential buildings are designed considering both investors and inhabitants in terms of interior area. Although they consist of 3 room (2 bedroom+1 living room) and

4 room (3 bedroom+1 living room) residences in general, 2 room (1 bedroom+ 1 living room) flats and studios are also frequently encountered to accommodate people living alone, families without children, students, white-collar employees or short-term business travelers. Due to the large openings on the facades, ventilation is usually provided by air-conditioning inside homes. Some high-rise residential buildings have internal gardens that belong to common use and are located within the structure. Fire escape areas are resolved in the common area inside the building, but it is very difficult to use these fire escape areas in buildings with 30 floors and above. Although most of high-rise residential buildings are designed in smart systems, excess energy consumption is still one of the most discussed issues. Inhabitants can also provide easy access to their cars directly from the elevators in front of their homes. In this period when sport centers have become the most important object of consumption, high-rise residential buildings without a gym are almost non-existent.

As in many parts of the world, the high-rise buildings in Istanbul are used as homes by many different segments of the society. People with a high social-economic level generally prefer high-rise residences; they serve both family life and individual life. It is seen that they increase rapidly both in the core areas of the city and the periphery zones recently. Apart from the question mark that high-rise residences were designed due to the need or supply and demand issue, their effects on the city silhouette continue to be ignored.

High-Rise Housing Marketing Strategies

Marketing efforts put a lot of pressure on the modern individual in today's world and endeavor to promise them more than their current lifestyle; it is one of the most important social tools that determine the lives of modern consumers (Becan, 2017, p. 297). Today, homes become objects determined according to the needs, fancy and financial situation of the consumer such as clothes and household goods. The transformation of the house into an object of consumption, unlike individual characteristics, are determined by consumption capacity, which determines social status. (Becan, 2017, p. 298). Elements such as who lives in it, what is around it, and the neighborhood it is located in, take the consumer to a certain world of meaning through advertisements (Becan, 2017, p. 298).

Branding is important for both the brand's position and perception in the market. The real estate sector attaches great importance to the branding process, just like other areas. They differ from their competitors and gain consumer trust because of their branding efforts. Brand image has gained importance as a result of the increasing competition in the housing sector in recent years. Therefore, marketing activities required for branding have become increasingly important for housing manufacturers. Today, housing manufacturers have moved away from traditional marketing methods and began to engage in consumer-oriented marketing activities (Öztürk and Batum, 2019). They select their target audience and discuss their lifestyles, psychology, routines, and many other habits. Housing brands that determine the consumer target audience work more effective in this way.

Luxury housing manufacturers do not abstain from allocating a high budget at this point. High-rise residences are generally designed for the upper-middle and upper socio-economic classes. Therefore, it is possible to evaluate the marketing strategies of high-rise residences as a luxury housing marketing strategy. The development of luxury residences has become a trend, especially in metropolitan areas (Gyourko and Linneman, 1993). People, who are getting richer in developing economies, inevitably want to own luxury homes. As a reflection of the expectations of the new wealthier classes, privileged and flamboyant housing has also emerged. The segregation strategy becomes the primary marketing factor in high-rise residences that can be classified as luxury residences. Even though the common feature of all them is similar, high-rise housing manufacturers want to be kept apart from one another. The marketing issue in high-rise residences is directly related to creativity, strategy, and financial situation. In order to appeal to high-income consumers, it is important to speak the same language as them. One of the important points of doing creative work is to target the right consumer at the right time (Öztürk and Batum, 2019, p. 113). Therefore, high-rise housing manufacturers should also analyze their consumers well.

The real estate market is formed because of the gathering of property owners, tenants, real estate professionals, architects, engineers, project developers, investors, and contractors (Deniz and Demir, 2017, p. 217). The change in the pricing mechanism during the purchase and sale of real estate products depends on the balance of supply and demand in the real estate sector (Çengel, 2013, p. 34). Businesses operating in the real estate sector should determine the current situation of the market, the size, and profitability of the market (Deniz and Demir, 2017, p. 218). The size of a market depends on the number of consumers who have ongoing needs, desire and ability to purchase, and are willing to change the resources produced (Küçükaslan, 2015, p. 224). Housing marketing consists of four variables namely price, product, promotion, and place (Koonzt, 2004, p. 3). The only factor that can generate profit among marketing variables is the price. For this reason, it is the most important factor that will affect demands and sales (Chuon et al., 2017, p. 34). Next, the product is a factor that meets the consumer needs. Promotion is the work done to convince consumers to buy.

Therefore, it is used to communicate about the service or product. Finally, the place is to carry out marketing communication activities of the product in the right place at the right time. It is one of the important ways to reach the target audience (Chuon et al., 2017, p. 35). For the real estate sector, we can describe 4P as below:

- “Product: What is sold? (real estate, service, idea)”
- “Price: Commissions or price list for real estate sector”
- “Place: Where and when is the real estate offered for real estate consumers? newspaper, radio, tv, magazines, web sites, apartment tax, public houses, mails, newsletters, telephone-address books, advertising board, automobile signposts, company cards, letterhead paper or fax cover pages”
- “Promotion: the design of advertising, propaganda, public relations and sales, and many other ways to inform and convince real estate consumers about products and services, according to company goals and target audience” (Barrel and Nash, 2005).

Although, four important factors of marketing are decisive in the context of this chapter, the concept of place forms the basis of the study. With the developing technology, the issue of which place the product is delivered to the target audience has been of great importance in recent years. The correct use of the place chosen as a marketing strategy, the quality of the visual and written messages in the place and the way they are conveyed to the consumer are important in the context of the study.

Assessment of High-Rise Residences in Istanbul and Other Metropolises

Today, many high-rise housing manufacturers attach importance to marketing efforts in order to have a positive impact on consumers’ perception and increase their sales. Especially in recent years, the rapidly increasing number of high-rise residences in Istanbul has led manufacturers to seek different and creative marketing methods. There are many methods such as the billboards, online advertisements, face-to-face sales, and many more. One of the most important factors in all these studies is the concept conveyed by the language used regardless of the media. Many different concepts addressing the consumer such as the promise of a life different from the current life of the consumer, the promise of status to the consumer and so on are included in these texts. These promises are often used in advertisements where marketing efforts are the most effective. Another area where they are used is the websites created by home manufacturers at the very beginning of the branding and construction process. Websites, one of the most important branches of marketing, are prepared with three-dimensional programs, filtered and equipped with the necessary visual material to impress the consumer. This visual feast is also adorned with surreal promises to be conveyed to the consumer. Considering that we are in the age of technology, the importance of these websites in the eyes of consumers is an inevitable fact.

Within the scope of the chapter, high-rise residential buildings of twenty floors or more that have been completed and entered the market in the last seven years will be examined. In order to analyze the differences between Istanbul and other metropol cities, this chapter will also include high-rise residences from Ankara and Izmir. The advertisement contents of twenty high-rise residences; ten in Istanbul, six in Ankara, and four in Izmir will be examined (Table 8.1).

Table 8.1: Assessment of High-Rise Residences

ISTANBUL	ANKARA	IZMIR
Spine Tower	Elmar Towers	Biva Tower
Skyland	Incek Bulvar Loft	Folkart Towers
Istanbloom	West Gate Ankara	Dap Izmır
Acarblu	One Tower Diplomatic	Mistral Izmır
Quasar Istanbul	Sinpas Marina	
Çiftçi Tower	Kuzu Effect	
IstMarina		
Pega Kartal		
Divan Bomonti		
Metropol Istanbul		

Source: Prepared by the author

In this chapter, the advertisements for the selected high-rise residential building projects published on their official websites will be subjected to visual and content analysis. In addition to the written material narrating the promises, the images used for envisioning this narration will also be analyzed and interpreted. While conducting the study, the following items will be taken as a basis:

- Headline types used in advertisements (Becan, 2017, p. 311)
- Basic promise in advertisements (Becan, 2017, p. 309)
- Frequently used words in advertisements (Becan, 2017, p. 309)

- Terms related to the home in advertisements (Becan, 2017, p. 309)
- Position of the housing in the city – location (Çınar, 2014, p. 496)
- The lifestyle presented (Çınar, 2014, p. 496)
- Social reinforcement where the housing is situated (Çınar, 2014, p. 496)
- Terms of payment and sales
- Highlights (family portrait, individual freedom, local)

The interpretation of high-rise residential building images on the websites designed to reach the target consumer was conducted through tables containing definitions and variables. In the tables below, the most common items, such as headline types (Table 8.2), frequently used words (Table 8.3), terms related to home (Table 8.4), location (Table 8.5), social reinforcement (Table 8.6), and the highlights (Table 8.7) of the high-rise residential buildings are examined in the cities of Istanbul, Ankara and Izmir. Detailed description and variable table examples of the examined high-rise residential buildings are in the appendices part of this chapter (Appendix A).

Table 8.2: Headline Types Used in Advertisements

	Headline Types Used in Advertisements
ISTANBUL	Information, curious, order
ANKARA	Information, curious
IZMIR	Information, curious

Source: Prepared by the author

Table 8.3: Frequently Used Words in Advertisements

	Frequently Used Words in Advertisements
ISTANBUL	Location, sustainability, designer
ANKARA	Investment, happiness
IZMIR	Design, environmental friendly

Source: Prepared by the author

Table 8.4: Terms Related to Home in Advertisements

	Terms Related to Home in Advertisements
ISTANBUL	Interior design, sustainable materials, terraces
ANKARA	Technology, design
IZMIR	Aesthetic

Source: Prepared by the author

Table 8.5: Location

	Location
ISTANBUL	Clearly emphasized
ANKARA	Unspecified
IZMIR	Unspecified

Source: Prepared by the author

Table 8.6: Social Reinforcement

	Social Reinforcement
ISTANBUL	Green area, gym, wellness
ANKARA	Kids play area, gym
IZMIR	Gym, pool

Source: Prepared by the author

Table 8.7: Highlights

	Highlights
ISTANBUL	Individual freedom, local
ANKARA	Family portrait
IZMIR	Family portrait

Source: Prepared by the author

Findings

After interpreting the visual materials of twenty high-rise residential buildings, remarkable issues that distinguish Istanbul from the other two metropolises were discovered. Primarily, the concept of family is frequently included, especially in the visual analysis of residences in Ankara and Izmir. Images of a father holding his child in his arms, mothers meeting with their children at gatherings for tea, children's room images, and family images walking hand in hand are seen in the high-rise residences in these two metropolises. Almost all projects have a family term in their web site catalogs. The situation is slightly different in high-rise residences in Istanbul. Emphasis was placed on family in only three projects. In fact, most of the texts on websites reflect many expressions such as individual freedom and the feeling of being unique.

Another remarkable issue in the high-rise housing examples examined is location. Locations of all residences in three metropolises are clearly stated.

However, the locations of almost all residences are defined separately and in a striking style of writing in a special area on the residences pages of the web sites in Istanbul. Different schemes have been drawn for many of them, and all the main roads, shopping centers, and popular districts in the vicinity have been explained to the consumer one by one. It is emphasized that almost all high-rise residences are in the center of Istanbul, regardless of whether the residence is located in Kartal or Zincirlikuyu.

The concept of the designer is another interesting topic in advertising analysis. All designers in Ankara, Izmir, and Istanbul have been published on their residence projects' websites. Yet, here, different distributions of foreign and Turkish architects and construction firms occur. Turkish architects and construction firms are the stakeholders of almost all high-rise residences designed in Ankara and Izmir. In Istanbul, both designers and construction companies, and contractors are based on foreign partnerships. Therefore, these designers are given a significant place in the official websites that have been examined in the Istanbul's high-rise residential building websites.

For a city as big as Istanbul with less usable green space, the provision of green or open spaces are often emphasized in advertisements. Almost all residences have their terraces, green areas, or balconies. In some high-rise residences, every home has its own interior garden. We do not see the green space theme this much in projects in Ankara and Izmir. However, it is possible to see at least three images of all the projects in Istanbul devoted to green areas and a few texts about feeling as if being in the middle of nature.

Finally, local icons are only found in high-rise residences in Istanbul. Although this is defined as the Bosporus in many structures, the old liquor factory in one residence and the cultural heritage concept that deals with the whole of Istanbul in another project appear.

Conclusion

Today, we encounter an increasing number of high-rise residences, especially in Istanbul. In recent years, many factors such as income level, different living conditions, changing economic class concepts made these buildings suitable for housing. Besides the general features of high-rise vertical buildings, each of them has different marketing techniques used to reach the consumer. These marketing techniques mentioned in the previous sections cover many variables such as the consumer to be addressed, the promise offered by the building to the consumer, and the location of the building. In this chapter, the metropolis of Istanbul and two other metropolises' advertisement contents of high-rise residences constructed in the past seven years were examined and compared. As a result of the chapter, several different features of high-rise residence advertisements in Istanbul from the high-rise residence advertisements in Ankara and Izmir were noticed.

Although there are no differences between Ankara and Izmir in terms of the marketing strategies used, the promises and prominent concepts such as lifestyles, and commitments differ than Istanbul. Luxury, prestige, and comfort have almost become a common language in high-rise residences in Ankara and Izmir. It is thought that especially the new living conditions of the people working in Ankara, their changing expectations and needs, and their relationship with diplomacy cause the term prestige to be used frequently in advertisement images. These advertisements, which promise the consumer to step into a more prestigious life than they have, also produce a number of themes based on the physical dimensions of the building. In Istanbul, besides offering different promises to the consumer, the situation of dealing with problems in the current conditions of the city has come to the fore. Location-based marketing is especially important for a city like Istanbul as its borders are expanding every day. Besides, the emphasis on green space stands out for the consumer who wants to own a residence in Istanbul.

The reason why Istanbul is a very crowded metropolis is due to many different reasons such as being an important trade center, the location of foreign affiliated companies, and the location of collages. Faster and more individual living conditions, different needs that should serve these living conditions, and the special emphasis of these needs in the advertisement visuals are very important for the marketing of high-rise residential buildings in Istanbul. Besides, it is possible to explain that the socio-cultural change in recent years, which has been explained in the previous sections, has a great impact on housing choices, as in many areas. The presence of high-rise residences, like all other housing types is increasing in all metropolises of Turkey. For this reason, the marketing strategies applied by housing producers to differentiate themselves from their competitors are developing day by day.

References

Barrell, D., and Nash, M. (2005). *Fundamentals of Marketing for the Real Estate Proffessional.* Dearborn Real Estate Education.

Becan, C. (2017). The Projection on Advertisements of Turning Urban Consumption Utopias into Dystopic Space: A Content Analysis on Luxury Housing Commercials. *Global Media Journal TR Edition*, 7(14), 295–319.

Bilgin, M. (2006). *The Place of Mixed-Use centers in Urban Life and Daily Life: Examples from Istanbul* (Master's thesis). Gazi University, Ankara.

CIAM (1928). *The International Congresses of Modern Architecture*, la Sarraz, Switzerland.

Chuon, A., Hamzah, H., and Sarip, A. (2017). Conceptualizing Luxury Residential Property for Marketing. *Malaysia Journal of Society and Space*, 13(2), 33–43.

CIAM (1928). The International Congresses of Modern Architecture, Switzerland.

Çengel, Ö. (2013). *Real Estate Management and Marketing*. Anadolu University Publishing, 1743(1), 9–34.

Çınar, C. (2014). Marketing Strategies in the Istanbul Housing Market. *International Journal of Housing Market and Analysis*, 7(4), 489–505.

Deniz, E., and Demir, B. (2017). Investigation of Marketing Strategies in the Real Estate Sector in the Light of Hedonic Consumption Concept: The Case of Izmır Folkart Towers. *The Journal of Academic Social Science*, 5(45), 213–239.

Erdinç, S., and Öymen Gür, Ş. (2007). A Research on "Rezidans" Culture: The Case of Istanbul. *Journal of Near Architecture*, 1(1), 68–90.

Gifford, R. (2011). The Consequences of Living in High-Rise Buildings. *Architectural Science Review*, 50(1), 2–17.

Gümüşeli, N. (2016). *Cihangir District and Art Deco* (Master's thesis). Istanbul: Istanbul Technical University.

Gyourko, J., and Linneman, P. (1993). Affordability of the American Dream: An Examination of the Last 30 Years. *Journal of Housing Research*, 4(1), 39–72.

Koontz, C. (2004). The Marketing Mix: The 4p Recipe for Customer Satisfaction. *Marketing Library Services*, 18(2), 3–6.

Küçükaslan, N. (2015). *Real Estate Marketing*. Ekin Publishing, Turkey.

Öztürk, M., and Batum, P. (2019). How Housing Brands Use Social Media in Their Marketing Communications?: A Content Analysis. *Journal of Administrative Sciences*, 17(33), 111–135.

Priwer, S., and Phillips, C. (2009). *Skyscrapers and High Rises*. Routledge Taylor & Francis Group, New York.

Sarkisian, M. (2016). *Designing Tall Buildings, Structure as Architecture*. Taylor & Francis Group, New York.

Stapleton, C. M. (1980). Reformulation of the Family Life-Cycle Concept: Implications for Residential Mobility. *Environment and Planning A: Economy and Space*, 12(10), 1103–1118.

Turkington, R., Van Kempen, R. & Wassenberg, F. (2004). *High-Rise Housing in Europe*. DUP (Delft University Press), Delft, The Netherlands..

Yüksel, U., and Akbulut, T. (2009). The New Products of Consumption-Oriented Architecture in Recent Years: Residences. *Megaron*, 4(2), 110–118.

Appendix A: Selected examples of variable tables among the high-rise residential buildings examined.

QUASAR ISTANBUL (2014)	
Headline types used in advertisements	no title
Basic promise in advertisements	unforgettable memories
Frequently used words in advertisements	location, liquor factory, center of the city, design
Terms related to home in advertisements	interior design, architect
Position of the housing in the city – location	clearly emphasized
The lifestyle the housing presents	unspecified
Social reinforcement where the housing is situated	museum, gym, office
Terms of payment and sales	unspecified
Highlight celebrity	unspecified
Highlight family portrait	unspecified
Highlight local	liquor fabric

SKYLAND (2017)/ISTANBUL	
Headline types used in advertisements	order type
Basic promise in advertisements	living life at the top
Frequently used words in advertisements	dream, peak, landscape, prestige
Terms related to home in advertisements	technology, experience, ceiling height, architect, smart home technology
Position of the housing in the city – location	clearly emphasized
The lifestyle the housing presents	freedom

Social reinforcement where the housing is situated	office, gym, wellness center, common semi-open spaces, hom design center, green area
Terms of payment and sales	clearly emphasized
Highlight family portrait	unspecified
Highlight local	unspecified

SİNPAŞ MARINA (2017)	
Headline types used in advertisements	curious type
Basic promises in advertisements	inside life, outside of what you know
Frequently used words in advertisements	marine, view, symbol
Terms related to home in advertisements	view
Position of the housing in the city – location	unspecified
The lifestyle the housing presents	peaceful living space
Social reinforcement where the housing is situated	marina, beach, kids play room, gym
Terms of payment and sales	clearly emphasized
Highlight family portrait	clearly emphasized
Highlight local	unspecified

FOLKART TOWERS (2015)	
Headline types used in advertisements	curious type
Basic promises in advertisements	our hearts beat high
Frequently used words in advertisements	prestige, creativity, icon, environmental friendly
Terms related to home in advertisements	technologic, aesthetic

Position of the housing in the city – location	unspecified
The lifestyle the housing presents	comfort
Social reinforcement where the housing is situated	mall, office, gym, pool, art gallery
Terms of payment and sales	unspecified
Highlight celebrity	unspecified
Highlight family portrait	unspecified

Part III
What Is Next? Future Reflections

Arda Çalışkan

9 Housing Preferences for Generation Z Students: A Case Study in Istanbul

Introduction

It is seen that "the generations" increases its importance day by day and is a concept that manifests itself in nearly all areas of life. The generation is defined as "a collection of people born in approximately the same years, who have shared similar difficulties and fates, and who have been obliged to similar assignments" (TDK, 2021). There are six different generations that live today. These are: Silent Generation, Baby Boomers, Generation X, Generation Y, Generation Z and Generation Alpha. Each of these generations has different characteristics, unique attitudes, values, and different world views.

As of 2020, 32 % of the whole population in the world, are incorporated into generation Z (Schroders, 2021). This group of people born between 1995 and 2010 has very different behaviors and desires than the previous generations. These different behaviors and desires bring with several changes. Many sectors such as technology, economy, marketing, education are doing researches to adapt to these changes. It is obvious that the field of architecture and housing necessitates such research as well.

The majority of the student groups studying at universities are mostly Generation Z in today's world. Housing can be a big issue for these students whether they live away from their family or not. Students' mental health, social relations and academic achievements may be affected by their accommodation types and choices. There are many different options for student accommodation, especially in metropolises like Istanbul. Residing next to a family, house-sharing with friends, living in micro/studio flats, private and state dormitories are just a few of these options.

Considering the variety of options in Istanbul and specific needs/wants of the new generation, this chapter focuses on two main questions: "Which of the many accommodation options offered for students is more suitable for Generation Z?", and "What kind of a place do they want to live in?". To think on these questions and to fill the gap in the literature on the reflection of generation differences on living places both in national and international literature; it is planned to conduct a field study on generation Z students attending a university in Istanbul, in order to better understand their wishes and desires, to make inferences on their housing preferences, and to see whether there is a change in these preferences depending on the generation's characteristics.

Within the scope of the chapter, a brief definition and overview of generation Z characteristics will be followed by literature review on the transformation and types of student accommodations around the world, Turkey and particularly in Istanbul. Then, the findings of a research conducted with generation Z university students in Istanbul will be discussed with some projections for the future.

Generations

The concept of generations has been defined differently in many different sources. When these different definitions are considered, it is possible to summarize "generation" as a human community born in certain year intervals, affected by common important events and having common characteristics related to these events. According to researches, it is difficult to talk about a situation where the year intervals of the generations are clearly defined. However, it was decided to use the year intervals determined by Seemiller and Grace (2019). They have done a very comprehensive research about generations and different year intervals and decided to define those born between 1925 and 1945 as Silent Generation, 1946–1964 as Baby Boomers, 1964–1980 as Generation X, 1981–1995 as Generation Y, and those born between 1995 and 2010 as Generation Z individuals. According to them, in most of the market research reports, 1995 was a commonly referenced starting year for Generation Z. Although it is seen that the generation Z is defined in different year intervals in some studies, in general, most of the studies are based on the year 1995.

According to Zemke (1999), community members are affected by events that have an impact on all of them. Major events that mark thresholds in the history be it wars, disasters, plaques; economic and technological advancements and social milieu have permanent and continues effects on upcoming generations. Hence, it becomes inevitable for each generation to have different characteristics. Today, generations come together and collaborate more than it was in the past. The importance of the generational difference is evident in the dialogs of teachers with their students, parents with their children. For this reason, it is very important that generations understand each other's characteristics and act according to these features. The basic characteristics of the generation Z are given separately in the following section. However, it is not convenient to make over generalizations and prototype people born between the specified year intervals. The environment in which the individual grows up, geography and family structure are effective in character formation, yet the zeitgeist of the twenty-first century is ingrained in Z generation.

Generation Z

Generation Z is formed by people born between 1995 and 2010. This generation is born and is growing with technology and mobile devices; thus, they have a good command of technology and its benefits. Due to the development of technology and the globalization of the world, they are a generation without geographical borders. They can access information in the easiest way and without any effort. In this context, it is seen that their way of communication is different than the previous generations. These individuals, who are very talkative and social in their communication on the Internet, cannot show the same features in face-to-face communication (Salleh et al., 2017). They can do many jobs at the same time. While listening to music on one hand, reading a blog on the internet and dealing with social media accounts on the other is just one example of what Generation Z individuals frequently experience. (Salleh et al., 2017). Because of these features, they are also called Generation M (multitasking: multitasking/processing) (Toruntay, 2011). It is the generation with the highest synchronization of hand, eye, ear, and motor skills compared to previous generations. It would not be wrong to say that social media is one of the most important parts of their lives. Face-to-face meeting has gradually lost its importance with the use of social media. As a result, excessive individualization and feeling of loneliness are increasing among young people (Öz, 2015). As claimed by Yücel, having none or few siblings also contributes to getting used to loneliness (2018). They prefer computer to book and text to speech. It can be said that generation Z caused major changes in the education system. Various researches have been designed and conducted to get to know them better and to teach them more efficiently (Yücel, 2018). Not only the education, but all of the other sectors are also trying to get prepared for this generation. They use different methods, different approaches to promote their "products" to them. As a result of the literature research (Toruntay, 2011; Öz, 2015, Salleh et al., 2017; Yücel, 2018) individuals of Generation Z have the following characteristics (Table 9.1):

Table 9.1: Generation Z characteristics

Realistic
Born into technology and more global world
Highly connected (Internet)
Too individual and lonely but wants to socialize when they want
Those who prefer computer to book and text to speech
Relatively weaker communication skills compared to other generations
Collaborator
Creative
Unsatisfied
Easy to adapt
Who prefer to spend time at home
Result oriented
Self-confident
Thinking about the future
Can use 5 screens at once (television, mobile phone, tablet, computer, etc.), multi-tasker
Impatient
Competitive
Independent
More demanding
Less focused (Low attention time)

Source: Adapted from Toruntay, 2011, Öz, 2015, Salleh et al., 2017, and Yücel, 2018.

Generation Z and Housing

It is a known fact that architectural spaces are constantly changing and transforming in accordance with the Zeitgeist of the eras and lifestyles. Such changes are very much related with the user groups, specifically generations having common desires, behaviors and needs to a degree. Therefore, the design of architectural products by considering the characteristics of that period and generational differences becomes important in terms of user satisfaction and the efficiency of the space usage. Architectures that address young generations, generation Z for today, allow us to make projections for the future. Therefore, creating the spaces of tomorrow and predicting what kind of spaces we may encounter in the future can be possible with understanding Generation Z (Tanrıkulu 2021).

The generation Z people, are now under 26 years old and they are mostly continuing their higher education. The period between 18 and 25 years old is very critical in human life since it refers to some serious changes and transitions in the life course; moving away from family/house, experiencing new lifestyles, and being included into new households; initial efforts to gain a living are only a few of them. Under these circumstances, understanding the accommodation and housing preferences and needs of university students seems crucial in terms of developing a vision for the contingent demands of generation Z for other architectures.

In the literature, there is not much research on the housing needs, expectations and wants of generation Z. In a study conducted on the housing preferences of the generations in Malaysia, it was seen that the most important factor in the housing choice of the Z generation was the house itself (physical qualities, rooms, largeness etc.), and then the neighborhood and its location (Ismail and Shaari, 2019). However, for the Generation X, the neighborhood where the residence is located is the most important factor in their preferences. Ismail and Shaari (2019) explained the reason for this situation as they think that younger generations will move to a separate house for the first time (rent or purchase), establish their lives in this house, and think that it will be a new starting point for them. Therefore, they want to do all of this in a house that satisfies them with its physical features. According to the same study, younger generations (Generation Y and Z) give importance to physical factors of the house more than the sense of belonging or place attachment which are important for older generations (Baby Boomers and Generation X). In this respect, it can be said that generations have different perspectives towards the housing unit.

In a study on Generation Z individuals and their perspective on home; it was seen that most of them want to live in detached houses with gardens. They give importance to the spaciousness, largeness, and comfort of the place they live in. The most important features they mentioned after these concepts are silence, tranquility, and peace. The location of the place also shows itself as another striking element. In the future, they want to live in low-rise, distant residences rather than high-rise buildings which are very close to each other. They want to live in areas close to nature, rather than living in the city, away from "green". In addition, they prefer their home to have a beautiful view (Tanrıkulu, 2021). In another research by La Roche, Flannigan, and Copeland (2010), they found that students of new generations have more expectations about housing than their parents. They are willing to pay additional fees for more options in their living environment. In the same study, they found that the most important factors in determining the accommodation preferences of the students are private bedroom, onsite parking, double beds, onsite laundry facilities, internet access, and proximity to campus. In another study that discusses how the generation Z uses common spaces, it has been stated that doing sports, visiting friends, and having fun are important for them (Düzenli and Alpak, 2019). They prefer common public spaces which they can fulfill these desires. In terms of housing program, they are interested in co-working spaces, creative spaces for hobbies/crafts and customization of space (Hommati, 2021). From this point of view, it is obvious that apart from sectors such as education, communication, shopping, traveling and entertainment, the housing sector should also be prepared for this new generation.

Housing Issue for University Students

We can talk about many challenges for students such as adapting to the university and the new systems, getting used to the new living environments/ accommodations or adapting their living in their family house to the new studying and socializing practices. The quality of the accommodation, to what extent it meets their needs and wants directly affects the life of the student (Kara et al., 2019). Situations such as the socio-economic status of the student or her/ his family, previous dwelling culture, and habits may be effective in their selection of the place to live. There are also more pragmatic factors that are influential in their preferences such as feeling comfortable, being close to the school, and being able to study comfortably (Çemrek and Filiz, 2007).

In a study conducted in Belgium that investigates the housing preferences of students, it was found that the most important preference factor is the type of housing. After that, rent price and the size of the room/house are listed as other factors. The most preferred housing type is studio flat. Arguably, this situation arises from the students' needs for privacy and freedom. The proximity of the accommodation to the campus showed itself as a relatively less effective consideration (Verhetsel et al., 2016). However, in the study conducted by Ersoy and Arpacı in 2003, it was determined that in the house preferences of the students, the rent of the house and the proximity to the school are important. In another study, it was seen that the new generation of students increasingly want to live in larger spaces. They also want greater privacy and personalize their living environments when they want (Khozaei et al., 2014). Debatably, achieving these conditions is inversely proportional to the number of people they live with. In a similar study, Şahinli and Kılınç (2014) found that most of the students prefer to rent a flat. More than half of the students staying in the state dormitory stated that they are not satisfied with the rules of the dormitory and therefore they want to rent a house. In another study with a similar subject, it was seen that the most important factors in students' housing preferences were having their own bathrooms, being close to the campus and room size. It is also interesting that the rent of the accommodation was of little importance for the students participating in the study (Oppewal et al., 2005).

All such experiences and accommodation options are very much related with a broader context, namely where the university is located; urban or rural area, whether it is in a small or a big city, even the location of the university within the city, be it in a central zone or periphery. The next part of the chapter will focus on the housing/accommodation options and experiences of university students in Istanbul.

Accommodation/Dwelling Options for University Students in Istanbul

Istanbul is one of the most populous cities in the world. It is a metropolis that attracts both domestic and foreign university students due to its job opportunities, location and cosmopolitan nature hosting different cultures. There are a total of 57 universities in Istanbul, including 13 state and 44 private universities by the year 2021. According to the data of Istanbul Governorship in 2020, the number of students enrolled in universities in Istanbul is 1.000.834 (İstanbul Valiliği Bilgi İşlem Şube Müdürlüğü, 2021). With its student population alone, Istanbul has a larger population than many other countries in Europe. This serious population is in constant search for accommodation. According to the news made by TRT Haber, 167.262 students settled in a university in Istanbul in the year 2020 (Son Dakika Haberler, 2021). However, it is known that 65.000 of these students are not in Istanbul by the year 2020 due to online education provided by universities as part of the measures against the Covid-19 pandemic. Yet these 65.000 students will come to Istanbul and look for a place to stay when this period is over. There are many different accommodation options for university students in Istanbul. However, there are still some doubts as to how effective these many options are for the Z generation, which has quite different demands and views compared to the previous generations.

When it comes to student accommodation, dormitories are the first to come to mind. KYK (Credit and Dormitories Institution) dormitories serve students living in Istanbul with a total of 33 dormitories, with 22 dormitories for girls and 10 dormitories for boys (KYK Yurtları, 2021). It is seen that the prices vary from 230 Turkish lira to 390 Turkish lira depending on factors such as the physical characteristics of the dormitory (being old or new), the number of students staying in the room, and social areas (UniBilgi, 2021). When looking at the general of KYK dormitories, depending on the student population in Istanbul, multi-person rooms are in the majority and the living standards are relatively low. In addition, since the capacity of KYK dormitories in Istanbul is 25.000, the remaining students must search other accommodation types such as private dormitories or houses.

There are also many private dormitory options in Istanbul for students who do not want to share a room with many others and want to stay in a new and cleaner place. The prices of private dormitories depend on the location of the dormitory, the number of people in the room, and the features of the dormitory such as pool, gym, socialization areas. It can be said that the dormitories on the European side are more expensive than those on the Anatolian side, and the price increases as the number of people in the room decreases (Eyurtlar, 2021). It is not hard to estimate that the current pandemic will most probably increase the demand for private rooms in private dormitories at least for a while.

Another option for students studying in Istanbul is to rent a flat. Research by Karabacak and Sayılı (2016) shows that students prefer dormitories in their initial years, then they tend to share a house with their friends. In the same study, they mentioned the factors that affect the student's choice of accommodation as gender, the monthly income, class of the student, the department of the student, average expenses, and the average monthly income of the family and the family's place of residence. Istanbul is an expensive city. According to the Turkish housing rent index data, Istanbul has the most expensive rents in Turkey as of 2021 (Endeksa, 2021). According to another report prepared, rental prices in Istanbul have increased by 38.4 % in the last 5 years, and the price per square meter has reached nearly 22 Turkish Liras (Zingat, 2021). Not only the rents but also all other living expenses cost much for students. Hence, students might tend to share a house with their friends for sharing the rent and all other expenses.

In Istanbul, it has been observed that the districts most preferred by students for accommodation are generally the areas where universities are concentrated. Beşiktaş, Üsküdar, Kadıköy, Fatih, Şişli can be given as examples. Rental fees vary within these districts. For instance, Beşiktaş where many universities concentrate, has the highest housing rents and residential real estate prices (Endeksa, 2021). In addition, that rents increase during the periods when schools are open and decrease relatively as these periods pass (Internet Haber, 2019).

A Survey on Accommodation Preferences of University Students in Istanbul

An online survey which consists of multiple choice and open-ended questions, is conducted to understand the dwelling/accommodation preferences of Generation Z university students in Istanbul. Considering the pandemic conditions, to reach the students in the fastest and most effective way, a document is created on Google Forms and shared with them. A total of 143 students from Bahçeşehir University, 126 (88,1 %) Turkish and 17 (11,9 %) international participated in the study. 118

(82,5 %) of these students are female, 24 (16,8 %) are male and 1 (0,7 %) marked the other option. All of the students participating in the survey are born in 1995 and after. The highest number are those born in 1999 with 42 people (29,4 %). 37 students (25,9 %) from the 1st grade, 53 (37,1 %) from 2nd grade, 44 (30,8 %) from 3rd grade and 9 (6,3 %) from 4th grade participated (Table 9.2). While 87 students (60,8 %) stated that they lived in Istanbul before, 56 students (39,2 %) stated that they settled in Istanbul after starting university. The three districts most students live in are Beşiktaş, Şişli and Kadıköy.

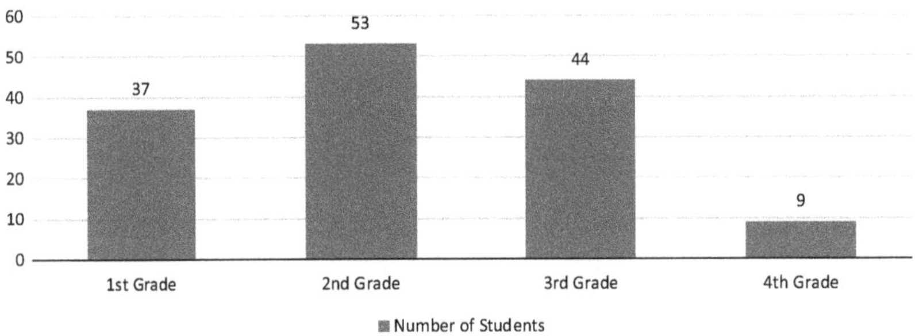

Table 9.2: Grades of the students who participated in the study

It is seen that 89 students (62,2 %) answered yes to the question of whether you like being alone, 44 (30,8 %) answered partially and 10 (7 %) of them said no. The emergence of such a result is not surprising for the generation Z who enjoy loneliness and spending time with themselves. However, only 24 students actually (16,8 %) live alone. 96 students (67,1 %) live in a house with their families, 16 students (11,2 %) live with a friend or sibling and 2 (1,4 %) students stay in an apart with others. It is found very interesting that only five students (3,5 %) accommodated in the student dormitory. Arguably, this situation is related to Covid-19 after seeing other answers. In addition, although most students like loneliness, it is seen that 70 % of the respondents describe themselves as social. 83 students (66,9 %) stated that they lived with 3 or more people. However, almost the same number of students (81) said that enough space is allocated for them in their accommodation. Similarly, 72 students (59,5 %) were found to have sufficient privacy. It can also be mentioned that more than half of the students live in a place where they were staying for 4 years or more.

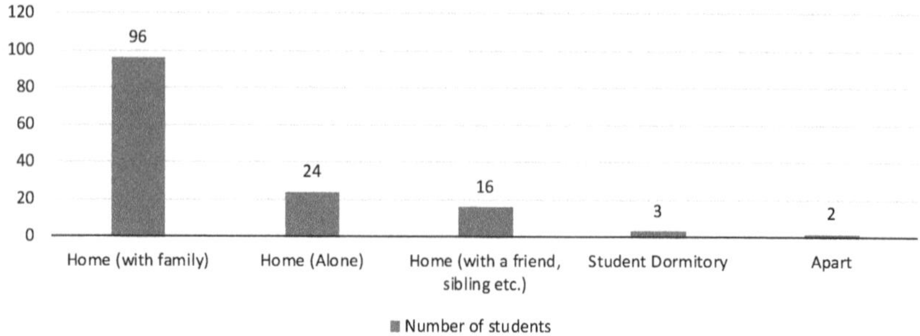

Table 9.3: "What is the accommodation you live in now?"

Regarding the accommodation type, the data revealed that 77 students (53,8 %) accommodated in flats, 21 (14,7 %) in a detached house, the same number of students in a gated community, 19 (13,3 %) in residences, and the remaining 5 (3,5 %) in dormitories (Table 9.3). More than half of the students gave the answer of "location" to the question that asked the main factor in choosing this accommodation. It is not surprising that this answer comes to the fore in a city like Istanbul, which is very crowded and has a serious traffic problem. After that, the most given answers are the facilities of the accommodation and security, respectively. It can be said that these two answers are the expected ones for Istanbul. The fact that economic reasons are the most important factor for only 12 (8,3%) students is not surprising considering that the students who participated in the study were studying at a private university (Table 9.4).

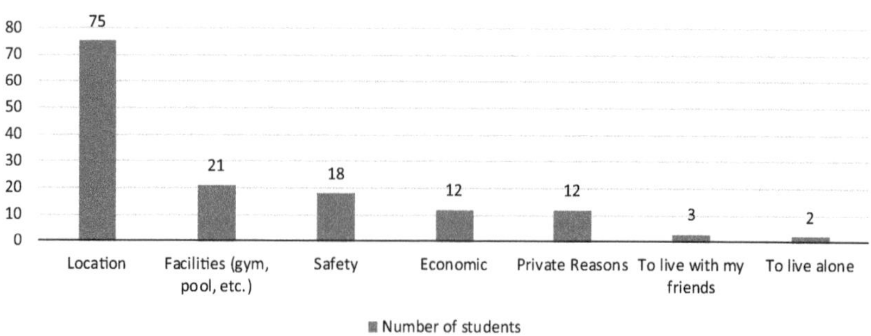

Table 9.4: "*What is the main factor in choosing this accommodation?*"

Similar answers were given to the question of which location would you like to live in. 37 (25,9%) of the students stated that they want to live close to the university campus, 37 (25,9%) to socialization areas such as cafes and restaurants, and 38 (26,6%)to friends and family. Some mentioned their preference about "being in the city center" and living in a location with "comfortable transportation" opportunities. In addition, 38 (26,6%) students answered the question of what is the most important factor in your living area as "a balcony". Yet, this answer might be related with the pandemic and increasing demand for open spaces in living environments.

"If you are staying at home, which area of the house do you prefer to spend your time in?" was one of the questions on the survey. Most students answered this question as their own room. They prefer to personalize their own rooms to feel more comfortable. However, it is another case that some of the students use the living room to socialize and spend time with their family and friends. For example, one student said, "*In the living room. I like spending time with my flat mate. Having someone with me while I study motivates me.*" Another student who thinks the other way around said, "*I prefer to spend time alone in my room, in an area that belongs to me. I do everything in my room. (Hobby, cooking, lesson, etc.)*" Another student said, "*When I'm alone, I prefer the comfortable sofa in the living room but otherwise my bedroom.*" Such answers lead questioning the household type that the students belong to. The use of the space, behavior patterns, privacy concerns seem to be very much related with the household type, whether the student is living with his/her parents, sharing a flat with a friend or living alone.

"If you had a choice, what kind of place would you like to live in during your education life?" is one of the most critical questions of this study. In the answers given, it is seen that more than half of the students wanted to rent a flat alone. Even students who do not live alone but think they have enough privacy and comfort have stated that they want to move to a separate house. One can say that their wants towards living alone manifest the free-spirited nature of the generation Z and their inclination towards loneliness. The most common response after renting a flat alone was renting a house with a friend. It is also interesting that rather than living in the same house with their family members, they prefer to live in different houses but in close distances.

Regarding their place of accommodation, they mentioned their preferences such as "having a balcony", "a place that has a story", "bearing historical traces", "open kitchen, light, mezzanine and high ceilings", "city and sea views", "green view", "safe", "not too large", "spacious". In these features they refer to, they talk about not only the place of accommodation but also their lifestyle preferences. If there are places, where they "have to" stay, in other words they are obliged but not very willing to such as student dormitories, they make changes as the space allows. They turn their beds and desks into places with more light and personalize their wardrobes. Another noteworthy element in the study was found to be the concept of temporariness. It has been seen that there are foreign students who consider returning to their countries after completing their university education, and similarly, Turkish students who will return to their family's houses in other cities after school is over. In the answers given, most of these students think that they were not permanent where they live, so there was no need to make any major spatial changes. Instead, they prefer to personalize their environment with small personal objects such as toys, blankets, decoration stuff etc.

Discussion and Conclusion

We see that the century we are in is witnessing a rapid change in many different ways that directly affect our lives, such as the devices we use, our working styles, our payment methods etc. It is an undeniable fact that a similar change occurs in the spaces we use. To what extend twenty-first century houses and accommodation types take their share form this change and are adapted to new generations is a critical question.

Prior to the study, it was assumed that generation Z might have a nomadic tendency and preference to live in motion rather than belonging to a place. The gradual change and digitalization of the concept of space might have negative impacts on the importance given to a house/and or accommodation and "having a place to go" loses importance day by day accompanied by a disregard for the spatial changes. However, the findings of this study imply that those assumptions are not entirely correct. Generation Z still attaches importance to the places they live in and prefers to change these places as much as they can. They like to make their living space a place of their own and personalize it. Only in this way they belong fully to that place and feel comfortable in there.

When evaluated in general, the perspective of Generation Z towards places and houses is not as different as expected from previous generations. However, it should be mentioned that they also have quite different features; and these features are also reflected in their approach towards housing. For example, it has been observed that the most important factor in choosing an accommodation unit for them is "location". Generation Z members who value their time and prefer to do many jobs at the same time do not want to waste their energy, their time in traffic. They prefer accommodation units that are close to where they study and work, usually within walking distance. Especially in a metropolitan city like Istanbul, this situation seems to emerge more clearly. Not only generation Z, but most of the people in Istanbul probably prefer to live close to where they work. However, their priorities may differ in the choice of their place of residence. When evaluated in this context, it is remarkable that location is the most important factor for Generation Z, and that all the other factors mentioned in the previous sections are not as important. However, this situation is not fully valid in the study of Ismail and Shaari (2019). In their research physical features of the housing unit were more important for generation Z. Such a discrepancy proves the importance of the context. From this point of view, it becomes clear how much of a determining factor the location is in a crowded metropolitan city like Istanbul.

They prefer to spend most of their time in their own rooms. For generation Z who love solitude and enjoy spending time with themselves, privacy is very important, that is also supported by their preference for "living alone". Basically, they are looking for units that meet their needs to socialize when they want and be alone when they don't. For this reason, flexible features in living spaces become more important than ever for this generation. It is a matter of debate how likely these issues are in Istanbul, which is getting crowded every day and prioritize financial gain to design qualities when it comes to housing supply.

Worldwide but in Istanbul specifically, the new generation of accommodations specially dormitories and housing units that address university students should offer the balance between private and social spaces in terms of spatial configuration. It cannot be denied that this generation, we know better each passing day, discover new features with, and grow up together; has some unique characteristics. Although this study concentrates on student accommodations as the initial place of transition for generation Z, it will be healthier to design the spaces that are being built now, considering the characteristics of the Generation Z as the users of tomorrow. More research is required in this field to gain insight into their needs, wants and expectations.

References

Çemrek, Z., & Filiz, Z. (2007). Üniversite Öğrencilerinin Barinma Sorunlarinin Uygunluk Analizi ile İncelenmesi. *Eskişehir Osmangazi Üniversitesi Sosyal Bilimler Dergisi*, *8*(2), 207–224. Retrieved from https://dergipark.org.tr/tr/pub/ogusbd/issue/10992/131547

Düzenli, T., & Alpak, E. M. (2019). Urban Open Space Usages of Z Generation. In *3rd International Symposium on Innovative Approaches in Scientific Studies*. Ankara, Turkey.

Endeksa (2021). Retrieved October 2, 2021, from https://cutt.ly/sb05FNJ.

Ersoy, A. F., & Arpacı, F. (2003). Üniversite Öğrencilerinin Konut Koşullarının ve Konutta Yaşamayı Tercih Etme Nedenlerinin İncelenmesi. Milli Eğitim Dergisi, no. 158, 181–191.

Eyurtlar.com. (2021). *Istanbul Öğrenci Yurtları*. Retrieved October 2, 2021, from https://www.eyurtlar.com/yurtara?sehir=40&ilce=0&yurttipi=0&universite=0

Hommati. (2021). *How generation Z will change the housing market (forever)*. Retrieved October 2, 2021, from https://www.com/blog/how-generation-z-will-change-the-housing-market-forever

Internet Haber. (2019, February 4). *Öğrencinin Olduğu Yerde Kiralar Artıyor*. Retrieved October 2, 2021, from https://www.internethaber.com/ogrencinin-oldugu-yerde-kiralar-artiyor-806193h.htm

Ismail, H., & Mohamed Shaari, S. (2019). The location, house, or neighbourhood choice preferences among Malaysian housing generations. *Journal of Surveying, Construction & Property*, *11*(2), 64–74. https://doi.org/10.22452/jscp.sp2020no1.6

İstanbul Valiliği Bilgi İşlem Şube Müdürlüğü. (2021). *Üniversite şehri istanbul*. T.C. İstanbul Valiliği. Retrieved October 2, 2021, from https://bit.ly/3os0Ubn

Kara, H. Z., Aykul, M., & Pulat, A. B. (2019). Neden Ve Sonuçlari İtibariyle Üniversite Öğrencilerinin Barinma Sorunu. *PESA Uluslararası Sosyal Araştırmalar Dergisi*, *5*(2), 78–91. Retrieved from https://dergipark.org.tr/tr/pub/pesausad/issue/47373/543139

Karabacak, M., & Sayılı, M. (2016). Üniversite Öğrencilerinin Barınma Yeri Tercihleri: Havza Meslek Yüksekokulu Örneği. *Çankırı Karatekin Üniversitesi Sosyal Bilimler Enstitüsü Dergisi*, *7*(1), 195–21. Retrieved from https://dergipark.org.tr/tr/pub/jiss/issue/25889/272746

Khozaei, F., Hassan, A. S., Al Kodmany, K., & Aarab, Y. (2014). Examination of student housing preferences, their similarities and differences. *Facilities*, *32*(11/12), 709–722. https://doi.org/10.1108/f-08-2012-0061

KYK Yurtları. (2021). *Istanbul'daki Kyk Yurtları*. Retrieved October 2, 2021, from https://www.kykyurtlar.com/istanbul-kyk-yurtlari/

La Roche, C. R., Flanigan, M. A., & Copeland, Jr., P. K. (2010). Student housing: Trends, preferences and needs. *Contemporary Issues in Education Research (CIER)*, *3*(10), 45. https://doi.org/10.19030/cier.v3i10.238

Oppewal, H., Poria, Y., Ravenscroft, N., & Speller, G. (2005). Student preferences for university accommodation: An application of the stated preference approach. *Housing, Space and Quality of Life*, 113–124. https://doi.org/10.4324/9781351156363-10

Öz, Ü. (2015). *XYZ Kuşaklarının Özellikleri ve Y Kuşağının Örgütsel Bağlılık Düzeyi Analizi*. (Master's Thesis). İstanbul: Atılım Üniversitesi.

Şahinli, M. A., & Kılınç, N. Ş. (2014). Karamanoğlu Mehmetbey Üniversitesi (KMÜ) Öğrencilerinin Barınma Sorunlarının Tespiti ve Değerlendirilmesi. *Karamanoğlu Mehmetbey Üniversitesi Sosyal Ve Ekonomik Araştırmalar Dergisi, 2014*(2), 87. https://doi.org/10.18493/kmusekad.83966

Salleh, M. S. M., Mahbob, N. N., & Baharudin, N. S. (2017). Overview of "Generation Z" behavioral characteristic and its effect towards hostel facility. *International Journal of Real Estate Studies, 11*(2), 9–67.

Schroders. (2021, April 8). *What investors need to know about Gen Z.* Retrieved October 3, 2021, from https://www.schroders.com/de/ch/wealth-management/insights/markte/what-investors-need-to-know-about-gen z/#:~:text=Gen%20Z%20is%20now%20the,cohort%2C%20with%202.5%20billion%20people.

Seemiller, C., & Grace, M. M. (2019). *Generation Z: A century in the making.* London and New York: Routledge, Taylor & Francis Group.

Son Dakika Haberler. (2021). *İstanbul'u Kazanan öğrencileri Bekleyen Yeni sınav: Konaklama Ve Ulaşım.* Retrieved October 2, 2021, from https://www.trthaber.com/haber/egitim/istanbulu-kazanan-ogrencileri-bekleyen-yeni-sinav-konaklama-ve-ulasim-515446.html

Tanrıkulu, E. (2021). Türkiye'de Z Kuşağı'nın Konut Algısı Üzerinden Geleceğin Konutlarına İlişkin Önermeler. *Online Journal of Art and Design.*

TDK. (2021). *Türk Dil Kurumu: Sözlük.* Retrieved October 3, 2021, from https://sozluk.gov.tr/

Toruntay, H. (2011). *Takım Rolleri Çalışması X ve Y Kuşağı Üzerinde Karşılaştırmalı Bir Araştırma.* (Master's Thesis). İstanbul: İstanbul Üniversitesi Sosyal Bilimler Enstitüsü.

Unibilgi. (2021, September 24). *Kyk Yurt ücretleri 2021–2022.* UniBilgi. Retrieved October 2, 2021, from https://www.unibilgi.net/kyk-yurt-ucretleri/

Verhetsel, A., Kessels, R., Zijlstra, T., & Van Bavel, M. (2016). Housing preferences among students: Collective housing versus individual accommodations? A stated preference study in Antwerp (Belgium). *Journal of Housing and the Built Environment, 32*(3), 449–470. https://doi.org/10.1007/s10901-016-9522-5

Yücel, G. (2018). Yiyecek-İçecek Hizmetlerinin Değerlenmesinde Kuşaklararası Farkların Belirlenmesi: Lara-Kundu Otelleri Üzerine Bir Araştırma, *Güncel Turizm Araştırmaları Dergisi.*

Zemke, R., Raines, C., & Filipczak, B. (1999). Generations at Work: Managing the Clash of Boomers, Gen Xers, and Gen Yers in the Workplace.

Zingat (2021). *Istanbul Emlak Endeksi, Analizi ve Bölge Raporları - Zingat.* Retrieved October 2, 2021, from https://www.zingat.com/istanbul-bolge-raporu

Büşra Atam

10 From School to Home: Changing of Home-School Relation in Architecture and Design Students in Istanbul with the Pandemic

Introduction

Home has the smallest boundary that includes physical and semantic features, where a person's relationship with the outside begins and ends. Also, it is the initial place that a person has experienced since childhood and learned, has semantic responses as well, as it is the place where one feels belonging and feels safe. Studies on dwelling and housing culture show that the home has played an important role in the lives of individuals from past to present (Hayward, 1977; Buttimer, 1980; Rapoport, 1982; Deprés, 1991; Mallett, 2004; Campbell and Vallerand, 2020).

With the pandemic situation, our living areas, our homes, and personal space have gained more importance, and they are also reshaped with "social distance". Transformation of space affects both home space, and public/semi-public space designs. Individuals who spend a lot of time at home, whether they live, work, study, or play, began to experience these settings differently than they did before the pandemic. Fitting their daily lives into a single home space, a sense of belonging to the home, and being/staying at home have all taken on new meanings for them. In addition to the function of the existing housing space, the home has also taken on the meaning and functions of working, learning, playing, feeling safer, opening up to the world, and exploring the environment virtually. Especially the relationship of working and studying people establish with the home and the arrangements they have made at home in this process are considered important in terms of transformed meaning of home for them. When this process is handled in the scope of the students, it is seen that the school-home relationship has gained a new home-centered meaning with the moving from school to home.

The student-home-school relationship is the main conceptual triad of this chapter. The interaction between some concepts such as home-school relation, sense of belonging, social interaction, and place-making practices affects this relationship. The discussion of the changes that this situation has undergone with the pandemic constitutes the conceptual background of the research and also provides its theoretical structure.

Meaning of Home: Transformation and Changes with Covid-19

A home is a sheltered place from the past to the present, containing all time and space, and also has meanings beyond that. The home is more than a shelter (Heidegger, 2008). Accordingly, the dwelling has a feature that protects, nourishes, and cares. The concept of home is different from a house with its temporal, spatial, and personal meanings. The home is a "place" with its social, cultural, and emotional dimensions as well as its physical structure and function (Easthope, 2004). The physical structure of the house, which we see as our private space, becomes our home with our experience and the relationship we establish. In this respect, there is an extremely close relationship between home and privacy. At the same time, discussing the importance of the sense of belonging to a place is critical when discussing the concept of home (Heidegger, 2008). Home is where we feel belonging that also belongs to us. At the same time, a home is a multilayered place and emotion where our dreams live (Gomez and Vannini, 2017). It changes, transforms, and gains meaning under our control. When we reinterpret Lefebvre's (1991) perceived-conceived-lived space triad within the context of the house, the home as the living space contains one's emotions, interventions, and experiences. The relationship between home and person can be explained by the term "topophilia" that Tuan (1990) defines as the emotional bond between person and place. Topophilia indicates a different level for each individual, as well as differs according to the place of residence and time. Accordingly, it is this effective bond that gives meaning to home and which we can define as belonging that is shaped by our experiences and life.

Home can also be defined as a place of memory that contains all times. Bachelard (1969) describes the home with the phenomena that include the past, present, and future. The relationship we establish with home, lives together with these accumulations that make sense with our lives and consist all times. This relation is not only established spatially. A home is a place that includes and participates in our social lives. With whom we live in our house and whom we invite to our house, also determine the limits of our social relations with both the home and other people. These boundaries can be shaped by the visible physical borders of the house, or they appear as invisible boundaries determined within it. Therefore, a home is a place that designates the state of co-presence or separation. This helps us to understand the perception of the home and the social dynamics as well as the spatial and individual dynamics of the relationship established with it. From this view, both the meaning attributed to the individual and the meaning of the home gained through social relations are tied together.

Considering the relationship between the house and the individual, the household structure gains importance here. The house has the feature of being together, sometimes for extended families or nuclear families living together. This situation is more common in traditional household structures. Today's shifting living conditions have affected the concept of home and the relationship built with it, as has the changing household structure. For nuclear families, it is seen that the house has certain meeting places within the framework of actions held together in limited times. These appear as living rooms, bedrooms, or dining tables on a smaller scale. Today, for individuals who live alone or live in a shared manner, the home offers personalized opportunities to spend time alone, to relax, and to spend time with the individual spaces it contains rather than its feature that brings people together. Personal space and personal time are becoming more important at home as household structures change. Especially for working and studying individuals, it is the smallest unit that includes an escape area after work/school, for personal time, and space. This change of place, its meaning, and use in daily life is an important dynamic that determines the leisure time perception of the person.

The meaning of the home, the relationship established with it, and the perception of the home are multi-layered structures woven together with concepts that are intertwined with each other. For this reason, it is thought that in this section it is important to convey this interactional structure before the discussion about the transformation in the meaning of the home experienced with Covid-19.

The house has a structure that changes/transforms both spatially and socially from past to present. When we look at the recent past, together with the consumption society brought about by the economic-political changes, the house was also affected by this situation. Alcocer and Martella (2020) explain this change in the house and household, with the expansion of the home beyond its physical boundaries with the feminist revolution after the 1960s, and the expansion of the household into the city while transforming into a self-referenced independent space. Considering the transformations experienced by the house both socially and spatially, first of all, the house started to be designed as smaller spatial units to be used only during the remaining time after work. Also, this transformation can be the reflection of individualization in-home space.

The change of household structure, the smaller scale of households, and the home that responded to new household needs also differed spatially. This situation is not only in the outer walls of the house but also in the change of the interior spatial setup. The decrease in the time spent in the kitchen has brought with it the design of the kitchens as the smallest volumes in the home. The balconies, which provide the relationship of the house with the public, and have been used and functioned widely in the past, have either shrunk or disappeared in this process. We can say that the time spent at home has given its place to time spent in public spaces in this process. All these social and spatial transformations also change the meaning and perception of the home for the individual.

In addition to the change in the house and household structure, there have been some separations in the multi-layered structure of the house. An example of this can be read through the relationship between workspace and home. Especially with industrialization, a sharper transformation has begun in the structure of homes and working spaces. From the hunter-gatherer lifestyle to industrialization, home-based work was more dominant, however, with the industrial revolution, the basis of the workplace had become offices and factories instead of the home. Along with all these, in recent past, the rapid development of technology and globalization have affected life in every aspect, and while increasing the access and communication opportunities of people, it has brought individualization to a different dimension. Together with the changing production systems and working styles with technology, the working spaces that shifted to offices and industries after the Industrial Revolution returned to homes (Toffler, 1981). Considering the effects of globalization and technology on the focus of home and place, Mittchel (1999) mentions the importance of new housing types that will provide the needs of both working and dwelling and that the spatial setup can change with working from home.

As it can be understood from here, although these issues have not recently entered our agenda, remote learning and working from home has become an urgent necessity with the Covid-19 pandemic. This sudden necessity brought about the effort to return homes, which are not ready for such a rapid transformation in spatial terms, into spaces that will allow for many other activities which ordinarily take place in the working space, school, and public space. As staying at home has become a necessity, the sheltered structure of the houses has become more readable. Homes, where we have been in limited times and perform limited activities before are now located in the center of our lives with the pandemic. Thus, with the pandemic, the new transformation process in the meanings attributed to the home begins.

The change in the effect of the home on our social relationships is one of these transformations. While our homes have visible or invisible boundaries that determine our social relationships, it can be said that physical boundaries are drawn strictly with the pandemic. In this process, the house, which was physically closed to the outside, turned into a more open place than before. Alcocer and Martella (2020) define the house after pandemic as a total center of human life. Likewise, the need for socialization of people has begun to be met in virtual environments in various ways with the adoption of technology by more people. Now homes are our new yoga studios, study areas, concert halls. The home, which has become more visible in this process, has become the physical source of virtual interactions, experiences, and spaces. With the inclusion of individuals in meetings and social activities from their homes, the perception of space-body-time has begun to gradually dissolve in the virtual environment. There is no longer a single house, a single place where we are together; instead, we invite many houses that are intertwined in a virtual environment and join these spaces.

Pandemic has transformed our homes into living spaces that can be anywhere and can be accessed by everyone, albeit limited. Thus, home spaces that are visible and accessible to everyone are transforming into places where many different functions overlap. For instance, while the bedroom takes place in the perception of home as a personal place where we rest and spend personal time, it has also transformed into a space where we work, attend lectures/meetings, and do sports. This situation shows the perceptual and semantic transformations of the spaces in the home, which we understand as personal space/personal time and can be associated with privacy. In this process, working from home and home-centered education have spatial effects and have caused changes in individuals' perceptions. For example, the place where we can work and feel comfortable at home is a place close to the modem. Before the pandemic, the home was the place of rest and privacy where the intensity of daily life ended and where we could relax. But with the pandemic, it has become the physical center of this intensity. Another effect of the pandemic on the perception of the home is that the concept of personal time has become more invisible and flexible with working from home and online education. Previously, leaving school/class, leaving work was the spatial equivalent of personal time perception. Now, living and working in the same environment has caused a loss of personal time and leisure time meanings attributed to home.

Considering the effects of the pandemic on home, the overlapping of many layers, both temporal and spatial, brings with the perception and consideration of the house as a new living space. These superposed meanings manifest themselves in the physical space, with the interventions and changes set up to enable different functions. While these arrangements may be temporary, the settings made in the home space for working from home and online education set more permanent and constant limits on the person-home relationship. As a result, the following section discusses the transformation of education, as well as the transformation of home settings and the meaning of home due to pandemics, in order to shed light on the student-home-school relationship.

Transformation of Learning Environment and Home-School Relationship with Home-centered Education

School is a learning environment that covers a large part of an individual's life. It is also effective not only in theoretical but also in the physical, cognitive, and psycho-social development processes of the individual. Many studies have shown that social relations are established since childhood in school, and these spaces that are freely discovered after a home are important both in the perception of space and the relationship established with space and in interpersonal relations (Rißler, Bossen, and Blasse, 2014). The transformation in the school space from the past to the present progresses together with the transformation in education. The fact that traditional dictating education methods are replaced by learning methods based on individuals' experience supports the internalizing of knowledge by discovering and discussing it. The rapid development of technology and the internet transform the traditional school space within the framework of educational activities, as well as change the relationship of education with the school space. The addition of educational content such as coding, software that will support the development of students as individuals who synthesize, interpret and use this change, or learning of nature and built environment based on experience can be given as examples of the change in educational activities. At the same time, the integration of technological tools and different approaches into the education model can be discussed through remote learning, online learning (e-learning), distance learning, and home-schooling in addition to hybrid/blended learning practices. Thus, with the transformation of the traditional education model, alternative learning environments to the traditional school space and new home-school relations emerged.

When looking at remote learning, it is seen that it has a structure that is independent from the school and traditional classroom space, where students and teachers are separated by distance and time, which can be in real-time or in more flexible times, with or without technology. Online learning, also known as e-learning or electronic learning, is a face-to-face training application in the classroom with digital tools. We can say that teacher-student and student-student interaction is higher in online learning compared to remote learning. Another type is hybrid/blended learning which is a system that uses digital and traditional learning methods together (Zook, 2018). In distance learning, students work from their homes, and teacher-student communication is performed digitally. One other learning system, which includes digital and physical activities in the home environment is defined as home-schooling. In this system, parents create education plans (The Critical Thinking Child, 2020). Until pandemics, these systems were mostly implemented in kindergarten, primary school, and high school education. Online learning and distance learning applications of universities were limited. However, with the pandemic, distance learning and online education have been adopted rapidly in all levels, and the current learning system transformed into home-centered education.

In the university context, changing education practices with the pandemic has resulted in the development of distance-learning or hybrid solutions. The type and process of education have also been significant factors in the implementation of these learning systems. Although the hybrid education model is similar to online and remote learning in some respects, it is a system based on conducting students' lessons both online and face to face on some days. The realization of the design education discussed within the scope of the study with distance learning, online or hybrid methods affected not only the students' working habits but also their use of space in home and school. Considering that design education consists of theoretical and studio courses, being in the studio and working together in the studio, constitutes the basis of the study habits of the students. During the pandemic, this situation disappeared and design education started to be carried out in a virtual environment. This shift influenced both the studio instructors' and students' perceptions of design education. Three-dimensional designs that can be physically perceived with all senses have left their place to digital representations that are perceived by the visual sensation.

The school, where students spend the majority of their time, is semantically not only a place of education, but also a place where social relations, a sense of belonging, and students' working habits can be established. Changes in the education system and studying from home affected the working habits of the students. Design students, who spend their time generally in the studio and working at school, started to use their homes as a working space. Thus, the physical studio environment which holds the potential to socialize has become an unused space. Therefore, the process of returning home from school forced the students' school-home relationship to transform perceptually, experientially, and semantically. In this process, students who returned from school to home, and from their student homes in Istanbul to their families' homes, lost their social environment and the habit of working together physically. Students who worked with their friends at school had to work alone at home. During this process, the school space, where they worked physically together and socialized, continued to exist in a virtual environment. The potentials of coexistence in the virtual environment are discussed in terms of how much it provides effective communication in comparison to the physical environment, as well as its advantages and disadvantages. Eventually, it is possible to say that it is an important communication channel and environment for design students who cannot experience the physical studio environment. This situation also affects the perception and the meaning of home. Home is no longer an accommodation space for the student used for limited activities after classes.

Home has a new and diverse meaning beyond the accommodation space with the articulation of the studio. In addition, the physical boundaries between home and school became blurry. Having more invisible physical boundaries change also the meaning and perception of the home. The transformation of the home into an alternative studio environment during a crisis is realized with personal arrangements and facilities. For this reason, we can say that although the meaning attributed to home by each student is basically similar in terms of sheltering need, the degree of transformation between the use of the house and the home-school space varies from person to person.

Reading of Changes in Home-School Relations of Architecture & Design Students

The changing home-school relationship of design students with the pandemic was discussed with a broader perspective in the previous sections. A survey has been conducted with a questionnaire to read the relationships of architecture and design students with home space through the concepts of place-making practices, personal space/personal time, sense of belonging, and social interaction. The findings of this survey is presented here to unfold the changing meaning of home for architecture and design students.

The reason why the faculty of architecture and design students are considered as a focus group is that they spend a large part of their days and even nights in schools and studios; they create both a working and living space for themselves with the arrangements they have made in the studios, and they go home to meet their limited needs. With the pandemic, previously perceived and used home space is transformed according to the changing needs in this process. Thus, we can say that in the case of belonging to a home that opens from home to studio, this time, there is a reverse flow. It is possible to say that the experience of a home-centered life by the students of architecture and design faculty who work in studios, rest, socialize, in short, spend most of their daily life experiences in and around the school space, causes more dramatic changes in the perception of home and the usage of home environment. This situation also affects social interaction. While the students were working together at school, they also had the opportunity to socialize. However, this studying environment that has been moved to homes has resulted with the individualization of students and the re-establishment of co-presence in virtual environments.

The questionnaire was conducted with 193 students that are 2nd (34 %), 3rd (38 %), and 4th (28 %) grades who are all studying at Bahçeşehir University Faculty of Architecture and Design in the 2020–2021 academic year. Participation of students from these grades to the questionnaire is considered important in terms of the time spent in the studio environment and their sense of belonging. Thus, the relationship that individuals who have recently adapted to the school and those with longer-term experience have established with school and home can also be understood. The reason why the focus group of the study excludes 1st grade is that; they didn't have face-to-face studio experience in the school.

The questionnaire is structured in three sections to cover demographic information, pre-Covid-19 pandemic, and Covid-19 pandemic process and consists of multiple-choice and open-ended questions. The questionnaire consists of home-school relation questions covering time spent at school and home, study place preference and working habits, place-making practices in the home space, the meaning of home, personal space, personal time and identity, the transformation in social interaction situations with the pandemic. Collected data has been interpreted with questionnaire response diagrams.

Perception of Home and Home-School Relation

Within the home-school relationship, it was examined whether and how the pandemic was effective on the frequency of students working at school (Figure 10.1). The data shows that most of the students used to work at school before the pandemic. Considering the frequency of working at home before and after the pandemic, the pandemic is effective on working at home. Most of the design students quit working at school during the pandemic. This situation indicates that there is a significant difference between working at school and working at home. It is seen that the pandemic affects the home-school relationship and students' working practices.

Figure 10.1: Working Space Distribution Before and During the Pandemic.
Source: Prepared by the author.

Place-making Practices and Sense of Belonging

Moving from school to home also changes students' place-making practices. When looking at the change of place-making practices, we can say that students used to make more spatial arrangements in the place they live in the period before the pandemic. It is critical to note at this point that, as a result of the pandemic, 60 % of the students have changed their working space (Figure 10.2). In this part, the question about the effect of online education and the return of students to their hometown is read through the short answers given to the questionnaire. According to this, it is seen that 20 of the 70 students whose working space has changed returned to their hometown. One student said "I moved away from my home and school and moved to my family living in another city" for the open-ended question about changing working place. In the answers of the remaining students, it is noteworthy that the keywords "working alone", "working at home/room instead of school", and "working at family home" are frequently used. For instance, one student remarked "While I was working with my friends at school or home before the pandemic, now I work alone in the family home". It is also thought that there are more areas of presence in the accommodation where they live individually or with their housemates than in their families' homes. Before the pandemic, students were more decisive about their working spaces, but with the pandemic, the impact of this situation has decreased. It can be said that the degree of dominance in the personal spaces of the students has changed as the boundaries of the working spaces narrowed and students moved to their families' houses while living alone or with their housemates. Likewise, it can be seen that students make arrangements by changing/transforming the new environment where they live and work and create their personal spaces.

Figure 10.2: Place-making Practices Distribution Before and During the Pandemic. Source: Prepared by the author.

The concept of personal space has been examined by specifying the students' working spaces before and during the pandemic. When we look at the questionnaire data, the students mostly work in the living room before and during the pandemic, and then they work in the bedroom, study room, and kitchen, respectively. Workshops, gardens, and balconies are rarely used as working spaces, contrary to the view that balconies have been used more effectively during the pandemic process (Gezici Yalçın and Düzen, 2020). It is noteworthy that students do not prefer these spaces as their working space. The answers show that students generally use more than one place at home as a study space. (Figure 10.3).

Considering the place usage before and during the pandemic, we can mention that the students started to use the bedroom and living room more often. This situation brings with it the question: "Did moving from their own homes to their family homes and starting online education cause a change in students' personal space?" Looking at answers given to open-ended questions one student said "I made changes in my working environment as I had to move to whichever room was available". Another student answered as "When I was in Istanbul I had my own workspace, now I have to use the common areas in the house where I live with my family". The other student remarked "I was living alone in Istanbul, now I live with my family, and since the internet only works in the living room, the space change affected me negatively". From these answers, we can understand that the pandemic and online education affect students' personal space in addition to their workspace.

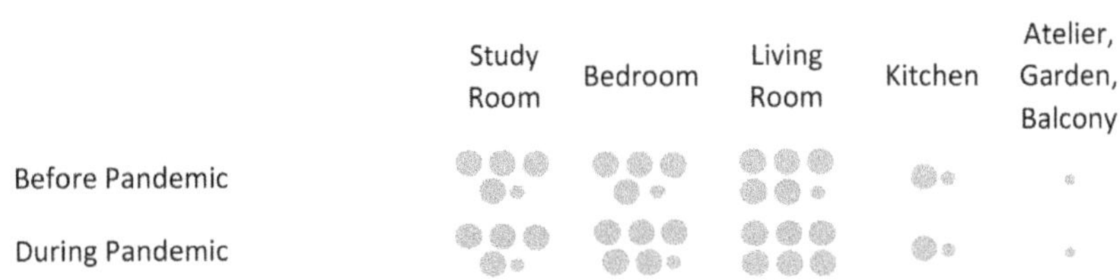

Figure 10.3: Distribution of Workspaces of Students Before and During the Pandemic. Source: Prepared by the author.

Open-ended and multiple-choice answers show that students organize their workplaces at home for online education for providing more privacy. However, it draws attention that the number of students who make arrangements in their backgrounds that can be seen during the online classes is not as high as those who make spatial arrangements. The reason for this is very few students are turning on cameras in online education (Figure 10.4). Students' open-ended answers are critical in understanding the boundaries of the home environment and articulations in opening to the virtual environment. One student said that "Usually I tried to prefer a minimal background and removed some decoration items. Photographs and some personal souvenirs and so on" for the open-ended question about the spatial arrangement of home-centered education. Another student remarked, "During the lectures where I had to turn on my camera, I removed the special items from the visible parts of the house and arranged them". Looking at the answers, we see that they generally made arrangements to prevent the living spaces and personal belongings from being seen. As understood from these quotes, privacy is effective in being visible or in background arrangements that are visible from the camera for people working or learning from home. These answers show that students tend to protect their personal space and privacy in a virtual environment. The sharpening of the physical boundaries of our homes and the fact that they are more visible and accessible in virtual channels brought along the re-definition of privacy in virtual environments.

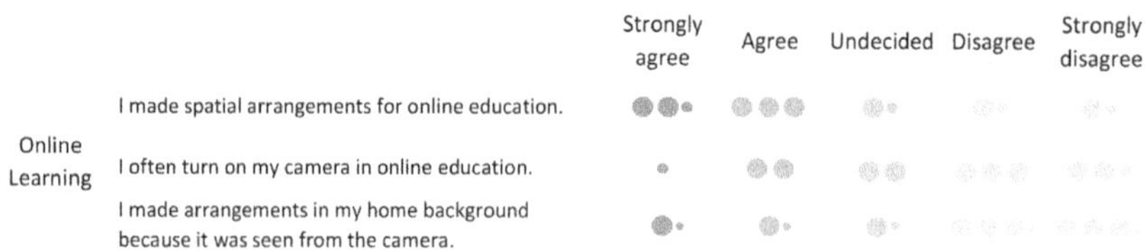

Figure 10.4: Home-centered Education, Place-making Practices and Privacy.
Source: Prepared by the author.

Students who work at home also created their personal time during the pandemic. Moreover, the increase in the time spent at home with the pandemic and the diversified uses of the house have changed the meaning of the house for students. But, when looking at answers, it can be said that in general, home-centered education does not affect the sense of belonging. Although it is not enough for making a general comment, questionnaire responses show that students' sense of belonging to their homes decreased by 5 % during the pandemic (Figure 10.5). It is thought that this situation may be related to the change of accommodation place and the number of people living together.

Figure 10.5: Distribution of Sense of Belonging, Personal Time and Meaning of Home Before, and During the Pandemic. Source: Prepared by the author.

Home-centered Life/Education and Interpersonal Relationship

The effect of home-centered education and life is also seen in the relationship between individuals in addition to home-school relations. Considering the change in students' habits of working together in the physical environment, it is seen that the rate of co-working decreased during the pandemic. However, the students came together and started to co-work in a virtual environment. The opportunity to work together in a virtual space supports the increase of virtual co-presence instead of physical co-presence. Thus, students communicate in a virtual environment and include virtual spaces in their out-of-school study space. Both the habit of working together and the situation of students being physically together outside of school have decreased during the pandemic. In this process, instead of meeting in a physical environment, students came together via virtual channels. Therefore, this chapter shows that the pandemic transforms both working and socialization habits in daily life (Figure 10.6).

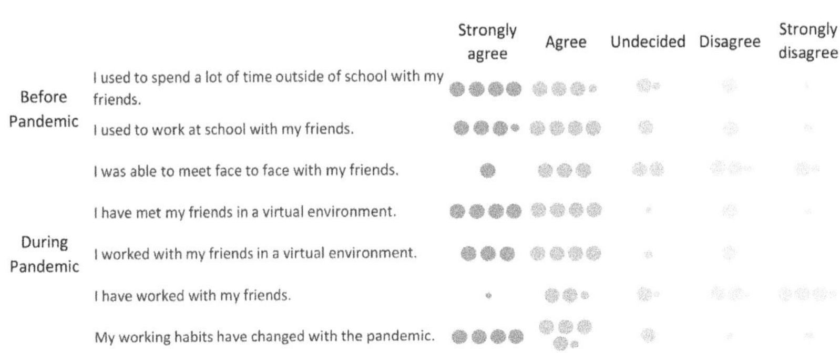

Figure 10.6: Working and Socialization Habits Before and During the Pandemic. Source: Prepared by the author.

Conclusion and Discussion

The effects of the pandemic which suddenly change and restrict our daily life habits cause us to rethink and create new possibilities for the home. This chapter examined how the transformation process brought about by the pandemic changes the home-school relationships of design students, how they perceive their homes, how it changes the meaning of their homes. It discusses the changes in their practice of making space as they began to use their place of accommodation/home as a working environment, the transformation of students' personal time-personal space perception and sense of belonging during the process, and the effects of home-centered education on interpersonal interaction and working habits.

Accordingly, the experiences of the students whose working environment have shifted from the school space to the home bring along both spatial and social, and perceptual changes. The most significant shift among them is the complete change of students' study habits during the pandemic period. The change in working habits also affected spatial and interpersonal interaction, and the students who used to work together in the studios started to work alone either at their own homes where they have been living or in the family homes that they returned. The fact that the pandemic eliminates physical experiences and opens the door to virtual experiences is seen in this chapter with the experiences of design students in virtual environments to socialize and work together.

Students returning home from school and spending more time in their home spaces in this process are expected to make more spatial changes. However, the questionnaire shows that students used to make more frequent spatial changes in their homes also before the pandemic. This situation suggests that the students, whose virtual presences are quite intense, when returning to their family's home during the pandemic, their physical spaces are restricted and their physical presence areas decrease. In addition, it shows that their sense of belonging to home decreases slightly. The reason for this can be that some of the students left their homes where they lived alone or with their housemates and moved to their family homes with the pandemic and continue their existence in a limited new place. When looking at the transformation of personal time and personal space concepts, it is seen that students spend more time for themselves. In contrast to the process of working from home professionally/remote working, we can say in this chapter that students manage to provide personal time while working at home. Likewise, Shamir and Salomon (1985) state in their study that working from home and its effects on employees are closely related to the blurring of the physical and temporal boundaries between work and home. Moreover, the same study mentions the diversity of roles at home and the effect of blurring these roles while working from home on the relationship between work and home. In this chapter, it can be interpreted that students having more personal time while they work from home is related to the decrease in their responsibilities in the family home. Hence, it is possible to claim that pandemic affects the working (professionals) and studying (students) groups differently. Moreover, it is important to investigate the effects of working from home and learning from home in terms of student-instructor relationship in design education in future studies. This chapter uncovers privacy implementations for ensuring privacy in the virtual environment. Students develop solutions to prevent their personal spaces from being seen. Thus it is seen that individual efforts are made to protect the privacy that becomes blurred in homes that are physically closed but open to larger environments through virtual channels.

In conclusion, the changing home-school relationship with the pandemic has been discussed in this chapter within the framework of the meaning of home and home-school interface for the students. There is no doubt that the long-term impact of the pandemic, which entered our lives at once and forces many things to change, including our daily life, will continue to exist in our lives and living spaces. Therefore, it is thought that this chapter will contribute to future studies in terms of examining the new meanings and potentials of the home and their reflections on interpersonal interactions.

References

Alcocer, A. A., and Martella, F. (2020, 06, 04). Public House: The City Folds into the Space of the Home. *Architectural Review*. https://www.architectural-review.com/essays/public-house-the-city-folds-into-the-space-of-the-home

Bachelard, G. (1969). *The Poetics of Space*. Beacon Press.

Buttimer, A. (1980). Home, Reach and the Sense of Place. In A. Buttimer and D. Seamon (Eds.), The *Human Experience of Space and Place*. Croom Helm.

Campbell, E. J., and Vallerand, O. (2020). Approaching Home: New Perspectives on the Domestic Interior. *Canadian Art Review*, 45(2), 7–14.

Deprés, C. (1991). The Meaning of Home: Literature Review and Directions for Future Research and Theoretical Development. *Journal of Architectural and Planning Research*, 8(2), 96–115.

Easthope, H. (2004). A Place Called Home. *Housing, Theory and Society*, 21(3), 128–138.

Gezici Yalçın, M., Düzen, N.E. (2020). Altered Meanings of Home Before and During COVID-19 Pandemic. Human Arenas. https://doi.org/10.1007/s42087-021-00185-3

Gomez, R., and Vannini, S. (2017). Notions of Home and Sense of Belonging in the Context of Migration in a Journey through Participatory Photography. *Electronic Journal of Information Systems in Developing Countries*, 78(1), 1–46.

Hayward, G. (1977). Psychological Concepts of Home among Urban Middle Class Families with Young Children. *(unpublished thesis)* City University of New York.

Heidegger, M. (2008). Building Dwelling Thinking. In D. Farrel Krell (Ed.), *Basic Writings*. London: Harperperennial. Modern Thought, pp. 343–364.

Lefebvre, H. (1991). *The Production of Space*. Blackwell Publishing.

Mallett, S. (2004). Understanding Home: A Critical Review of the Literature. *The Sociological Review*, 52(1), 62–89.

Mitchell, W.J. (1999). E-Topia: "Urban Life, Jim-But Not As We Know It". MIT Press.

Rapoport, A. (1982). Identity and Environment: A Cross-Cultural Perspective. In J. S. Duncan (Ed.), *Housing and Identity*. Homes and Meier.

Rißler, G., Bossen, A., & Blasse, N. (2014). School as Space: Spatial Alterations, Teaching, Social Motives, and Practices. *Studia Paedagogica*, 19(4), 146–160.

Shamir, B., & Salomon, I. (1985). Work-at-Home and the Quality of Working Life. *The Academy of Management Review*, 10(3), 455–464.

The Critical Thinking Child (2020, 05,14). *The Difference Between Remote Learning, E-learning, Distance Learning and at Home Schooling*. https://www.thecriticalthinkingchild.com/the-difference-between-remote-learning-e-learning-distance-learning-and-at-home-schooling/

Toffler, A. (1981). *The Third Wave*. Bantam Books.

Tuan, Y. (1990). *Topophilia: A Study of Environmental Perceptions, Attitudes, and Values*. Columbia University Press.

Zook, C. (2018, 11, 15). *How Is Blended Learning*. https://www.aeseducation.com/blog/what-is-blended-learning

Suzan Girginkaya Akdağ

Berna Sayar

11
Smart Transformation of Housing in Istanbul as a Resilience Response to Crisis Scenarios

Introduction

Cities have become vulnerable due to rapid growth and rapid urbanization. The growing world population and unsustainable consumption of ecological resources have ended up in the deterioration of ecological balance, climate change and an increase in the number and intensity of natural disasters. To avoid the risks and the crisis that these global problems might cause on the social, political, and economic systems, metropolises have been investing in smart city technologies and smart city branding. Authorities aim to use the Information and Communication Technologies (ICT) efficiently and effectively to turn the critical components (infrastructure, security, energy, management, education, health services, building and transportation/mobility) and services of the city into more conscious, intelligent and interactive features (ITU-T, 2014). Thus, the technological (digital) revolution penetrates human and city life in an integrated way. In addition to smart city applications, smart buildings and smart spaces using advanced ICT enabling sustainable design, construction, operation and maintenance of buildings are increasingly becoming a necessity. At this point, the high investment cost technologies raise the economic concerns and the dilemma of luxury versus necessity even though it is for the sake of people and their living environments which are facing several risks and crises scenarios.

Currently, almost all recent luxurious housing projects are designed to be smart so that they can fulfill "environment and energy", "user comfort", and "safety and security" criteria and increase the life quality of their users. They can minimize human control through automation and optimize several qualities through the use of advanced digital systems. A smart home comprises the installation and use of advanced and integrated building technology, such as building automation, safety, telecommunications, user systems and facility management systems. Research by a global real estate consulting brand showed that according to most people, a home could be considered "smart" if it owned smart security, temperature, lighting, and safety systems (URL-7). Specifically, 60 % thought that for a home to be smart, it needed to own at least three categories of smart products with security and temperature control in priority. Besides, consumers were open to using more advanced smart home services that recognized them, their lifestyle and their needs (Mozer, 2005).

According to the statistics on the smart home market, household penetration will be 12.3 % in 2021 and is expected to hit 21.9 % by 2025 (URL-1). In Turkey, the consumers' lifestyles and expectations from IoT (Internet of Things)-based smart home technologies were found to be parallel (URL-2). According to Başarır Özel, the preference of the participants in terms of smart systems was found out to be home security systems (78 %), smart home appliances (75.5 %), home automation (74.6 %) and home entertainment systems (71.7 %). The leading factors affecting consumer attitudes were multi-functionality and "design" in the home appliances sector, "speed of return on investment" in the energy sector while "prestige" came to the fore in the construction sector. Professionals, regardless of their industry, underlined the importance of smart home technologies in terms of the "ease of use and installation", as well as the "comfort", "security", "time-saving" and "entertainment and enjoyment" advantages on consumer decisions. The research also examined the link between consumers' character traits and their attitudes towards smart home technologies. The survey participants stated their attitudes towards technology as optimistic (72 %), open to technological innovations (68 %), sensitive to the environment (64 %), having a healthy lifestyle (60 %) and having a tendency to see the house as a reflection of their selves (65 %). Therefore, the smart home has become a key solution for fulfilling different customer needs and expectations including sustainable (active-passive), green, environmental-friendly, certificated, age-friendly, assisted and/or healthy housing and architecture along with urban development. Hence, in the shift from automated home to next-generation technologies, it is essential to understand the available practices, consumer needs and preferences, and future market trends for setting further adoption strategies.

This chapter investigates the impact of safe life scenarios on the smart housing market and trends in Istanbul. It focuses on the "smart" transformation of housing in Istanbul and conduct a pilot study in Anatolian side district Kadıköy, which is located along the Istanbul-Baghdad railway line that has always been an indicator of the modernization process of the city. As the first station of the railway line, Haydarpaşa Train Station has connected various centers of Anatolia to Istanbul since the early twentieth century and served as an arrival point for immigrants from rural Anatolia who came to work in the city.

Especially after the 1950s, within the framework of the economy and industry, besides offering employment and livelihoods, Istanbul has become a center of attraction for those with dreams of wealth, rising class, and luxurious life.

Based on the relationship between technological advancement and standards of living, this chapter explains the transformation of housing architecture in Istanbul to smart and intelligent buildings as a resilience response to crisis scenarios. Initially, it explains the rising concept of smart homes and intelligent building technologies in the information society. Then, it introduces the major disasters that are soon awaited to take place in Istanbul to reveal the factors that shape people's preference for smart homes. Accepting the 1999 earthquake as a milestone that has reset the local and national building codes, the pilot study inspects three smart housing projects that were built in ten-year time intervals on the Anatolian side. These projects are similar in terms of their scale and promise of smartness for upper-income groups. All data about the projects are taken from a national real estate information and marketing platform (URL-1) and the official websites of their construction companies (URL-4, URL-5 and URL-6). Then, for each project, existing building facilities are mapped with the ten "Quality Environment Modules" (QEMs) proposed by So et al. (1999), Chow and Leung (2005) and Omar (2018) respectively. These quality modules are used as a definition and evaluation criteria for intelligent buildings, that consider the architectural, environmental, and socio-economic dimensions of sustainable and resilient architecture. Hence, the availability and variety of the modules in a project will indicate how efficient its promise of smartness has been to meet the users' needs. The outcomes of the mapping and comparison of projects will demonstrate the strengths and weaknesses of the existing smart home and intelligent building practices in responding to disaster scenarios, as well as the opportunities and threats in the real estate market.

The Concept of Smart Home in the Information Society

Back in the 1950s–1970s, the idea of a smart home was pervasive throughout science fiction literature and movies. In Ray Bradbury's book and several Disney films, homes were depicted as being full of robots and wall-to-wall devices, where all that was required was to push a button, and the smart technology throughout the home would automatically fulfill the user's request. The first home automation machine, which dated back to 1966, was the ECHO IV, a machine capable of creating shopping lists, adjusting the temperature, and turning off appliances (URL-8). In the 1970s, a smart building had a building management system (BMS) comprising of disconnected subsystems or "silos" that were automated at the level of individual functioning. The ’70s X-10 Powerhouse and the ’90s Hal 2000 were designed to do what modern smart home systems do. They controlled various home devices from a central location over the home’s power lines from a central control unit, later by a PC with MS-DOS. Thus, 1970s smart home technology proves that Alexa and Google Home technologies are not new (Coward, 2017).

Smart home technology has come a long way since the 1980s and has gained a whole new meaning (Buckman et al., 2014). Currently, any BMS is highly integrated and wirelessly connected to the internet. The connected segments are controlled and automated either with mobile solutions such as smartphones and tablets or stationary control modules with touchscreens. The “server” module monitors all the activities and provides users with feedback and error messages when necessary through telecommunication. The networking module enables programming facilities and increases the level of user comfort in the home. Facilitated by advanced analytical software and data processing equipment, users have access to large amounts of information that they can use to make intelligent decisions for enhancing building performance thus improving their quality of life.

In the current market, “smart” homes are mainly used for automated units with several smart devices (i.e. door lock, thermostat, light switch) (Batov, 2015). These devices are typically controlled through a mobile app from the residents’ smartphones. Most commercial products are limited with the ability to use remote control and predefine the behaviors of different engineering systems. It has been shown that there is no intelligence in such systems and despite their promise for convenience, money savings and energy efficiency, they can even discomfort inhabitants (Balta and Ozkan et al., 2013). Moreover, the utilization of integrated automated systems may consume more energy than necessary (Reinisch et al., 2011). The benefits of current “smart” homes are wider than just remote control. Donated with an intelligent building system, a smart home essentially programs itself by monitoring the environment and sensing actions performed by the inhabitants. A smart home owns learning ability and self-adjustability (Yang and Peng 2001; Wigginton and Harris 2002; Wong et al., 2005; Kaya and Kahraman 2014) due to innovative technologies such as cloud computing (for virtual and thin client computers), embedded sensors (for personalization and real-time feedback), smart materials, self-healing and low embodied high-performance energy (for energy efficiency), biomimetics (for economic use of materials and energy), robotics (for maintenance and internal surveys) and other forms of convergence technologies in the Internet of Things (IoT). Today, IoT-oriented smart home aims to collect human-machine interaction, then analyze, predict, and utilize information in solving life problems. Smart homes can provide user comfort, energy-saving, time-saving, safety, security, expert systems, health and care, and assistive technologies. Thus, their incentive towards eco-friendly, user-friendly and cost-effective solutions to personal and societal problems has started new business and service models for smart and sustainable living. The timeline of the key drivers of smart homes in Table 11.1, reveals the evolutionary character of smart living technologies that support smart city initiatives in reacting to global challenges of sustainability and creating resilient environments and communities.

Table 11.1: Key drivers for smart homes in history. Source: Prepared by the authors

Era	Key Drivers of Smart Homes
The 1950s	Technological Utopianism
The 1960s-1970s	Computation Building Management systems
The 1980s	Integrated Technology
The 1990s	Information and Communication Technologies and Connected Homes Automation
The 2000s	Embedded Intelligence for Users Interaction and Quality of Life Investment Return
The 2010s	Building Information Model Embedded Intelligence for Sustainability, Monitoring and Climate Resilience Policies
The 2015s	Innovation and New Design Initiatives on Environmental, Economic and Social Perspectives Sustainability
The 2030s (URL-9)	Artificial Intelligence Energy Efficiency Adaptable Homes The Privacy Trade-off Between Personal Data and Access to Services Cyber Security Virtual Realities

Smart Housing as a Response to Crisis Scenarios in Istanbul

Throughout history, Istanbul has always been exposed to natural disasters and its built environment has suffered serious damage in this direction. Today for crisis scenarios, smart buildings stand out with their promise to perform better than traditional buildings, support sustainability goals, and make cities more resilient to environmental, economic, social and cultural shocks. In all global cities, striving for resilience, authorities have developed and implemented mitigation programs, activities, and initiatives covering local plans and regulations, structure and infrastructure projects, natural systems protection, education programs, preparedness and response actions. Through strong incentives for the efficient, fast, and consistent development of the city and its built environment, they shift the barriers to high-quality and affordable housing for low and medium-income groups. In this sense, the urban transformation has been regarded as a chance for getting prepared for the crisis scenarios and improving the quality of housing stock in Turkey (Türkoglu and Kundak, 2011).

Today, one of the key drivers of the growing smart home market and trends is the need to increase urban resilience against housing vulnerabilities in Istanbul, which is at the risk of several disasters (URL-10). Among them are major earthquakes, rapid climate change, new migration waves, recurrent pandemic waves, and subsequent economic crises, which require solutions and strategies for development planning. According to Odabaşı, mayor of Kadıköy district, the future city should be considered in light of two significant problems which are global warming and earthquake after the pandemics are over (URL-11). The need for smart cities and buildings with increasing intelligence is urgent for all cities in Turkey and Istanbul due to the three main disaster scenarios given below:

Major Earthquakes

Turkey's most populated city Istanbul and the cities nearby are expected to be hit by an earthquake with a magnitude of at least 7.0 on the Richter scale. The previous 1999 Marmara earthquake showed that about 60 % of the building stock in Turkey was vulnerable to the earthquake due to a complex and active system of tectonic activities by the Anatolian and Eurasian tectonic plates. The 1999 Marmara earthquake caused a major demolition on the built environment and economic activity, necessitating many measures to be prioritized and new building safety laws to be enacted. Municipalities were given the power to initiate Urban Transformation Projects to rehabilitate urban areas or to mitigate disaster risk (Yönder, 2006; Yönder and Türkoğlu, 2011). To prepare Turkey for an earthquake and at least to lessen the damage, the demolition of 500.000 houses a year and constructing earthquake-resistant houses have been devised by Ministry of Environment and Urbanization. In Istanbul 50,000 buildings are at risk of collapse that will affect the lives of 1.2 million people (URL-12).

Rapid Climate Change

The urban transformation in Istanbul has also been considered as an urgent obligation according to the Climate Change Action plan of the Republic of Turkey (2011–2023) (URL-13) and the Strategic Plan of the Istanbul Metropolitan Municipality (2015–2019) (URL-14). Istanbul is one of the European cities most vulnerable to climate change, thus adaptation activities have priority. Since 2010 Turkey has been experiencing its driest years. In the summer of the same year, heavy rainfall and severe hail events have affected the transportation infrastructure and caused significant damage to homes and vehicles. According to a study that assesses the potential economic damages of extreme weather events in 15 European coastal cities, Istanbul ranks first (URL-15). Turkey's most economically significant city, Istanbul, as the most vulnerable metropolitan city in Europe, is under the threat of several damages that are expected to increase radically until the end of the century. The risks imposed by climate change on the city's municipal services and investments, economy, ecosystem, and social and cultural assets require action from all actors in Istanbul (URL-11). Table 11.2 reveals high risks and medium risks that shape the city's physical, economic, and socio-cultural dimensions. Under several risks, citizens require higher-quality housing that meets the global standards for a safe, energy-efficient, healthy, accessible and affordable life.

Table 11.2: Risk categories for Istanbul in the climate change analysis report. Source: URL-16 (Open source)

High Risk	Medium Risk
• Energy • Public Infrastructure • Land use, Forestry, Biodiversity & Agriculture • Health • Water Resources Management	• Waste Management • Buildings • Tourism, Trading & Socio-Cultural Structure • Industry • Transportation

New Pandemic Waves and Immigration Flow to the Metropolis

Throughout history, Istanbul has always been a center of attraction due to its economic, social and cultural identity. Especially after the 1950s, the intense and various internal migration waves and their socio-economic impacts became apparent in the built environment. The state was incapable and reluctant to cope with these masses/immigrants and to offer formal solutions to the scarcity of housing in Istanbul. This caused informal housing which in time created zones that would be subjected to slum/squatter settlement clearance/urban renewal, something that has whetted neoliberalism's appetite for construction and unearned income. The patchwork urban morphology and creation of build-and-sell systems and apartments, gated communities, and satellite cities are among the results of this situation (Akcan and Bozdoğan, 2012). Several economic, social and political issues raised due to urban–villager conflicts and cultural segregation, victimization and the rise of arabesque culture, changing rents and social diversity, varying property rights and zoning, so on. After 1980, concepts such as security and sterility affected the apartment areas. The residential pattern that developed as single apartments in single plots turned into secure apartment complexes over larger plots. Closed housing or gated community settlements, that used to be located in the city's periphery spread towards the city center (Arıkan, 2013). Since then, gated community settlements have been introduced to consumers as solutions to safe, secure and prestigious life by isolating their residents from lower classes. Today, smart homes are not addressing these local immigrants who triggered the urban transformation of the city but middle/high-income groups, ironically including a group of wealthy foreigners even asylum seekers/immigrants who acquire citizenship via buying a house. Liberal policies, globalization and the expansion of the upper and middle class in developing countries have increased the demand for gated community settlements. This demand for secure living has been welcomed by the construction industry, which has diversified its products in the housing market and promised privileged and smarter lives through infrastructure systems and services.

Nowadays, smart homes can be built quickly with developing technology and several public and private institutional loans for "green housing". Following international sustainability standards, financing incentives for zero-carbon-footprint energy-efficient buildings play a leading role in the rise of the smart home market. However, affordability is still a determiner for the adoption of smart home technologies. The industry has reached the majority of early adopters and technology enthusiasts and is now targeting an increasing number of mainstream users. In developing countries such as Turkey, the high initial cost of technology and high property values in Istanbul limit the smart home market with the upper-income customer segments. Therefore, smart homes represent a new form of spatial discrimination in the city (Akalın, 2016) under the concept of "luxury housing", with promise of new technologies and tailor-made solutions for their residents.

Smart Home Projects and Safe Life Scenarios in Istanbul: A Pilot Study in Kadıköy, Feneryolu Neighborhood

Since the 1999 earthquake, urban transformation and the new stock of smarter, safer, and more sustainable buildings have been acknowledged as ideal solutions for building a resilient city and a community towards increasing disaster risks in Istanbul. To display the rising importance of crisis scenarios and the smart transformation of housing as a resilience response, three prestigious housing projects, that were built in 10-year intervals in one of the most popular residential districts of Istanbul and have been marketed as smart houses are compared according to their facilities in this part (Figure 11.1).

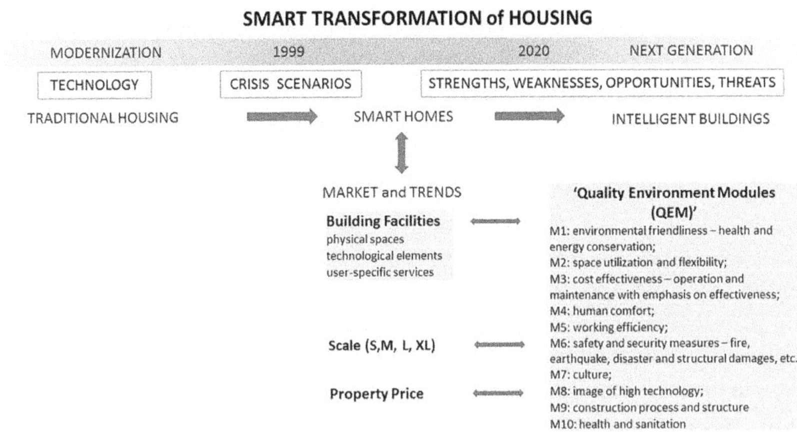

Figure 11.1. Model for comparing the projects using QEMs. Source: Prepared by the authors.

A Popular Residential District in Istanbul: Kadıköy District and Feneryolu Neighborhood

In this chapter, Kadıköy is selected as the pilot area since it always takes its place among the top five districts with the most housing sales, according to figures. Located on the Anatolian side on the northern shore of the Marmara Sea, Kadıköy district developed as an extension of the modernization breakthrough from the late nineteenth century to the early twentieth century. Owing to the construction of the Baghdad railway line and its first train station Haydarpaşa (Bilgin et al., 2010), Kadıköy district has always been the gateway for migrations to Istanbul and has triggered the demographic transformation between the village and the city and between the cities themselves. The transformation of the region, which used to host the prestigious summer residences of the upper-income groups, into a permanent settlement could be explained by the expansion of the transportation network. The start of ferry services in 1843 and the suburban train and piers built in the coastal districts in the 1870s made this line accessible and habitable. In those periods, the type of vehicle used played an important role in the spatial distribution of income groups. Upper-income groups were settled on the coast due to maritime transportation, which was considered being more respectable, while middle and upper-middle-income group settlements were settled around the suburban train line. Supplied with gas in 1892, electricity in 1921, and tram and bus in 1928, the Kadıköy district hosted the first neighborhoods where apartment-type buildings were seen in Istanbul (URL-17). The original residential pattern comprising of low-rise reinforced concrete houses with gardens began to disappear after 1965 due to new zoning regulations and emerging conservation problems.

Feneryolu neighborhood is located in the Kadıköy district of Istanbul and is bordered by Baghdad Street in the north and Fahrettin Kerim Gökay Street in the south. It has been a residential area since the end of the nineteenth century, thus has spatialized the ideological, economic and social ruptures of a geographical place with almost no resistance (Arıkan, 2013). Thus, from its built environment and different housing typologies, all spatial fragmentations that took place in the last hundred years can be read. Settlements in Feneryolu first started in the second half of the nineteenth century with wooden mansions located in large gardens, and over time, they turned into detached houses varying between two and three floors. Since the 1940s, the density of the housing pattern has increased rapidly. Following the detached house period, the planned construction period started with new development rights that allowed an increase in the density and height of buildings. Plans dated 1952 and 1964 initiated the transition to apartment typology (Arıkan, 2013). The formation of the residential pattern began to be determined by zoning regulations and/or land and property prices rather than user preferences. Since then, in the Feneryolu neighborhood, several large-scale housing projects have been built in line with global trends. Their promise for a safe, secure and peaceful life with social facilities and more green spaces have been purchased by upper and upper-middle-income groups demanding luxury and comfort (Figure 11.2).

To understand the changing concept of smartness on the housing market, three projects which are similar in terms of prestige and socio-economic level of their residents in Feneryolu neighborhood are analyzed (Table 11.3). The reason for selecting these projects is that each was built in 10-year intervals (1999, 2008 and 2018 respectively) after the 1999 Marmara Earthquake (URL-4, URL-5 and URL-6). Thus, all have been built according to new building regulations that met the required standards at their time of construction. Today, they all are recognized on the market for their smartness that was enabled by the advanced building technologies of their decades (Figure 11.3).

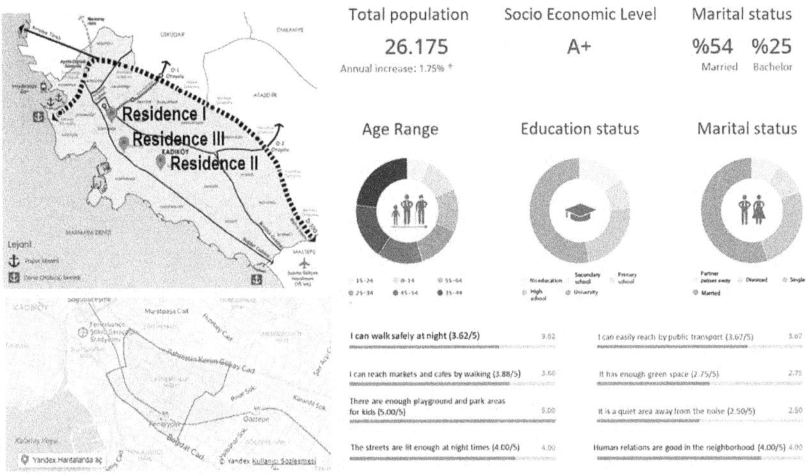

Figure 11.2. Map of Kadıköy District, Feneryolu Neighborhood with socio-demographic characteristics and evaluation by real residents. Source: URL-1 (Open source).

Table 11.3: Info about the three residential projects chosen for QEM analysis. Source: URL-4, URL-5 and URL-6 (Open source)

	Residence I	Residence II	Residence III
Date of Construction	1999	2008	2018
Number of Apartments	110	520	52
Number of Blocks	3	4	2
Number of Floors	16	44	13
Flat Area	220 m^2	87 m^2 to 1050 m^2	196 or 380 m^2
Land Area	12000 m^2	4400 m^2	3500 m^2
Green area	1100	4100 m^2	3500 m^2
Specific Info	An initial example of high-rise housing projects in urban transformation after the 1999 Marmara earthquake.	Subject to public concerns for being built over public land.	Includes an architectural heritage shopping complex which is dated back to the Early Period Modern Turkish Architecture.

Figure 11.3. Views from the three residential projects chosen for QEM analysis. Source: Prepared by the authors.

Methodology: Mapping Smart Housing Project Facilities with QEM

The definition of smart homes and intelligent building practices have intertwined. In the current market, "smart" homes are mainly used for automated units with several smart devices meanwhile "intelligent" buildings can be defined as buildings that are "designed and established based on a suitable selection of 'Quality Environmental Modules' that satisfy the user's requests by mapping this module with appropriate building facilities to attain lifelong building values" (So et al., 1999; Chow and Leung, 2005, Omar, 2018). In Table 11.4, the multi-criteria framework by Chow and Leung (2005) is given. In Table 11.5, for each project, building facilities are mapped with the ten "Quality Environment Modules (QEM)" evaluation criteria that cover architectural, environmental, and socio-economic dimensions of Intelligent Buildings. The data used for exploring the projects' existing QEMs, concerning their physical spaces, technological elements, user-specific services, are derived from a national real estate information and marketing platform (URL-1) and the official websites of their construction companies (URL-4, URL-5 and URL-6). The number of checks given shows the relative intensity of the number of constituents that the project meets.

Table 11.4: Definition of QEMS (Chow and Leung, 2005). Source: Chow and Leung (2005) (Table prepared by the authors based on the previous research named New Intelligent Building Index for Buildings Around the World)

Quality Environment Modules	Constituents in a building
M1: Environmental Friendliness	Lift & Escalators, Lavatories and Provisions of Appliances, Thermal Comfort, Electrical Services, Heating services, Ventilation and Air-conditioning, Lighting, Drainage, Waste Disposals, etc.
M2: Space Utilization and Flexibility	Architectural Design, Carpark and Transportation, Flexibility in Internal Arrangements, Building Provisions, etc
M3: Cost-Effectiveness	The life cycle cost of a building
M4: Human Comfort	Architectural Design, Lift, Lavatory and Provisions of Appliances, Thermal Comfort, Ventilation and Air-conditioning, Lighting, Access, Acoustics, Colour, Entertainment Facilities, etc.
M5: Working Efficiency	Architectural Design, Lift & Escalators, Lavatories and Provisions of Appliances, Thermal Comfort, Lighting, High Technology, Sign and Directory, Carpark and Transportation, Building Facilities, etc.
M6: Safety and Structure	Earthquake Monitoring, Building Structural Condition Survey, Structural Monitoring, Tile Debonding Monitoring, Terrorist Attack Precaution Plan, Fire Protection, Electrical Safety, Elevator Reliability, Public Announcement, Total Egress, Escape Plan, Essential Electrical Power, Preventive Maintenance of Building Systems, Indoor Air Quality, Safety Management System, Settlement Monitoring, Risk Management, Security and Crowd Control, etc
M7: Culture	Soft elements such as Feng Shui, Entertainment Facilities, Privacy Requirements, Colours, Interior Decoration, Food and Beverage, External Landscape and View, Indoor Plants, Religious Facilitation, Culturally Based Interior design, Promotion Activity, etc
M8: An Image of High Technology	Broadband Internet, Electrical Services, Office Automation, Electronic Facilities, Artificial Intelligent Control, Webpage, Hotlines, Telephone Provisions, Fibre-optic Network, Building Services Automation, Mobile Phone Coverage, Advanced Carpark Facilities, etc.
M9: Management Practice and Security	Building Management Practice, Building Services Operation and Maintenance, High Technology, Security and Monitoring, Controls, Management Planning, Water Supply and Drainage, Environmental Protection,
M10: Health and Sanitation	Potable and Flushing Water System, Drainage, Toilet, Carpark and Lift Ventilation, Odour, Cleanliness, Refuse Handling, Pest and Mosquitoes Controls, Filtration in Swimming Pools, Jacuzzi and Sauna, etc

Table 11.5. Mapping smart housing project facilities with QEM. Source: Prepared by the authors

Modules	Residence I (1999)	Residence II (2008)	Residence III (2018)
M1: Environmental Friendliness	✓	✓✓✓	✓✓✓
M2: Space Utilization and Flexibility	✓	✓✓✓	✓✓
M3: Cost-Effectiveness	✓	✓✓	✓✓
M4: Human Comfort	✓	✓✓✓	✓✓
M5: Working Efficiency	✓	✓✓	✓✓
M6: Safety and Structure	✓	✓✓✓	✓✓✓
M7: Culture	✓	✓✓	✓✓✓
M8: An Image of High Technology	✓	✓✓✓	✓✓
M9: Management Practice and Security	✓	✓✓	✓✓
M10: Health and Sanitation	✓	✓✓	✓✓

Findings and Discussion

Different types of buildings are defined to be smart through varying sets of QEMs. According to So et al. (1999), the most important criteria for residential buildings were to be human comfort (M4), culture (M7), safety – fire, earthquake, disaster and structure (M6). However, analyzing the physical spaces, technological elements, and user-specific services of the three prestigious residential projects in Istanbul has revealed the changing criteria of smartness in line with the disaster scenarios. Given below are the major quality factors involved in the resilient housing design in Istanbul.

According to the comparison of QEMs in Table 11.5, M6, which is the safety and security measures for earthquake, disaster and structural damages, has come out to be the major criteria for all projects built in Istanbul since the 1999 Big Marmara Earthquake. After the disaster, the building codes were changed to trigger the urban transformation with an increase in built area and maximum height. This new vertical development was reasoned with green land use as in Residence II. However, this latter project was built on public land and aroused major conflicts in the public discourse and media. Its high-rise and high-density residential typology was reasoned with the "environment and energy criteria" of the 2010s and was enabled via intelligence modules such as M1 (environmental friendliness), M2 (space utilization and flexibility) and M4 (human comfort), which aim to minimize the effects of "rapid climate change" as indicated in Table 11.4. The M3 (cost-effectiveness) has always been an important criterion in Istanbul since in the context of its vulnerable economy, safe and secure houses with smart and sustainable solutions are regarded as a type of investment for disaster scenarios. Among the three projects, the Residence Project I owns less advanced systems owing to its construction date thus the operational costs are higher. However, a low-carbon retrofitting would optimize its energy and water use and would make it more cost-effective.

Istanbul has been staging a massive urban transformation since the 1999 Marmara Earthquake. To be discernible among the huge and new building stocks, these projects had to be conceptualized with new meanings. They employed M7 (the culture) which refers to the soft/non-technical components of design that suit residents' changing lifestyles and behaviors and M8 (an image of high technology in the built environment). On these terms, Residence Project III is remarkable in terms of preserving the old shopping center building, which is an architectural heritage building of the Early Period Modern Architecture in Turkey. On the other hand, Residence II inherits the curtain wall design of futuristic high-rise towers (Table 11.3).

Around the second half of the 2010s, alienation of citizens to the new built environment and immigration flow to the metropolis imposed new initiatives on environmental, economic and social sustainability (Table 11.1). Besides their advanced smart home automation systems, Residence II and III have been highlighted on the real estate marketing platform (URL-3) for providing expat-friendly environments and opportunities for citizenship rights to their owners. The child-friendly and/or pet-friendly environments, sports and well-being facilities have stood out for the high standard of their living conditions.

Among the ten QEMs, M9 (management practice and security), M5 (working efficiency) and M10 (health and sanitation) are found to be the last intelligence criteria among the preferred constituents by users in the context of a smart house since they are more technical features that could only be grasped after a duration of residence/use. However, the current and future scenarios of the pandemic have increased the importance of M10 (health and sanitation), M5 (working efficiency) and M9 (management practice and security) together with M2 (space utilization and flexibility), to fit the new normal of living and working, socialization and distancing.

Based on these outcomes, it can be concluded that the choice of QEM modules by the building contractors is not only related to a building typology but also depends on the context. Therefore, the selection of QEM modules might differ according to location, date of construction and urban and/or environmental dynamics, which are the disaster scenarios for Istanbul in this chapter. Therefore, new QEMs are to be added to the list (Table 11.4) in the near and distant future since smartness and/or intelligence are related to the user's benefits and how well the indoor environment meets their requests. Since the real estate market and trends will be shaped by smarter homes as a resilience response to crisis scenarios, the architecture, engineering and construction (AEC) industry shall build its business strategies on the integration of requested QEMs in the housing projects.

References

Akalın, M. (2016). Mekânsal Ayrışmanın Bir Yeni Biçimi Olarak Kapalı/ Kapılı Siteler: Akkent Konutları Örneği, Hitit Üniversitesi Sosyal Bilimler Enstitüsü Dergisi, Yıl 9, Sayı 2, Aralık 2016, ss. 923–956. [Closed/Gated Sites as a New Form of Spatial Segregation: The Example of Akkent Residences, Hitit University Journal of Social Sciences Institute, Volume 9, Issue 2, December 2016, pp. 923–956].

Akcan and Bozdoğan (2012). Turkey. Modern Architectures in History. Reaktion Books.

Arıkan, B. (2013). Kentsel Mekanın Değişimi ve Konut Dokusunda Katmanlaşma: Feneryolu Mahallesi Örneği, İTÜ, Fen Bilimleri Enstitüsü, Yüksek Lisans Tezi, İstanbul. [Change of Urban Space and Stratification in Housing Texture: The Example of Feneryolu Neighborhood, ITU, Institute of Science and Technology, Master Thesis, Istanbul].

Balta-Ozkan, N., Davidson, R., Bicket, M., and Whitmarsh, L. (2013). Social Barriers to the Adoption of Smart Homes. *Energy Policy*, Vol. 63, pp. 363–374, ISSN 0301-4215, https://doi.org/10.1016/j.enpol.2013.08.043

Batov, E. İ. (2015). The Distinctive Features of "Smart" Buildings. *Procedia Engineering*. Vol. 111. https://doi.org/10.1016/j.proeng.2015.07.061

Bilgin, İ., Akın, G., and Güvenç, M. (2010). *İstanbul 1910–1010 Kent, Yapılı Çevre ve Mimarlık Kültürü Sergisi*. İstanbul: İstanbul Bilgi Üniversitesi Yayınları. [*Istanbul 1910-1010 City, Built Environment and Architecture Culture Exhibition*. Istanbul: Istanbul Bilgi University Publications].

Buckman, A. H., Mayfield, M., and B.M. Beck, S. (2014). "What is a Smart Building?", *Smart and Sustainable Built Environment*, Vol. 3, No. 2, pp. 92–109. https://doi.org/10.1108/SASBE-01-2014-0003

Chow, L. K. H., and Leung, A. Y. T. (2005). New Intelligent Building Index for Buildings Around The World – A Quantitative Approach In Building Assessment Experience With Hong Kong Tallest Building, Two International Finance Centre. The 2005 World Sustainable Building Conference, Tokyo, 27–29 September 2005 (SB05Tokyo), pp. 2302–2309. DOI: https://doi.org/10.1142/9789812701480_0142. https://www.irbnet.de/daten/iconda/CIB3885.pdf

Coward, C. (2017). *'70s Smart Home Tech Proves Alexa and Google Home Are Nothing New.* https://www.hackster.io/news/70s-smart-home-tech-proves-alexa-and-google-home-are-nothing-new-a4b94f4b639b

ITU-T (2014). Technical Report on Smart Sustainable Cities: An analysis of definitions United Nations, International Telecommunication Union (ITU-T), Focus Group on Smart Sustainable Cities (FG-SSC).

Kaya, I., and Kahraman, C. (2014). A Comparison of Fuzzy Multicriteria Decision-Making Methods for Intelligent Building Assessment. *Journal of Civil Engineering and Management*, Vol. 20, No. 1, pp. 59–6. https://doi.org/10.3846/13923730.2013.801906

Mozer, M. C. (2005). Lessons from an Adaptive Home. *Smart Environments: Technologies, Protocols, and Applications*, edited by D. J. Cook and S. K. Das. ISBN: 0-471-54448-5, John Wiley & Sons, Inc.

Omar, O. (2018). Intelligent Building, Definitions, Factors and Evaluation Criteria of Selection. *Alexandria Engineering Journal*. https://doi.org/10.1016/j.aej.2018.07.004

Reinisch, C., Kofler, M., Iglesias, F., and Kastner, W. (2011). Think Home Energy Efficiency in Future Smart Homes. *Journal of Embedded Systems*, Vol. 2011, pp. 104617. https://doi.org/10.1155/2011/104617

So, A. T. P., Wong, A. C. W., and Wong, K. C. (1999). A New Definition of Intelligent Buildings for Asia. *Facilities*. https://doi.org/10.1108/02632779910293488

Türkoglu, H., and Kundak, S. (2011). *Urban Transformation as a Tool for Disaster Mitigation*, ERSA conference papers, European Regional Science Association. Retrieved from https://www.researchgate.net/publication/254457532_Urban_Transformation_as_a_tool_for_Disaster_Mitigation

URL-1. Statista. Smart home. https://www.statista.com/outlook/dmo/smart-home/worldwide. Accessed 1 September 2021.

URL-2. How are smart home technologies transforming life? https://haberler.boun.edu.tr/tr/haber/akilli-ev-teknolojileri-yasami-nasil-donusturuyor. Accessed 3 September 2021.

URL-3. Feneryolu, Kadıköy, Istanbul Regional Report (Feneryolu, Kadıköy, İstanbul Bölge Raporu). Retrieved form https://www.zingat.com/kadikoy-feneryolu-bolge-raporu?mode=demographics. Accessed 20 March 2021.

URL-4. https://www.tasyapi.com/tr/kiziltoprak-kuleli-kosk-konutlari-0936. Accessed 10 January 2021.

URL-5. https://www.tasyapi.com/tr/bagdat-caddesi-four-winds-residence-09406. Accessed 10 January 2021.

URL-6. http://www.cakirkayayapi.com/tr/projects/burc-sitesi. Accessed 10 January 2021.

URL-7. https://wondrwall.co.uk/intelligent-homes-are-the-evolution-of-smart-homes/. Accessed 25 September 2020.

URL-8. Bravas, How Far We've Come: The Evolution of Smart Home Automation. Retrieved from https://bravas.com/bravas-blog/item/how-far-we-ve-come-the-evolution-of-smart-home-automation. Accessed 11 January 2021.

URL-9. Andrew Lucas, What Will the Smart Home of the Future Look Like in 2030. https://1sd8cp36yiis47168hvghagm-wpengine.netdna-ssl.com/wp content/uploads/2017/10/2030-White-Paper.pdf. Accessed 11 January 2021.

URL-10. Disaster Resilient Urban Planning and Building. http://www.guvenliyasam.org/wp-content/uploads/2016/02/ADSPY.pdf. Accessed 06 January 2021.

URL-11. http://www.gazetekadikoy.com.tr/gundem/odabasi-kadikoy-avm-istemiyor-h16446.html. Accessed 2 February 2021.

URL-12. 50,000 buildings in Istanbul at risk of collapse: Environment minister. https://www.hurriyetdailynews.com/50000-buildings-in-istanbul-at-risk-of-collapse-environment-minister--108582. Accessed 4 February 2021.

URL-13. Climate Change Action Plan 2011 – 2023 Republic of Turkey. https://webdosya.csb.gov.tr/db/iklim/editordosya/iklim_degisikligi_eylem_plani_EN_2014.pdf. Accessed 10 December 2020.

URL-14. İBB Strategic Plan 2015–2019. http://www.ibb.gov.tr/en-US/Organization/Birimler/StratejikPlanlamaMd/Documents/stratejik_plan_2015-2019.pdf. Accessed 10 December 2020.

URL-15. Istanbul Climate Change Action Plan Summary Report 2018. https://www.iklim.istanbul/wp-content/uploads/%C3%96zetRapor%C4%B0ngilizce.pdf. Accessed 09 December 2020.

URL-16. Istanbul Climate Change Action Plan Climate Change Risk, Opportunity and Vulnerability Analysis Report (İstanbul İklim Değişikliği Eylem Plani İklim Değişikliği Risk, Firsat Ve Kirilganliklar Analiz Raporu). https://www.iklim.istanbul/wp-content/uploads/analizraporu.pdf. Accessed 25 January 2021.

URL-17. Kadıkoy Province Web Site. http://www.kadikoy.gov.tr/kadikoy-ilce-tarihce. Accessed 18 May 2021.

Wigginton, M., and Harris, J. (2002). *Intelligent Skins* (1st ed.). Routledge. https://doi.org/10.4324/9780080495446

Wong, J. K. W., Li, H., and Wang, S. W. (2005). Intelligent Building Research: A Review. *Automation in Construction*, Vol. 14, Issue 1, pp. 143–159. ISSN 0926-5805, https://doi.org/10.1016/j.autcon.2004.06.001

Yang, J., and Peng, H. (2001). Decision Support to the Application of Intelligent Building Technologies. *Renewable Energy*, Vol. 22, Issues 1–3, pp. 67–77. ISSN 0960-1481, Doi: https://doi.org/10.1016/S0960-1481(00)00085-9

Yönder, A. (2006). Disaster Mitigation or Gentrification? Urban Transformation Projects in Istanbul. Paper Presented at the 47th Annual ACSP Conference in Forthworth, Texas. November 7–12, 2006.

Yönder, A., and Türkoğlu, H. (2011). "Post 1999 developments in Disaster Management in Turkey: The regulatory frameworks and implementation of land use planning for disaster risk reduction in Istanbul." Case study prepared for ISDR Global Assessment Report 2011.

Gizem Akdemir

12
Tiny Living in a Megacity: Exploring the Emergence of Tiny-House Movement in Istanbul

Introduction

The tiny house movement is steadily gaining popularity in public, and it is becoming a valid topic amongst recent housing discussions. Originated in the U.S, the movement can be considered as one of the alternative living ways that should be mentioned during the times of Covid-19 pandemic (Byrne, 2020). It is possible to track down the reasons for the growth of tiny houses to its media coverage and its emergence as a new lifestyle centered around concepts such as freedom and living a simple life. Motivations such as environmental concerns, the cycle of debt-related with contemporary, primarily American lifestyles, frustration concerning excessive materialism, and its potential as a small structure for housing the homeless and poor are considered as reasons for the growth of the movement (Gauer, 2004; Anson 2014; Heben 2014; Evans, 2018). Similarly, in Australia, dissatisfaction with unsustainable housing development, rising debts, and a rejection of the idea that ties home ownership and citizenship together caused the movement spread more (Penfold et al., 2018; Shearer & Burton, 2019; Weetman, 2018; Wotton et al., 2018). But the affordability is presumably the biggest reason behind the attraction to tiny houses. This also affected the increase of tiny houses in Turkey and in its most crowded city, Istanbul. Tiny houses became an alternative tourism option, which according to Galip Ölmez, the founder of Yako Groups, people preferred them for their close relationship to nature with an option for a healthier and more isolated life, in addition to comfort and convenience (Ölmez, 2020). Tiny houses on wheels as second homes or holiday houses are also seen in European countries with Germany appearing to be the pioneer, as a response to high rental prices (Shearer and Burton, 2019). Sustainability is a major factor for the rise of the movement, including possibilities of reducing the environmental impact and individual spatial footprint (Ford and Gomez-Lanier, 2017). Also, it proposes solutions for a type of mobile housing for travelers with tiny house on wheels (THOWs) (Shahani, 2015; Ford & Gomez-Lanier, 2017; Evans, 2018), temporary housing, and as a solution for housing in urban areas that host large populations in limited space (Priesnitz, 2014; Maghribi et.al., 2015; Ford & Gomez-Lanier, 2017). Even though these motivations behind the growth of tiny house are still relevant, the movement has been criticized for promoting an overly romantic outlook for down-sizing, sustainability, and affordability. With that, legal barriers including zoning regulations and uncertainty of tiny houses as a typology in urban environments cause problems that withhold the lifestyle from achieving its promised potential (Ford & Gomez-Lanier, 2017).

The conditions of the pandemic which led to the construction of a new relationship with the meaning of home (Byrne, 2020) can also cause a rethinking of the tiny house as a relevant typology. Although it is widely covered in electronic media primarily in U.S (Anson, 2014) and Australia (Penfold et al., 2018; Weetman, 2018), there are fewer studies on the tiny house itself as a typology. As a typology, Shearer & Burton (2019) mentioned two specific types as mobile and permanent. Yet, there is a lack of studies that discusses its course in non-English speaking countries such as Turkey.

Therefore, this chapter mainly aims to understand the tiny house movement and its manifestations in Istanbul. After providing a brief history of the concept's emergence, the study elaborates on the motivations that drive people to join the tiny house movement around the world as well as the legal barriers and criticism towards the movement. It intends to explore how the situation differs or reflects in Istanbul with a short survey about Istanbul's leading tiny house developers. It is hoped that a discussion will be initiated about the future of tiny homes, current customer profiles, motivations, and concerns of users.

Emergence of Tiny Houses and Motivations Behind the Movement

As a relatively new housing typology that has emerged in the USA, the tiny house revolves around "minimizing, de-cluttering, and downsizing" that originated in nineteenth century romanticism (Anson, 2014; Ford & Gomez-Lanier, 2017). Similarly, the idea of small houses is not new as it is encountered often in American history and several Western countries. Nevertheless, as a more recent movement, tiny houses gained significance with the initial manufacturer companies such as Tumbleweed Tiny House Company and Small House Society and rapidly multiplied by the development of other USA companies, eventually turning into an international movement (Mutter, 2013; Boeckermann et al., 2019). Before the advantages of modern banking systems and zoning regulations, small houses such as bungalows, cabins, and cottage houses meant affordability and design revolved around local building materials, landscape, and climate

(Downing, 1969; Mcalester, 1984; Evans, 2018). Also, small housing units on the property of larger main houses were common as well; they provided living quarters for family elders, newlyweds, guests and servants or slaves, and rental income for main homeowners (Hunter, 1999; Evans, 2018). Affordability continued as a driving force for small houses to be built after World War 1 (WWI), when there was an affordable housing shortage. American companies such as Sears and Roebuck produced home-kits with mail delivery via train, which included necessary building elements (Wentling, 1995; Evans, 2018), while organizations like the Architect's Small House Bureau provided plans for small houses around 800–1,000 square feet for potential home builders (Hunter, 1999; Evans, 2018).

Shortly after, mass-produced mobile houses became immensely popular, especially within low-income groups. Now, the term mobile home is accepted as being synonymous with "manufactured home" to describe small houses produced modularly in factories and assembled on-site (Hunter, 1999; Evans, 2018). This production and placement system like the tiny house garnered negative reaction for the final products deemed unattractive and of low value for their design and related with increased problems rooted in poverty such as crime (Chernoff, 1983; Genz, 2001; Fischel, 2004; Boudreaux, 2011; Mandelker, 2016; Evans, 2018). This situation caused municipalities to create separate parking zones and thus, small houses were not completely integrated into the urban texture. On the other hand, they have persisted, and the typology has evolved, as they represent a part of the " 'American dream of owning a detached dwelling" as opposed to being a tenant and are perceived as more desirable affordable housing than apartments (Evans, 2018).

With affordability, the concern around excessive materialism and the current economic system resulted in searches for alternative lifestyles. It is argued that concepts like downsizing have re-emerged and are attracting people who want to take steps to adopt small living, which emphasizes more meaningful personal relationships and work without compromising quality of life (Evans, 2018). One example of that is the alternative communities developed around the 1960s and 1970s for objectives and desires on achieving more simple but meaningful lives (Manzella, 2010; Evans, 2018). These communities pioneered similar designs to tiny houses and built small structures such as buses converted into dwellings, geodesic dome houses, and hay bale homes (Evans, 2018). According to the research done by Mangold and Zschau (2019), the search for a good life can be related to the tiny house lifestyle. The possibilities of removing oneself from existing infrastructure and daily urban life, while experiencing freedom in a relatively secure way can be amongst the fascinations of tiny houses. The conceptual model describes the appeal of the tiny house lifestyle for reasons including financial security, freedom and autonomy, meaningful relationships, simple living, and new experiences (Mangold and Zschau, 2019). The term "'micro-living" explains another corresponding trend that revolved around shrinking living spaces and emerged as a solution to the affordable housing crisis (Harris and Nowicki, 2020). Although this lifestyle includes urban living spaces of small self-contained units, co-living tenancies, converted and subdivided shared spaces (Harris and Nowicki, 2020), its branding and attraction can be argued to be like tiny houses.

The problematic housing situation in the United States, caused by increasing housing sizes and urban density along with the environmental impact it is responsible for, has been indicated as an important reason for choosing tiny living. However, like mentioned, home-ownership still is a relevant motivation in the US, and it has been found to impact housing satisfaction, thus, overall life satisfaction, along with housing size, greenspace, and surrounding environment (Boeckermann et al., 2019). Murphy (2014) a tiny-house owner, verifies that one of the major motivations for her was the opportunity for house ownership amongst rapid rise in the real estate market (Murphy, 2014). Another reason she chose a tiny house lifestyle was the desire for a simpler life and the sense of empowerment that comes with owning a home that she built using recycling and refurbishing methods (Murphy, 2014). Related to the housing problems, concerns about the environmental impact of the unsustainable lifestyle culture of American consumerism became a major driving force for tiny house development (Mutter, 2013; Pflaumer, 2015; Boeckermann et al., 2019). Individual carbon footprint reduction as an immediate effect of downsizing and incorporating more sustainable design choices such as recycled materials, rainwater collection systems, energy sources (i.e., solar panels) are cited as primary motivations as well (Mutter, 2013; Boeckermann et al., 2019). The freedom that comes with the flexibility to not be dependent on a certain location or the existing urban infrastructure, especially for tiny houses on wheels (THOWS) (Evans, 2018), has become one of the most prominent attractions for the tiny house lifestyle (Mutter, 2013). As mentioned, the desire to be a part of an alternative group of people who are enthusiastic about tiny living that began in the 1960s and 1970s provided a sense of community (Mutter, 2013), despite the fact that these populations are very widespread and diverse globally (Evans, 2018). It is possible to argue that the flexibility of tiny houses is a design feature. Instances, where homeowners are directly involved in the design of the house, are as common as tiny house developers, and this potential of customization is considered an important motivation (Muttter, 2013). Additionally, several organizations in the United States have begun to use tiny houses as homeless shelters (Mingoya, 2015).

Therefore, the prominent motivations for choosing tiny houses were stated as affordability, living a simple life or in other words, down-sizing, freedom including mobility, flexibility, and the possibility of new experiences, environmental sustainability, sense of community, its design in addition to a sense of empowerment via home-ownership and autonomy (Ford & Gomez-Lanier, 2017; Boeckermann et al., 2019; Mangold and Zschau, 2019). It is worth noting that the media coverage created a sensation around the tiny house lifestyle and is steadily raising awareness about the typology itself. Acclaimed publications such as The New Yorker, Architectural Digest, and National Geographic include stories about the movement, while several movies, YouTube channels, and social media groups promote the lifestyle (Anson, 2014). These motivations are slightly related to the user profile but have no effect on the variety, which includes seniors, students, retirees, and young adults in addition to people interested in tiny living communities (Mutter, 2013; Boeckermann et al., 2019). Mingoya suggests people with high incomes who decide to downsize are highly associated with the simplicity of the movement, but the profile varies according to the cost, and size of the house (Mingoya, 2015).

Typologies of Tiny Houses

There are no definite measurements for tiny house designs. Many promoters assert that tiny houses are a maximum of 400 square feet, approximately 37 square meters (Evans, 2018). Definitions about their typology are also vague, changing from “a house built on a trailer that suits to the maximum trailer sizes that carry shipping containers and caravans” (Murphy, 2014) to “individually built, not just molded or assembled dwellings”; (Mitchell, 2014), and “…effective use of space, relies on good design, a vehicle for the desired lifestyle”. (Mitchell 2014; Shearer and Burton, 2019). Therefore, tiny dwellings have a large range of models that differ in size, mobility (tiny house on a trailer, wheels or skids), tenancy (holiday house, tourist cabin), construction methods (container house, converted shed, bus or truck, yurts), legal status, form, etc. Shearer and Burton (2019) who defined certain characteristics and created a list of tiny house typologies state that tiny houses are generally built on a mobile foundation and in a temporary location, but the most important factors are size and mobility. According to their study, it is possible to define two specific types of tiny houses: mobile and permanent (Shearer and Burton, 2019). Type 1, mobile tiny houses, include sub-types such as an iconic tiny house on a trailer, relocatable tiny house which can be moved to a site then fixed, or semi-permanent tiny house (Shearer and Burton, 2019). Examples of these sub-types are prefab, cabin, shipping container, mine hut, kit home, and etc. Fava Camp, a mobile housing park in the Pendik district of Istanbul, is a recent development that serves as a recreational accommodation and a local example (Fava Camp, 2021). Type 2 is permanent or non-mobile houses and includes sub-types of purpose-built tiny house/cottage, converted non-residential buildings (sheds, garages, barns), and tiny house villages (apartment complex/cottage/townhouse in the intentional or co-housing community). The latter subtype is also used as an affordable housing option to improve homelessness (Jackson et al., 2020).

Legal Barriers and Criticism on Tiny House Lifestyle

Although they are now frequently encountered, legal barriers to tiny houses persist. The major obstacles to the proliferation of tiny houses are the dependence on local zoning regulations and building codes (Anson, 2014; Murphy, 2014; Priesnitz, 2014). Because tiny houses represent an undefined combination as an emerging typology of a mobile home, recreational vehicle, or a caravan and a home, generally they do not fit completely to any of the existing legal categories (Ford and Gomez-Lanier, 2017). In Turkey, tiny houses under the term caravan can be an attractive alternative as a building on the zones where there is no building permit. The important thing is that they must not be built on a foundation, rather they must be built as a vehicle (Istanbul Metropolitan Municipality, 2018). The Vagoon House Company in Istanbul states that their products are not legal buildings, but vehicles and they are subject to the Highways Traffic Regulations and can be placed on the plot of the desired zoning plan without requiring a zoning permit (Vagoon House, 2021). In this case, tiny houses are defined as a legally parked caravans. In other words, they must be designed and manufactured to be carried on a trailer. Electricity and water connections, on the other hand, are solved with the facilities created within themselves, for example, electricity can be provided by solar panels and the house can contain water tanks. With that, water must be added to the water tank at regular intervals and the drain must be pulled by the sewage truck. Taking advantage of the legal gap, these houses can be placed on land without a construction permit while they do not have permanent infrastructure (Özlem, 2020). This off-grid system paves the way for many companies to create recreational centers or resorts with small houses. Even so, as Anson (2014) states, when viewed as mobile homes, many regulations restrict where homes can be legally parked – and mobile home communities (caravan parks) and recreational vehicle communities do not always allow small homes. Similarly, Mary Murphy, who built a tiny mobile house in Central Vermont, USA faced the difficulties of a possible violation of building codes (Murphy, 2014). Because tiny houses are accepted as homes, they are also affected by the zone established by many American states which regulates the minimum square meter area code for a home to be considered habitable. Murphy (2014) stated that she had challenges in designing a small space that works well with wide corridors, wide doors, and many other regulations on detail requirements and that putting wheels on the tiny houses possibly creates a way to take advantage of the "legal gap" that exists around the small house construction (Murphy, 2014; Ford & Gomez-Lanier, 2017). By utilizing it with a recreational car trailer, her tiny house was covered by vacation vehicle laws which eliminated the need to comply with a minimum habitable space requirement, excess energy use and payments such as real estate tax, and flexible permits were made possible (Murphy, 2014; Ford & Gomez-Lanier, 2017). The legal barriers considering tiny houses have started to diminish slowly as few places in the U.S such as Fresno, California are taking legal measures to recognize them as a form of housing rather than trying to adapt to existing regulations. The law allows a small house on wheels to legally park on a property as a permanent residence (Ford & Gomez-Lanier, 2017).

The tiny house movement and the lifestyle are criticized for promoting an overly romantic world view and presented as a more affordable way of gaining freedom, mobility, and environmental sustainability. Anson (2014) argues that even though the cost of maintenance and expenses of tiny house dwellings are lower, the ownership and development process of a tiny house still requires a substantial amount of savings for most people. On top of legal difficulties related to land regulations, most banks refuse to provide construction loans because of the uncertainty for potential tiny homeowners (Anson, 2014). Contrary to media coverage on the long-term benefits of the movement, mostly tiny houses are used short-term and as a source of rental income. Anson (2014) defines their design aspect, which started as a major motivation for tiny homeowners, an aesthetic appeal that a profit-driven economy around tiny houses relies on. From this perspective, it is possible to remark that tiny houses differentiate from the prior small housing typologies such as manufactured houses by their differences in aesthetic and class associations (Anson, 2014). There are also preventative aspects on the sustainability benefit of tiny house lifestyles, such as long-distance driving, and, frequent eating-out, caused by generally very limited storage space and kitchen (Anson, 2014). Lacking temperature regulation due to the lack of more contemporary appliances leads to excessive energy use during the heating and cooling process.

Tiny houses in Istanbul are relatively new and the regulations and criticism around them have yet to be developed as it is mentioned before. Therefore, there is a lack of tiny house communities as a presence in social media and other sources. To begin to shed light on the situation in Istanbul, a study was conducted with selected leading manufacturing companies that have been established recently.

Case Studies

A survey was carried out with three tiny house companies based in Istanbul to understand what motivates people to choose the tiny house lifestyle, to potentially own a tiny house, and to discuss the future of the movement in Istanbul. Companies were chosen based on web research and considering their online media presence. In January 2021, a survey containing seven multiple-choice questions and one open ended question was conducted using Google Forms. Participants were the three companies' founders and owners or CEOs. They were chosen for their knowledge of the company's history, communication with customers, and responsibility for the company's strategy and vision. The participants were informed about the content of the study and the protection of their personal information. The survey started with an open-ended question about the future of tiny-house movement in Istanbul. Then, the participants were asked about user's age range, education, working status and household type. Afterwards, questions about the tiny house users' motivations in choosing tiny houses (freedom, mobility, down-sizing, being in nature, affordability, environmental sustainability, escape from extreme materialism, design, removal from the urban environment, and social media influence), how long users prefer to use tiny houses and for what kind of settlement (as a long-term or a short-term residence, weekend get-away home, a fixed summer vacation home, and a mobile travel home), their concerns about tiny living (cost, design, security, location, comfort, availability of necessary equipment such as electricity, water, availability of the compulsory appliances, transportation, and communication) were asked.

Vagoon House

Vagoon House identifies itself as the pioneer tiny house company in Turkey and promotes tiny living as "extremely useful living spaces for people who are accustomed to modern city life, who want to live with nature but do not want to leave comfort" (Vagoon House, 2021). They claim that their products contain all the necessary comfort conditions that will make life easier, and this comfort will be anywhere the customer demands. Like the majority of tiny house companies in Istanbul, Vagoon House works with providing traffic permits, license plates, and caravan licenses and specifies that their product will provide the benefit to experience many protected areas and lands where construction is not allowed in the country (Vagoon House, 2021). They produce customized designs as well as modifying ready-made models and plans they present online, according to customers' wishes and preferred aesthetic style. Currently, their website presents seventeen ready-made models of various sizes, including models for café, atelier, office, and residential spaces (Vagoon House, 2021). The facilities are also provided by the company, including ready-made septic tanks if there is no wastewater connection available in the parking zone (Vagoon House, 2021).

In their survey responses, the founder of Vagoon House Cem Demirer stated that the "tiny house movement will become widespread with an increasing graphic over time". He specified that their customers are in their 30s and they are university and master's graduates. Significantly, the households interested were families of three or more which gives a slight clue about the attraction of tiny houses to families with high education levels. He stated freedom, downsizing, being in nature, affordability, design, and being removed from the urban environment were the primary motivations of their customers and they use them as a long-term residence, as a weekend home, and a summer vacation home. Finally, customers' concerns were design, cost, and the location of tiny houses.

Gorgor House

Before renewing their brand and began to manufacture tiny houses, Gorgor House was a carpentry company that mainly uses Black Sea region wood, which is a local material. The company emphasizes the minimalistic and sustainable qualities of the tiny house movement (Gorgor House, 2021). They promote living in nature, the highest quality in service, materials, and craftsmanship, and affordability with their products. They produce four models of tiny houses on trailers belonging to the type 1 (mobile) category of tiny house typology and offer different measurements for each model, slight customization in adding different energy systems like solar panels and its vehicle license along with the product (Gorgor House, 2021).

The owner of Gorgor House, Ibrahim Zorlu, participated in the survey and claimed that the future of the movement is not clear. According to Zorlu, it is not possible to say much about Istanbul especially because of the higher demand in the Aegean region where possibly the cost of the products varies and said, "For Istanbul and Turkey in general we think it will have a very different place after five years as what we understand from the current supply and demand interest".

He specified their customers in ages between 30 and 49 years old, having a high school, university, and doctorate education, and working. The household types of customers are small families of two or three, and two people living together. He stated freedom, mobility, and being in nature were the top motivations, which is possible to comment on the coherence with the company's branding. The customers use their products as mainly long-term and short-term residences and as a weekend home while their concerns were the cost, design, and availability of necessary equipment.

Yako Groups

Yako Groups distinguishes among other examples with their tiny house camping area; Yako House & Park in Polonezköy, one of the periphery neighborhoods in Beykoz district that is 30 km from the historical center of Istanbul. It is a company branded as a new generation event agency, activity, training, and tourism company, and among their several sub-brands, they produce tiny houses as Yako Tiny House (Yako Groups, 2021). They produce wooden caravan-type houses and offer accommodation in the company's land, also used as a tiny house park and license. They also have a Facebook page where they started a community around their product (URL-7). The company offers eight models that differentiate in design and size for accommodation and sales, which are produced also with trailers.

About the course of the tiny house movement in Istanbul, the CEO of the Yako Groups Galip Ölmez who participated in the survey said that "The popularization of more minimal and freer living concepts will positively affect the future of tiny houses". He specified a younger demographic profile of their customers, ranging in age from 18 to 49, and stated that they have a university education and work in general, while being mostly families of two. He stated freedom, mobility, being in nature, affordability, removal from the urban environment and social media influence as the main motivations of their customers and they use tiny houses for all accommodation options and residency types. Lastly, the customers' concerns revolved around cost, design, comfort, and availability of necessary equipment.

Discussion and Conclusion

In this chapter, a better understanding of the tiny house movement was aimed, and the topics related to global aspects of tiny houses were examined. Establishing a clearer connection between the emergence of tiny houses and prior housing types and cultural movements was deemed important for further studies as well. The motivations behind choosing tiny living were also discussed for grasping its potential as a global movement and thinking about its relevancy in the future. The existing tiny house typologies were mentioned although there are lots of variations in size, design, and form.

To gain insight into the development of the movement, a survey was conducted with three major tiny house developers in Istanbul. According to the findings, the customers' motivations rely heavily on the concepts of freedom and being in nature. They mostly use tiny houses as long-term residences and weekend homes and their concerns are primarily about cost, design, and availability of necessary equipment in tiny houses. The user profile of these companies are generally in their 30s, have a university degree, and working while being a part of small families.

Compared to the motivations suggested by research done globally or primarily in the United States, the concept of down-sizing is not considered to be one of the main factors for investing in tiny houses. Mainly, the opportunities to move away from existing infrastructure and everyday urban life while experiencing freedom in a relatively safe way can be seen as the attraction of the tiny house movement in Istanbul. Similarly, the concerns revolving around the environmental impact of unsustainable urban living and consequently, the desire to remove oneself from the existing consumerist culture did not appear as an outcome of the survey. This factor, which is considered a fundamental reason for the tiny house movement, can be accepted as not being a powerful motivation for users in Istanbul for the time being. Nevertheless, the flexibility to not be dependent on a certain location or the existing urban infrastructure, thus, to become distant from the city and urban lifestyle, is one of the major motivations of users in Istanbul as well as users globally. The flexibility aspect of the mentioned motivations is also accepted as a design feature, and can be associated with the tiny house typology itself. Although the individual design alterations and choices of the houses became a popular topic amongst the movement's community and over social media, the participants of the survey did not state it as being the major motivations of users in Istanbul. This situation can be correlated to the fact that companies that participated in the research are mainly producing the models designed and marketed in-house. Again, the users' input to the design or user customizations were not mentioned, but the design of the tiny house models was stated as one of the primary concerns while investing in a tiny house. The significant media coverage of tiny houses and social media popularity did help the rise of the movement in Istanbul and it can be said that the movement is expected to grow even further.

The user profile of the tiny houses in Istanbul was found to be not as varied as in global market, which includes seniors, students, retirees, and young adults as mentioned earlier. This can be explained by the movement's popularity on social media appealing to the younger generation who use social media intensively. Still, it can be said that the argument suggesting that people with high incomes are more common in the movement by choosing tiny house investment through down-sizing is also somewhat valid in Istanbul, with the profile that manufacturers most frequently indicate about tiny-house users. While the major motivations does not include down-sizing for users in Istanbul, it is understood that currently, more educated, and higher income people are involved in this movement. It can be said that affordability, which is presumably the biggest motivation for the tiny house movement, is incompatible with the motivations and the profile of the users in Istanbul. It was also possible to say that a certain typology in Istanbul, Type 1 (mobile) became more widespread than the other types. This situation can be interpreted as an outcome of the state regulations and legal barriers that inhibit building a non-mobile tiny house. The general use of the tiny houses were stated as a primary or weekend home and it is not consistent with the use of the houses globally, which is majorly a short-term house or an income source as a rental house. This can be considered as progress on the acceptance of tiny houses as a new residential typology, but also it can be explained by the general user profile and their other motivations for choosing the tiny houses primarily as a meaningful investment and a lifestyle change.

Despite the popularity of tiny houses and the sudden rise in the market, the movement remains relatively small compared to other countries. As it can be seen in the survey results as well, the future is not very clear in terms of the attraction of this lifestyle. Although most users choose small houses as their long-term residences, the possibility of the movement becoming widespread as a generally accepted lifestyle remains uncertain. On the topic of the criticism of the tiny house movement and tiny living, it appears that it is soon to remark on the negative aspects and it is difficult to reach a certain group of people or community of tiny house owners or users. Nevertheless, it is important to state the remaining questions about the future of tiny houses in Istanbul, including whether they can inspire to be a major alternative to affordability crises, broader production, and found a place in zoning regulations within the urban limits of Istanbul.

References

Anson, A. (2014). From sustainable to resilient cities: Global concerns and urban efforts. *Research in Urban Sociology*, 289–313. Doi: https://doi.org/10.1108/S1047-004220140000014013, iii. https://doi.org/10.1108/s1047-004220140000014022

Boudreaux, P. (2011). *The Housing Bias Rethinking Land Use Laws for a Diverse New America*. Palgrave Macmillan. Stetson University College of Law Research Paper No. 2012-01

Boeckermann, L. M., Kaczynski, A. T., & King, S. B. (2019). Dreaming big and living small: Examining motivations and satisfaction in tiny house living. *Journal of Housing and the Built Environment*, *34*(1), 61–71. https://doi.org/10.1007/s10901-018-9616-3

Byrne, M. (2020). Stay home: Reflections on the meaning of home and the Covid-19 pandemic. *Irish Journal of Sociology*, *28*(3), 351–355. https://doi.org/10.1177/0791603520941423

Chernoff, S. (1983). Behind the smokescreen exclusionary zoning of mobile homes. *Washington Journal of Urban and Contemporary Law*, *25*(January), 235–268.

Downing, A. (1969). *The Architecture of Country Houses*. New York: Da Capo Press.

Evans, K. (2018). Integrating tiny and small homes into the urban landscape: History, land use barriers and potential solutions. *Journal of Geography and Regional Planning*, *11*(3), 34–45. https://doi.org/10.5897/jgrp2017.0679

Fava Camp. (2021). Sıkça Sorulan Sorular. *Fava Camp Website*. URL: https://favacamp.com/. Accessed: 28.01.2021.

Fischel, W. A. (2004). An economic history of zoning and a cure for its exclusionary effects. *Urban Studies*, *41*(2), 317–340. https://doi.org/10.1080/0042098032000165271

Ford, J., & Gomez-Lanier, L. (2017). Are tiny homes here to stay? A review of literature on the tiny house movement. *Family and Consumer Sciences Research Journal*, *45*(4), 394–405. https://doi.org/10.1111/fcsr.12205

Gauer, J. (2004). *The New American Dream Living Well in Small Homes*. Eugene, New York: The Monacelli Press.

Genz, R. (2001). Why advocates need to rethink manufactured housing. *Housing Policy Debate*, *12*(2), 393–414. https://doi.org/10.1080/10511482.2001.9521411

Gorgor House. (2021). Sıkça Sorulan Sorular. *Gorgor House Website*. URL: https://www.gorgorhouse.com/. Accessed: 23.01.2021.

Harris, E., & Nowicki, M. (2020). "GET SMALLER?" Emerging geographies of micro-living. *Area, 52*(3), 591–599. https://doi.org/10.1111/area.12625

Heben, A. (2014). *Tent City Urbanism: From Self-Organized Camps to Tiny House Villages*. Eugene, Oregon: The Village Collaborative.

Hunter C (1999). *Ranches, Rowhouses, and Railroad Flats*. New York: W. W. Norton & Company.

Istanbul Metropolitan Municipality. (2018). Istanbul Zoning Regulation. *Resmî Gazete, 30426*. URL: https://www.resmigazete.gov.tr/eskiler/2018/05/20180520-4.htm. Accessed: 02.02.2021.

Jackson, A., Callea, B., Stampar, N., Sanders, A., De Los Rios, A., & Pierce, J. (2020). Exploring tiny homes as an affordable housing strategy to ameliorate homelessness: A case study of the dwellings in Tallahassee, FL. *International Journal of Environmental Research and Public Health, 17*(2). https://doi.org/10.3390/ijerph17020661

Maghribi, L., Wakatsuki, M., & Defterio, J. (2015). Tokyo's Big Idea: Can Micro-Homes Offer a Housing Solution? CNN. URL: https://edition.cnn.com/2015/11/03/asia/tokyo-japan-micro-home/index.html. Accessed: 22.01.2021.

Mandelker, Daniel R. (2016). Zoning Barriers to Manufactured Housing. *Washington University in St. Louis Legal Studies Research Paper Series*. No. 16-08-01. Available at SSRN: https://ssrn.com/abstract=2828268

Mangold, S., & Zschau, T. (2019). In search of the "Good Life": The appeal of the tiny house lifestyle in the USA. *Social Sciences, 8*(1). https://doi.org/10.3390/socsci8010026

Manzella, J. (2010). *Common Purse, Uncommon Future: The Long, Strange Trip of Communes and Other Intentional Communities*. Santa Barbara, California. Praege.

Mcalester, V. S. (1984). *A Field Guide to America's Historic Neighborhoods and Museum Houses: The Western States Great American Houses and Their Architectural Styles*. Knopf Doubleday Publishing Group.

Mingoya, C. (2015). Building together. Tiny house villages for the homeless: A comparative case study. *Department of Urban Studies and Planning in Partial Fulfillment of the Requirements for the Degree of Master in City Planning Massachusetts Institute of Technology*, 1–89. https://dusp.mit.edu/sites/dusp.mit.edu/files/attachments/news/mingoya_2015.pdf

Mitchell, R. (2014). *Tiny House Living Ideas for Building and Living Well in Less Than 400 Square Feet*. Betterway Home.

Murphy, M. (2014). Tiny houses as appropriate technology. Communities. 165(Winter), 54–59.

Mutter, A. (2013). Growing Tiny Houses Motivations and Opportunities for Expansion Through Niche Markets. *Lund University IIIEE Theses*, 2013:01.

Ölmez, G. (2020) Tiny House'lar pandemiyle birlikte Türkiye'de yaygınlaştı. *Platonline.* URL: https://www.platinonline.com/emlak/tiny-house-lar-pandemiyle-birlikte-turkiye-de-yayginlasti-1075379. Accessed: 25.01.2021.

Özlem, K. (2020). İnşaat izni olmayan arsalar için uygun mobil evler. *Homify.* URL: https://www.homify.com.tr/yeni_fikirler/5134983/insaat-izni-olmayan-arsalar-icin-uygun-mobil-evler. Accessed: 25.01.2021.

Penfold, H., Waitt, G., & McGuirk, P. (2018). Portrayals of the tiny house in electronic media: Challenging or reproducing the Australian dream home. *Australian Planner*, *55*(3–4), 164–173. https://doi.org/10.1080/07293682.2019.1632360

Pflaumer, D. H. (2015). *Tiny House Handbook.* Ball State University.

Priesnitz, W. (2014). Tiny Houses, Tiny Neighborhoods. *Natural Life Magazine* (March/April 2014), pp. 12–19. URL: http://naturallifemagazine.com/1404/tiny-houses-tiny-communities.htm. Accessed: 24.01.2021.

Shahani, A. (2015). Could a Tiny Mobile Studio Solve Your Housing Crisis? *NPR's All Tech Considered.* URL: https://www.npr.org/sections/alltechconsidered/2015/11/02/453975501/could-a-tiny-mobile-studio-solve-your-housing-crisis. Accessed: 05.02.2021.

Shearer, H., & Burton, P. (2019). Towards a typology of tiny houses. *Housing, Theory and Society*, *36*(3), 298–318. https://doi.org/10.1080/14036096.2018.1487879

Vagoon House. (2021). Sıkça Sorulan Sorular. *Vagoon House Website.* URL: https://www.vagoonhouse.com/. Accessed: 23.01.2021.

Weetman, V. M. (2018). Resistance is fertile: Exploring tiny house practices in Australia. *Australian Planner*, *55*(3–4), 232–240. https://doi.org/10.1080/07293682.2019.1636837

Wentling, J. (1995). Housing yesterday. In *Designing a Place Called Home* (pp. 1–18). New York, NY: Chapman & Hall.

Wotton, J., Skates, H., & Shutter, L. (2018). Tiny House–when size matters. *Australian Planner*, *55*(3–4), 209–220. https://doi.org/10.1080/07293682.2019.1634112

Yako Groups. (2021). Sıkça Sorulan Sorular. *Yako House Website.* URL: https://www.yakogroups.com/. Accessed: 23.01.2021.

www.ingramcontent.com/pod-product-compliance
Ingram Content Group UK Ltd.
Pitfield, Milton Keynes, MK11 3LW, UK
UKHW020153290926
15471UKWH00005B/850

9 783631 854914